Praise for The Mother of All Makeovers

"Hollie's writing is as fabulous as the way she lives her life… unapologetically raw, full of entertainment and beautiful storytelling that keeps you laughing and wondering what's going to happen next!"

— *Jennifer Bertrand, HGTV Design Star Winner (Season 3) and Military Makeover Designer, Lifetime Channel*

"A chic, happening, successful designer in cheetah print, open-toed heels, Hollie Gyarmati never would have imagined the turns her life would take when, after marrying Detroit's most eligible bachelor, she rapidly had more babies than a day care. In her achingly funny, brave, tell-it-like-it-is memoir, Hollie takes us along in the stroller as she trades high-style couture for jeans with elastic stomach panels, becomes a round-the-clock milk machine, makes a medal-worthy run for the diaper Olympics, and reels after the recession hits her hometown of Detroit, taking with it her husband's lucrative livelihood and 'life as we knew it.' A triumph of resilience and a testament to the indomitable spirit of motherhood, *The Mother of All Makeovers* is like an ice bucket dumped on your head. It will wake you up, bring you to your senses, and make you laugh and cry at once. In her debut book, Hollie Gyarmati has written the mother of all comeback stories."

— *Marni Jameson, nationally syndicated home columnist, and author of* Downsizing the Family Home.

"Hollie sparkles irresistibly like a Tiffany box, and charms when you untie the pretty ribbon. Hollie has a gift for finding humor in everyday challenges, creativity and style without a wink of sleep, and energy when the gas tank is empty. In no time, she will become your go-to girl for style and design tips, this I promise. Untie the ribbon and find the gift of Hollie!"

—Lucy Penfield, Interior Designer, Minneapolis

"I knew from the moment I met Hollie that she was a shining star. Tom and Hollie's personal strength and courage is inspirational!
—Cindy Obron Kahn, Realtor, Detroit

Julie -
Thank you for your kindness!
Happy Reading & God Bless!
Hollie

THE MOTHER OF ALL MAKEOVERS

A Memoir of More, Less and Making Busy Beautiful

Hollie Gyarmati

The Mother of All Makeovers / Hollie Gyarmati — 1st ed.

ISBN 978-1-7337995-0-8 (pbk)
ISBN 978-1-7337995-1-5 (eBook)

Published by Sheldon Books

Cover illustration by Nicole Jarecz
www.nicole-jarecz.com
Instagram: @nicolejareczillustration

Author photo by Jennifer McKinstry
www.canopycreativeprofessionals.com

I have tried to recreate events, locales and conversations from my memories of them. In order to maintain their anonymity in some instances I have changed the names of individuals and places, I may have changed some identifying characteristics and details such as physical properties, occupations and places of residence.

For Tom. They never said it would be easy.

CONTENTS

FOREWORD

Straight from the heart, *The Mother of All Makeovers* transforms the unforeseen circumstances surrounding the housing crash of 2008 into a path of renewed faith and bold authenticity. Chock full of humor, humility, and chutzpah, Hollie Gyarmati intimately details the enormous effort she and her husband undertook to parent five kids under five years old and ultimately thrive in abandoned and declining Detroit.

A must-read for anyone who aspires to create a life of substance, *The Mother of All Makeovers* is a true testament to maternal instinct and the unrelenting resolve of the human spirit. You will laugh, cry, then wonder why it took this emerging writer so long to share her brilliant, heart-felt story.

— *Mark Brunetz, Emmy Award winning TV host, author, and social entrepreneur*

PROLOGUE

I know Vegas is called *Sin City*, but as I hugged my Prada into my hip in the back seat while thinking about a decade of diapers, design, and the dreams of a girl who just wanted to be a mom, I felt closer to Heaven than I ever thought possible. Nothing in my life had happened the way I had planned. It wasn't even the life I'd ever wanted, if I'm being honest.

If Saint Peter himself had appeared before me and said, *"Hollie, you are going to marry the man of your dreams. The two of you will have seven years of feast and seven years of famine. You will leave your career to bring five children into this world in less than four years. You will be a wife, a mom,* and *the homemaker of a house with seven bathrooms. You will change over 27,000 diapers, lose all your material assets, prepare for over seventy-seven house showings for which you will vacate your estate, leaving it looking like your family— including your dog—do not exist, and you will cry alone in your closet more than seven hundred times.*

You will experience "for richer or poorer." You will experience "for better or worse." You will go through things and wonder how you can survive another day. But even though there will be much worry and stress, you will never lose hope. Instead, you will decide to dream bigger than you did, even as a little girl. You will be a broken-down, almost middle-aged woman, yet your dreams will be filled with passion and purpose. They will keep you strong and your faith will not waiver. In the end, God will make your crooked roads straight and your chaos calm. He will bless you with divine strength and love to carry out all things according to His will. And you will see His hand at work through all His creation. You will be blessed beyond your wildest dreams and filled with more love than your heart ever thought possible. And you will find your happy ending in the most sinful city on earth, Las Vegas," I would have thought it impossible. I looked down at my weathered luxury bag and laughed at the irony of my life…

CHAPTER 1

THIS GIRL IS ON FIRE

Detroit 2015

Air travel. You either love it or hate it. I haven't loved it for at least a decade, but on this day, I didn't just love it. If I'd had an overhead sound system blasting Alicia Keys and some moves, I would have started a viral-worthy flash mob in front of the intermittent water feature centered in the main atrium of the Delta terminal. Always on time and usually early, I glided through the crowd with an inner happiness I'd never before felt. It was some kind of "life moment happy," and I didn't expect to feel it alone at the airport. But there it was, and I owned it.

Not because of my fear of escalators and fast-moving transport, I decided to walk to my gate, allowing plenty of time to casually sip a skinny latte while enjoying my favorite pastime: people watching. A quick-witted skill passed down from my grandparents, I thrive on creating storylines for those moving around me. When I was little, my Grandpa and Grandma Foss used to lounge in the screened-in front porch of their village two-story during happy hour and assess the neighborhood activity. They would discuss the comings and goings of husbands and wives, boyfriends and girlfriends, nosey mothers-in-law... You name it, they had a story for everyone else's business before getting to their own. I would listen in as I savored my own cocktail, Squirt with a splash of grape juice, admiring their all-American sport as I worked on my latest drawing with a No. 2 pencil. It's no wonder I love interviewing clients, discovering stories, and putting my observational techniques to good use. My solo walk through the expansive airport brought me back to my inherited roots and my "happy" with full attentiveness.

This January Monday morning boasted an easy-moving crowd. A lot of businessmen with very little enthusiasm over their nine-to-five. A couple of young families led by frazzled moms pushing strollers and dads lugging car seats and endless bags of survival gear for their flight. *I'm glad those days are over,* I thought. A few old ladies with bronzed skin, short bleached hair, and quilted fabric carry-ons were selecting the first-come seats at their gate as early arrivals. They were returning to Naples or West Palm after flying in for a family emergency or eightieth birthday celebration. As I smirked at the predictability, I was immediately taken with a group of college boys triumphantly striding toward me, dressed in prep school attire and carrying large bags that concealed hockey or rugby equipment. Regardless, they were athletes, and their victorious, playful camaraderie reminded me of great, inspiring sports movies like *Rudy* or *Remember the Titans* where the underdog wins and the anthem-like theme song at the end makes you so happy you want to run outside and scream to the world that anything is possible if you have the faith and endurance to see it through to the end.

Then it hit me: what I felt that day was anthem happy.

I arrived at my gate with twenty minutes to spare, which was just enough time to run to the ladies' room and organize my carry-on. I had a small, black pull-behind and my beloved Prada bag, both meticulously stuffed to the outer corners with two days' worth of business casual/evening wear that took me hours to figure out. Like a pro, I always wear bulky layers for travel. This morning it was a comfy, black, long-sleeved T-shirt, black leggings, brown riding boots, and the fifteen-year-old DKNY denim jacket I'd purchased from Marshall Field's when I worked there. A soft cashmere scarf wrapped itself loosely around my neck because I knew it would come in handy when I needed an in-flight pillow.

I also had clean make-up for travel day because you can always add, but you can never take away. Since I began air-travel, I learned that straight hair endures a long day of head-resting and is easy to freshen up if you fall asleep. Straightening my hair became my night-before-travel ritual over the years, so when I walked out of the bathroom that morning with my shoulder-length highlighted waves loosely curled, my husband gave me a disapproving look. He was so accustomed to my straight hair travel routine that he immediately questioned the motive behind my change. I explained that my goal was to go from day to night and possibly endure the whirlwind trip without a wash, thus eliminating the need for hair utensils. Humored by my thoughtful yet predictable consolidation strategy, he gave me the "Oh geez" smirk I've grown to love over the years.

With plenty of seat options, I relaxed into a classic black tandem sling seat and scoped out the scene. The gate area was filling in. The Delta crew was prepping the boarding counter, and the crowd around me was predominantly male. Forty-to-sixty-something casually dressed professionals. They were Monday morning travelers but not regulars or executives. Canvas luggage. Many seemed to know each other. I reached into the front zipper of my bag and pulled out my boarding pass. I was in the third group; we all had unassigned seats. With the details set, I decided to scroll texts to look busy. Everyone knew where I was and my message file had been emptied, but it was better to look busy than get sucked into conversation.

"Are you going for the KBIS show?" a sixty-something man wearing a striped polo and khakis probed. I glanced up and smiled politely.

"No." This was exactly the kind of person I had no interest in chatting with. With a slight frown, I returned to my phone as though I were missing something big at the office.

"Are you going for business or pleasure?" Chatty it is!

"Business." The kind of business I could only have dreamed of three years ago.

"What do you do?" You seem like a nice guy, but I love *alone* right now.

"I'm a designer." I hate that there are not seat assignments.

"Oh, you look like a designer!" I know, right? Wait, is that alcohol emanating from your breath? Gross! Straight from the airport bar, trade show bound, and taking full advantage of a warm weather adventure. Please have friends to sit with on the plane...

At that moment, I was rescued from Mr. 8AM Cocktail by the boarding process. Whew!

The business class passengers quickly boarded, then rows through the twenties and beyond. My ticket was scanned, and my travel anxiety lifted, as this confirmed that I was officially accepted onto the aircraft, that I had made it to the right place, my rusty travel skills had sufficed, and I could now focus on rolling my balanced bags down the drafty ramp and onto the plane. Then it happened.

"I thought all the beautiful girls were in Vegas, but I think they're on this flight," my new friend belted out about ten feet behind me. My cheeks started to burn, and my palms began to sweat at the thought of sitting anywhere near this man for over three hours. I needed to find a female-friendly seat. As a beautiful blonde flight attendant welcomed me, I rounded the corner to a sea of men occupying window and aisle seats, making my selection a little tricky. Praying my way to the back, I slid into an aisle seat next to a young couple who appeared to be madly in love. The "first six months" kind of love. They were snuggled together, hand-in-hand, headphones on, absorbed in a movie on their tablet. *Score!* I'd successfully dodged all in-flight socialization, which gave me free rein to dig into my secret travel pharmacy for half an Ambien. My Ziploc stash would be a lethal party cocktail if it made its way into the hands of a buzz-craving teen. It was loaded with Ambien, Valium, Xanax, Tylenol, and Azo bladder pills. I snapped my little white pill in half and prepared to splurge on three hours of peaceful rest so I could enjoy every moment of my once-in-a lifetime adventure. And that's exactly what I did.

Roused by the pilot's voice announcing our descent into Las Vegas, I was pleased that I'd somehow managed to sleep with my head straight back against the seat—hopefully without my mouth hanging open—and was relieved that the snugglers were still in love, unaware of my presence. A smooth landing and exit off the plane had me walking through a bustling airport with nary a clue as to where I was going. I've never had to catch a cab by myself, so my female Venus logic quickly had me asking a nice valet how I might find a fast cab. Of course, he directed me to the opposite exit, a football field away. With no time to spare, I picked up my pace and zipped against the sea of travelers to large sliding doors that spit me into the longest cab line I'd ever seen.

It was over a hundred people long, four rows deep, and roped off along a dusty sidewalk that ran the length of the airport. White taxis, yellow taxis, minivans, you name it; every driver was on a mission to load, drive, and reload as fast as possible. Time was money. In my case, time was not money; it was evening attire prep! The thought of being late to my event made me light-headed. In my nanosecond worst-case-scenario vision, I would be in this line for two hours, get dropped at the wrong hotel, and miss it entirely. Inhale. *Enjoy* this time alone. Own Design Hollie. Late will not happen. God has brought you here for a reason; be anxious for nothing. Exhale. I focused my attention on the sights surrounding me in line.

The Vegas air was a cool sixty-five degrees and smelled of exhaust and cigarettes. High-rises across the street were covered with billboards that screamed Sin City. A forty-foot tall pair of luscious Victoria's Secret style red lips seduced one to nightlife at a casino. The visual stimulation was provocative and exciting, and by the time my eyes rested on the crowd I was twenty paces in. I quickly forgot about time as I became immersed into what looked like a melting pot of every social gathering in the United States. I had never seen such a mix of interesting people. Two tall, stocky men in front of me were cowboys. They were wearing ten-gallon hats, button-down shirts, Wranglers with oversized belt buckles, and cowboy boots. The business casuals from my flight were chatting in front, and mingled in were women from all walks of life who were much more recreational than men to check out. I immediately become Stacy London. Eighty percent need to tone it down. Too much cleavage, not enough support. Wrong hair color, just all-together wrong. Oh honey, you are pushing fifty, stop trying to look thirty! And those heels are a size too small; your baby toes are squashed like crescent roll dough waiting to be popped from their cardboard container. Finally! Some sweet young twenty-somethings with on-point travel style. Effortless long hair, oversized sunglasses, slouchy cotton T-shirts, and minimal jewelry. Skinny-washed jeans and cute wedges. Oversized, structured leather handbags. Louis Vuitton. I missed my twenties and blamed grunge flannels and Dr. Martens for stealing this coveted look from my youth. I secretly wanted to be these girls for a day. Maybe two. My daydream of glory days was cut short when a young Latino valet nicely directed me past the ropes. Fastest long line I'd ever moved through.

"Please stand on number five," he smiled, swiftly motioning me to a faded yellow number at the edge of the curb. In the same beat, a white cab pulled up with its trunk popped. With swift rhythm, my luggage was loaded and I was ushered onto the slippery black leather backseat with my Prada.

"Where to, Miss?" the driver asked through the rearview mirror. He was an older gentleman with dark eyes and a thick head of hair.

"Mandalay Bay," I politely replied. "I'm on a tight schedule. If you have a faster route, that'd be great," I added. The receptionist at my dentist's office told me to always be in a hurry and act like you know where you're going or they'll take you on a scenic tour to run the clock. He nodded his head, stepped on the gas, and within a couple of minutes we were on the strip. I've always been amazed by the way taxi drivers always manage to keep moving even if traffic is at a standstill. It had been almost twenty years since I'd seen the city, and it was bigger and more sparkly than I remembered. As we passed New York New York and its infamous roller coaster, I held up my phone and captured an image for my daughter, Emma. She didn't believe that a hotel could be graced with the Statue of Liberty *and* a roller coaster.

A sharp turn slid me into my bag, and I squeezed the worn leather handles. I looked down at its over-stuffed, boxy shape. Besides needing a new shoulder strap to replace the original thick padded nylon that had started to fray, this bag had stood the test of time.

After a decade of use, I'm still deeply moved by the story it has seen me through and believe a stranger may find it all unimaginable. The inverted triangular Prada logo still looked like new and it was filled with new cosmetics, an evening clutch that Tom gifted me for our first black tie event when we were dating, my phone, "the stash," and a brand-new pair of terra cotta Tory Burch suede heels covered with butterscotch jewels. At sixty percent off from Nordstrom Rack, they were my splurge purchase for this trip. I smile when I think about the fact that I've never felt guilty about a splurge because I make them so infrequently and so intentionally. The loyal bag sitting next to me was proof of that.

CHAPTER 2

BEFORE...

May 2005

"If you love it, just buy it," my husband said as he rolled the doublewide stroller forward and back. I smoothed my hands around the thick nylon gym bag and ran through every reason it should be mine. The size was right: it was fourteen inches wide by thirteen inches high and about ten inches thick. It had two top zippers, a front and back zipper, and a side zip pouch. I deemed its understated design acceptable for men or women (because I *would* be ditching Tom with it at times), and the quality would last a lifetime. It was Prada. I envisioned how often it would be scrubbed with soap and water over the next few years. Lined with black leather piping and heavy silver-tone hardware, it boasted textured black leather zipper pulls that could handle even the craziest twin mom frenzy. There were leather top handles and a detachable shoulder strap that would allow for a cross-bodied look. I knew I had to buy it. It would fit everything I needed and stay organized while holding six baby bottles, eight diapers, wipes, cloth diapers, extra changes of clothes, toiletries, personal items, and my wallet. I extended the shoulder strap to make sure it would fit over the handle of my front-to-back double stroller at home. It would nestle right under the rear infant car seat without banging against my knees as I pushed. Ergonomic perfection for a busy mom on the go.

"This is the one I want," I stated, as if I had a crowd of media on edge, waiting for my reply. "It will be my diaper bag, luggage for vacations, and a briefcase when I'm designing again." I made this clarifying statement to justify spending the hefty $1,100 on a bag. My husband, relieved that he was finished shopping in Naples for the day, smiled his big Hungarian blue eyes at the Neiman Marcus saleswoman, and handed her his Amex. Tom never told me no. He knew I was low-maintenance for the wife of a successful automotive dealer, and he didn't flinch at the price tag. I was the frugal one. I had no problem selling $30,000 rooms as a designer, but spending $1,000 on a bag that would get trashed daily was something I had to come to terms with. As I watched it being placed in a dustcover and secured in a large Prada box, my "want" transformed to a "need," and I carried it out into the hot Florida sun with twin mom pride and a vision of the perfect happily ever after as a stay-at-home mom living in the suburbs of Detroit.

* * *

We live in prestigious Bloomfield Hills. It's about seventeen miles north of the city, covered with lushly wooded rolling hills and small lakes. It's the heart of upscale living. A five-minute drive in any direction has you on most major expressways, yet a scenic tour down a side street could have you in the neighborhood of a CEO, professional athlete, or Motown legend. The city is sprinkled with gated communities, country clubs, private schools, multi-million-dollar mansions, and upper-middle-class homes coveted by doctors, automotive executives, and anyone wanting to live in Detroit's finest.

Our story is nothing short of a Cinderella tale, and if you were enjoying a glass of Merlot on a Monday night you might hashtag #bachelornation with confidence that our whirlwind romance happened long before reality TV existed. It was 9PM on a Sunday, and *my* eligible bachelor (Tom) had migrated from china shopping for his sister-in-law to the furniture department in hopes of finding the

Barbara Barry bedroom collection he'd seen in an *Architectural Digest* ad the year before. Delayed by an elderly saleswoman (who detected a bored thirty-three-year-old with no intention of making a purchase), he decided to take her lead and wait to speak with a designer. He will tell you that when I stepped through the heavy glass door of the studio (in lieu of the limo used by the reality TV show of the moment), he knew that I was the kind of girl he wanted to marry.

I was twenty-six, a Cum Laude university grad with a statewide award-winning portfolio and an up-and-coming designer for the fabulous Marshall Field's department store. Today, it stands as Macy's, but back then it was Marshall Field's (think State Street, Chicago), and for a century before that, it was Hudson's Department Store, the *only* high fashion retailer in Detroit, or Michigan at all for that matter. Ask anyone old enough to remember downtown Detroit before the seventies, and they will reminisce about the iconic, high-rise J.L. Hudson building and its reputation for cutting edge design, fashion, and impeccable guest service.

I grew up listening to my mom's stories of taking the city bus in the early sixties to shop there with my Grandma VanPachtenbeke. My grandparents immigrated to Detroit from Belgium after the second World War and brought with them Euro style and talent that I proudly wear in my "gene" collection. Grandma loved Hudson's, Parisian fashion, and everything for the home. She, like so many women of her generation, was an impeccable seamstress. Within a few weeks of her department store preview, she'd be sporting her own collection, hand-sewn in the little bungalow where she lived with her family of seven.

Some of my earliest childhood memories were of passing through the beautiful department store hand-in-hand with my mom and grandma. I may have been hauled along to try on Hush Puppies in the mall, but strolling past the glass cosmetic counters anchored by gold encrusted chandeliers and giant escalators leading up and down provided eye candy for my soul.

It took me fifteen years, hundreds of hours doodling floor plans, perspectives, and a dabble in graphic design and architecture to discover that interior design was in fact the career I had fallen in love with at the tender age of three. I'll never forget the crisp fall day I marched next door (Grandma and Papa lived next to us on a dirt road on the outskirts of town) and sat with my grandma at her kitchen table to share my exciting news. She, of course, was thrilled, and it was that day that she told me about the exclusive designers who worked behind the glass doors of J.L. Hudson's furniture department. It was that day when the vision was planted in my soul, and it was that moment I would remember as the last I'd spend with the woman I related to most on earth. She passed weeks later at only sixty-six due to complications from a routine valve replacement, breaking our hearts but not the dream she'd left in mine.

While my bachelor was running through his checklist of wife qualities in that moment outside the studio doors, I was deeply focused on the $14,000 bedroom suite he was in search of, and wondering if this intriguing single sporting an old flannel and work boots could possibly qualify as a lucrative design client. I was in search of luxe projects, not love, and what followed was an eight-month long professional relationship filled with lengthy phone calls that began with business and moved to the kind of soulmate-style conversations that would have you pouring that second glass of wine in hopes of a first date or even a kiss.

You see, when the universe intersects two lives that are meant to become one, something magical happens, and anyone who has experienced lifelong love will tell you that *when you know, you just know*. After he first turned the key in the door of his five-star bachelor pad decorated with the finest furnishings, floorcoverings, and amenities available in 2001, he turned to me, his designer and now best friend, and invited me to lunch. I knew that was it, and after our first kiss (to top off that great bottle of red), we began a courtship that would have even Chris Harrison waiting for an interview to discuss all the details.

That summer, I was spotted coming and going from Marshall Field's with stars in my eyes and stories of whirlwind romantic getaways to tropical islands, world-renowned ski resorts, fishing trips in Alaska, and quick flights to Chicago as co-pilot of Bachelor Tom's Mooney airplane. I was completely undeniably madly in love, and nothing much mattered except spending every moment with my client-turned-beau. As any epic season finale would have it, the solidifying moment came on Valentine's Day the following year as we coupled with cold drinks at the adult pool at the Grand Wailea resort in Maui.

I was reading an article in *Glamour* magazine (still an acceptable read if you were under thirty) about college girls abducted by devil worshipers while on Spring Break. Completely immersed in the horrifying story, I heard, "Will You Marry Me?" I set the magazine down on my sweaty thighs and looked up. Tom was sitting up in his lounge chair looking at me with sparkling eyes.

"Really? *Right now?* Are you serious? Because if you are, you should know that I am reading about devil worshipers chopping up girls! This will be etched in my memory forever!" I exclaimed, a little perturbed that this was obviously an impromptu moment that would not be locked in with a diamond.

"I know I don't have the ring, but yes, I'm serious," he replied as if I might jump into the ocean and turn into a mermaid, disappearing from his life forever if I didn't say yes. (This is where you find yourself teary-eyed with your empty glass, tweeting about how this love story is going to go down in #bachelornation history.)

"YES!" I answered with an uncontainable smile. He embraced me in a prince-like kiss, and that is where our marriage began.

CHAPTER 3

GLORIA

"Why are you cutting the tops off the strawberries?" my husband inquired as he sat at the kitchen island with a glass of Guinness. I was working my way through an oversized container from Costco and not in the mood for an interrogation.

"I've cut the whites off my entire life; nobody likes the white part," I stated, eyeing his pile of mail, toiletries, mints, and gadgets that had collected overnight on the other half of my workspace. The honeymoon (in Paris, of course) was over. I'd become a domestic goddess over the course of our first year and took great pride in everything from design (fluffed, puffed, and accessorized), homemaking (ironed sheets on the bed), gardening (front porch perfection), and cooking with the TV on (*Rachael Ray* and *Everybody Loves Raymond* rounded off my repertoire), which brings me to this moment slicing strawberries in my gourmet kitchen.

"Huh. My mom only pulled the greens off. You're wasting half the strawberry," he schooled. Ugh. His mother—God rest her soul—was a woman I'd never live up to, and since he was basically an only child (his older brother—and employer—was thirteen years his senior), he knew nothing other than the perfection of Mary Gyarmati caring for his every need. I say this very sincerely; she was everything I could have asked for in a mother-in-law, and Tom and I agreed that my Belgian grandma and his Hungarian mother were up in Heaven celebrating the victory of our union. His dad would have come to my defense if he were sitting with us. I knew I would have loved my mother-in-law because I adored my father-in-law, who lived on the other side of the city. He was our third wheel and joined us frequently for breakfast, dinner, and walks around the lake.

"That was your mom. This is me. Live with it," I retorted, as he moseyed to the library. I wondered what little Tom Gyarmati was like as a kid. I knew he was resourceful, creative, and an animal lover. As I layered my berries in a glass bowl, I smirked at the thought of him coaxing that chipmunk into the back of his parents' station wagon so he could take him home as a pet. He loved boating, fishing, and making money (he grew up on a canal, and his favorite game was Stocks and Bonds). He would have been my best friend if we'd grown up together and were the same age. I used to catch fish with the neighbor boy who was a year older than I was, and I guess I was also entrepreneurial. I *did* publish the Hensell Herald (named after the road I grew up on) and sold artwork to the neighbors. Even if we did grow up in the same hometown, we wouldn't have been friends. As fate would have it, we were eight years apart in age. To the day. And eight years, when you are ten and he is eighteen is not just an age gap, it's a generation gap.

Example: "Do you remember the Pringles commercial when they first came out?" he asked as we lay on our hammock in the backyard.

"I never knew life *before* Pringles," I answered

No response.

"Didn't you love Reagan?" he'd ask during dinner conversation.

"I was six. I was in love with Bo and Luke Duke."

Nothing.

"Everything But the Girl was so good when they first came out, don't you agree?" he'd inquire in the car.

"I was listening to whatever Casey Kasem was playing on the Top 40 countdown. Tom, I was just a kid when you were in college." This reminder was usually followed by him rolling his eyes, and that was that. My point had been made. We were not meant to be until I was all grown up. These little differences made it hard to reminisce together, but we shared the important things that formed a solid foundation in any marriage: religion, politics, family values, dreams. The big things made it easy to envision the life we would build together. The boy, girl, boy (BGB as we'd refer to them when we were dating) we would have, each planned two years apart. I never second-guessed leaving the store to start a family. As much as I loved my name on that Hudson's business card, I knew it didn't define my "who." I would be a designer forever. But at that point in time, I was embracing the idea of a family and longed to be a stay-at-home mom. It was perfect. Tom would someday own a dealership, giving us the financial security to continue our standard of living, pay for private schools, give faithfully to our church and community, and embrace all the bountiful things life had to offer.

* * *

Almost two years later, I found myself standing next to my hospital bed glowing at the sight of my newborn twins dressed in their homecoming outfits. Emma in pink and Noah in blue. Our "BGB" plan was fast-tracked when we found out we were having twins, and I was very fortunate to have had a healthy nine months to read up on how to keep these little people alive like a pro. I was recovering from a C-section, had spent four days in the hospital, and while I was nervous and weak, was ready to be pushed from the nest of on-call nurse help. The babies had been fed, my bags were packed, the discharge papers were signed, and my nurse, Darla, had me stocked up with all the baby supplies I might need during my first few days at home. I was dressed in my coming home outfit: gray active pants with a matching T-shirt and zip-up jacket layered proudly over my new nursing bra.

I was shocked by what these babies had done to my body. Everything was big, and I didn't feel like and certainly didn't *look* like me. I'd lost my 34Cs and my Victoria's Secrets had sadly been exchanged for granny panties from Kmart. Having the unplanned C-section sent me over the edge. The second day at the hospital, the nurse broke the news to me that I'd have to wear underwear that would cover my incision. She then looked at Tom and said, "Honey, go buy a pack of underwear for her. Full coverage underwear from the women's department."

"Size small," I added, just to feel like I still had something good going on down there. I cringed. Then I jotted down a few more items onto the list: lip balm, hand cream, Trident Original chewing gum, and the latest issues of *In-Style* and *People* magazines. An hour later, my husband was spreading an array of old lady underpants on my bed.

This might be a good time to mention that the "less is more" girl married the "more is more" guy. The first hint of this quality of his came when we were dating, and I mentioned that my favorite perfume had been discontinued. The following week, he gifted me with every bottle of eau de toilette spray he could find—worldwide—through eBay. At first, I thought it was sweet and romantic, then a little annoying that I'd have to find a home for a twenty-year supply of perfume. That was just the beginning of what would become a lifelong battle of what the "right" quantity was for all purchases. Money was no object for Tom. If he found one shirt he loved, he bought five more. The same rule applied to such things as toiletries, flashlights, and olive oil. He liked knowing that he was prepared at all times. This topic would be one that we'd haggle over for years to come, but in the moment of needing ugly old lady underwear, I was grateful for the five different varieties my husband was offering me. I so loved this man, and I was therefore ready and willing to merge my less-is-more approach to his more-is-more and live happily ever after.

As it turned out, the thought of doing that was slightly less stressful than the reality, as I would discover over the next several years.

Ready to bring home the babies, I was standing in my room, ready to go and waiting for the man I love to arrive. He was running at least fifteen minutes late. I'd had everything ready at home for weeks. Tom's only job was to figure out the car seats from the super *amazing* travel "system" I'd purchased from Babies R Us (I say amazing with sarcasm because I despised the baby registry process and all the gear that would clutter my home for the next couple of years). The safety racket over the car seat installation deemed it the perfect dad job since he was, after all, at the dealership every day, and the guys in the service department could do the work as well as provide a quick tutorial on car seat safety. *He'd better get here soon because these babies are going to need to eat again in less than an hour,* I thought. At precisely that moment, he walked in with a car seat in each hand.

"Hi!" he said as he greeted me with a quick kiss.

"I can't wait to get out of here. Are the seats ready?" He plopped them on the hospital bed. They looked ready to go. The five-point harness was buckled on each one. I unlatched one, and it popped open. It looked right, but there wasn't any slack on the shoulder or leg straps. They were pulled tight against the back of the seat. In fact, they were so tight you couldn't even strap a Barbie doll into the them. "How do you loosen these straps?" I asked. He grabbed the seat and fidgeted around with it for a minute. Clueless. His cover was blown. He hadn't done his homework and came unprepared to take his babies home from the hospital. My postpartum blood was boiling. I ask him to do one thing. *One* thing over the course of nine months to prepare for this moment, and he didn't take it seriously. *I can't believe I married this irresponsible human being. Jerk,* I thought. He looked at me in silence. This was *not* the time to do the guy thing where you're too embarrassed to ask for help.

"FIND SOMEONE TO HELP YOU. NOW," I commanded. Without question and full of guilt, he took the seats and walked out into the silent hallway. There wasn't a nurse in sight.

I was seething, hands on my hips and working worthless Lamaze breathing to keep from vomiting. The thought of keeping these babies alive on my own was freaking me out. The fact that my partner was a knucklehead was freaking me out even more. *My life is over.* Still silence penetrated the hallway. The hallway had been packed with nurses for four days straight, yet the moment I needed them, they vanished. While having my silent meltdown, my sweet and polite husband managed to stumble upon a nurse in an empty room.

"Excuse me," he asked. "Can I ask you a question about this infant car seat?" The nurse, who I am convinced was an angel, knew well the look of panic on Tom's "new dad" face, and what happened next was the best dose of reality anyone at Beaumont Hospital could have possibly given him. Her name was Gloria, but everyone called her "Glor." She was in her late fifties and, if I had to guess, had been married a couple of times. She was beautiful yet weathered and had sultry auburn dyed hair that was styled a little big for the times. Her brown eyes were lined heavily with makeup, and she wore rusty red lipstick. Her overall look screamed Ann Margaret and was opposite every other plain-Jane nurse we'd encountered. I'll bet Tom's cheeks and ears turned red just looking at her. She noticed he had two seats.

"Honey, let me guess. You're here to take your brand-new twins home and you're stressed out enough as it is and the last thing you need is to have to dick around with this *damn* car seat," she said as she took one from him and flipped it upside down on the bed.

"Exactly! The straps are too tight, and we can't fit the babies in!" he confirmed, relieved that this angel was there to save his marriage.

"Well, the directions don't tell you, but you have to lift here and pull from the front to create the slack you need. Like this," she demonstrated, just as she'd done for many other stressed out new daddies over the years.

"You have no idea what you've saved me from," Tom smiled.

"Let me tell you something. I've been here for almost thirty years, and everyone is overwhelming you with crap you don't need to know. The right and wrong way to do *everything*. What you really need to do is get your new family home, break open a bottle of wine, and relax. Everything will be fine!" Gloria marched my husband into our room and helped us strap in Noah and Emma. I loved her and her grit. By then, nurses had appeared seemingly from everywhere, and we had three or so escorting us out as I sat in a wheelchair being pushed by a sweet, old hospital volunteer. Tom proudly carried a car seat in each hand. We stopped in front of the revolving doors of the hospital entrance for a family photo before driving off to our happy home and what I would soon discover was my own perpetual Tomorrowland.

CHAPTER 4

TOMORROWLAND

Many know it as the futuristic world at The Magic Kingdom, created by the one and only Walt Disney, the home of Space Mountain, the Carousel of Progress, and all things beyond today. Ask a new mom what *Tomorrowland* means and she may burst into tears of exhaustion before telling you it represents the unspoken reality of her world. Starting with twins is absolutely double the work, but the phenomenon holds true for every new mom of any number of babies. And it never goes away. It's the reality of being The Mom that women forget to pass along via giant neon warning signs to those of us who are preparing to enter this new dimension of life. Maybe they know that if they tell us the truth, we may back out of the whole thing and life will not go on.

Let me explain: when you are The Mom, you not only have to work tirelessly to care for your baby (or babies), you also have to live one day *ahead* of them and everyone else you may be caring for if you want even a chance of survival. The more people you care for, the more planning is required, and therefore, the more work you must do each day to ensure you are prepared for the next. Every mom with her game on lives in Tomorrowland. The ones who choose not to cross over pay for it tenfold and can be spotted a mile away. They have the endlessly screaming toddler at the grocery store at 1:30 in the afternoon. They are late to every scheduled appointment or social gathering. They are ordering Chinese food twice a week because they didn't meal plan. They are beyond stressed and feel as though parenthood has done them wrong. But it hasn't. They just took a wrong turn. Or maybe they missed the neon sign and the secret passageway into Tomorrowland. Or maybe they just ignored it. But whatever the case, I understood this phenomenon within the first twenty-four hours of being home with my newborns and embraced the power I had as The Mom and what would be required of me to make our home a happy place to be.

My first hurdle was healing from the knives that had sliced through my abdomen, the ones that had sounded better than superhero natural childbirth. It would take six weeks to heal, and I felt like an old lady walking around because I couldn't stand up straight without feeling the pain. The second hurdle was the torrid "breast is best" theory. I wanted with every duct in my body to give the best to my babies, but whenever I'd consult with a breastfeeding expert, she'd overwhelm me with the idea of demand feeding and the ease of nursing two babies at once. These women were not my kind. They belonged to a different tribe—the one that pushes babies out in bathtubs, eats homegrown vegetables, and uses cloth diapers. I fell prey to their boob hype, but when I kindly asked them to *show* me exactly how I was supposed to latch on two babies at once, they couldn't.

"Oh, the football hold or cross them over one another," they'd say with a smile that made me want to throw a football at their faces. I would ask about milk production, pumping, feeding at the same time versus feeding separately. I was a front row star student in baby care logic; I needed to know how, why, how long, and what the protocol was if all of my "what ifs" happened so I could write my lists and plan my days. They, along with all the twin pregnancy books, fed me the same line: "Feed your babies on demand and you'll give your little bundles all they need (*leaving zero time for taking care of the house*). Sleep when your baby sleeps (*fifteen two-hour naps a day?*), and take advantage of all the help your friends and family offer you (*if those offers haven't come rolling in, does it mean that I'm a new parent loser?)*"

Let me clarify that, over the years, I've asked many twin moms if this was their experience, and none has confirmed this prescribed scenario to be realistic. Clearly, the job I had ahead of me required more hours in the day than existed, and I was the only person in my family and social circle who had twins. All I knew was what my mom and grandma told me about babies, and I had to make do with that.

"You'll figure it out, every new mom does. At least you have disposable diapers; we had to use cloth diapers," they lamented. They made it sound easy, all the while knowing that they'd hidden their neon signs because they wanted grand and great grand-babies! I decided to be a designer pioneer of moms of multiples. All I had were the "breast is best" ladies rooting me on to be a human milk machine and my mom by my side for moral support (for only two weeks, because my dad whisked her off to Florida every winter). Thank goodness Tom proved to be the greatest newbie dad I could ever ask for. He learned how to change little diapers in the hospital and followed my lead through the whole adventure. He didn't take time off work, but he recognized that I couldn't do it alone on three hours of sleep a day, so he insisted that I call my cousin to come a few times a week until my mom returned in the spring.

The "friends and family" plan the books talked about whereby these people were supposed to bring meals and hours of help were non-existent. We were financially secure, so people must have assumed that we'd hire help. And that was okay, however the real problem was that it wasn't in my nature to *need* help. I come from a long line of hard-working middle-class parents and grandparents, so nanny was *not* in my vocabulary.

There was one book I found helpful (besides Jenny McCarthy's *Belly Laughs*) called *Baby Wise*. It taught me how to encourage the coveted sleep-through-the-night schedule. It went against all the "breast is best" rules, and that alone was enough to light my fire. Noah and Emma ate every three hours from the moment they woke up in the morning until they went down for the night. No demand feeding here; I was in control. They ate. They played, which meant they were awake for an hour. They slept. I stuck to this routine so religiously that had it been the P90X program, I would have been infomercial success story royalty. During the first few weeks, I encountered every feeding problem imaginable. In the end, after receiving some good advice from my neighbor who was a mother of four, I boxed up the ugly nursing bras and settled on formula bottle-feeding.

Firing the breasts changed everything, and I started to feel like myself within a month. Before long, I could feed, burp, and change diapers during an episode of *Everybody Loves Raymond* in the middle of the night without waking up Tom. After eight very long weeks, all four of us were getting our zzz's. I was proudly taking care of everyone, making family meals, doing laundry, working-out, and running my errands with the babies in tow.

A month later, we were back in Naples, prepared to make the aforementioned Prada purchase. This trip marked my official graduation into motherhood. I embraced my neon sign and accepted the mission of being The Mom. This was something I could do—not without stress, but I knew that if I stayed one step ahead, I'd get through, just like a Friday night rush during the years of waiting tables. As a time period of fast-paced, overwhelming, and (sometimes near panic attack) multi-tasking, my new career was an eternal Friday night rush. I was expected to be attentive and kind, meet every need, think fast during emergencies, bus and clean everything to the point of exhaustion, and be prepared for the two-minutes-til-close diners at all times. The only difference was that I was in love with my patrons, and my tips consisted of sweet gummy smiles, squeaks of joy, content moments holding sleeping babies, and the peace of mind that came with knowing that they were happy and healthy, and my list was getting tackled.

The Friday night rush in Tomorrowland served as the real root of my desire for that beautiful Prada bag. I'd never worked so hard in my entire life or looked so unlike "me." I needed that bag to get me through whatever was coming next. Besides epic diaper bag shopping, Naples introduced us to the phenomenon of old lady stalkers and unwanted publicity. Whether by water, kiosk, or a romantic table by the pier, females over sixty-five were twins magnets. The double infant car seats were like catnip to these weathered women, and they quickly became a nuisance as they interrupted our family time with zero hesitation and a scripted line of questions.

"Are they yours?" *Of course, why would we be dining out with someone else's newborns?*

"Are they twins?" *No, they are a year apart.*

"Are they identical?" *Okay, ladies, identical twins are always the same sex; think about how ridiculous this question is!*

"Did you use fertility treatments or are they natural?" *Check please!?*

At my breaking point, I'd create a baby emergency that signaled that the interview was over. The attention was very kind, however it was depleting us of both niceness and time, so we came home from Florida with old lady scare tactics and rules for public outings. Our new pace was fast, and we didn't stop for anyone. If we saw the matching activewear coming our way with rouged cheeks and set hair, we immediately engaged in very important spousal conversation. This course of action worked every time and saved us hours of paparazzi questions in enemy territory.

Summer quickly approached, and Tom and I embraced our instant family of four during the warm months. Our evenings were filled with long walks around the lake, enjoying bath and bedtime routine with the babies, and getting them tucked in right on schedule, leaving us with time to sit on the patio with a glass of wine or watch a movie in our home theater. Life was good. My parents had migrated back from the south, and my mom came over a couple of days a week to help.

Little Emma needed physical therapy for Torticollis, a condition she developed in utero because her head was lodged in my pelvis. Poor baby, her brother was a uterus hog *and* woke her up even before she was born. My mom and I would take the babies to therapy, go to the mall, and stop at Whole Foods for a week's worth of groceries. During one of these outings, I remember buckling myself into the driver's seat of my Dodge Durango and turning to Mom in a moment of gratitude.

"I'm fortunate to be able to shop here and buy healthy food for my family. And go to the mall when I need something without worrying about a budget. And live in such a beautiful home that is practically paid for. Tom told me that if the world came to an end and he didn't have a job, he could work at McDonald's and still support us. That's how financially stable we are," I said, feeling a little guilty over such an admission, but I could tell my mom anything. She smiled, and we pondered that reality for a few seconds in silence. As I sat in my leather driver's seat, in control of the schedule, the babies, and the grocery budget, a flash of the worst-case scenario invaded my moment, and I prayed it away like a bad dream.

CHAPTER 5

ABOUT FACE

They say you make your first impression about someone within seven seconds. When I met Tom, I could *feel* his goodness. As we walked through his new home and undertook the design process, I admired who he was based not on his success but his integrity. I cringed when I found out that he lived at home because the over-twenty-five cellar-dweller bracket meant "lazy freeloader" or "student loan lifer." Tom debunked my theory when he shared the real reason he'd stayed with his father since graduating from college. After they lost his mom, his dad had triple bypass surgery. His elderly grandmother lived with them and needed care as well. I envisioned him helping his frail Biggy in and out of the house or running to the grocery store every week. This man put the needs of his family in front of the late twenties bachelor scene he could afford, and it sealed my "goodness" vibe in an instant.

We were only a couple of years into our marriage and experiencing the circle of life in ways we prayed for (starting a family), ways we accepted (it was a *lot* of work), and ways that topped anyone's list of worst nightmares. A few months before Noah and Emma were born, our lives had changed in an instant with a phone call from Tom's brother while we were vacationing in Traverse City. Can you imagine answering the phone only to hear, "Dad's dead"? He did instruct his brother to pull off the road before he delivered the shocking news. It was devastating, and I can't imagine the shock that was running through his brother's body. You know that instinctive worst fear that creeps into your gut during moments of high alert? I can attest to the fact that the accidental death of a parent is one of the most painful tragedies we had to endure, and it left my sweet husband without his best friend, co-worker, and the grandfather of his children. The last trimester of my pregnancy was dark for Tom, and a decade later I am inspired and filled with admiration when I reflect on how beautifully he handled new fatherhood, taking such good care of two lives that came into the world after such a horrible loss.

When Noah and Emma were seven months old, we found out that our number three was on the way and embraced that new life with pure joy. My mom mojo cranked through another healthy nine months as I chased my cruisers around the house. I had one hiccup, an appendectomy fifteen weeks into the pregnancy. One step forward, two back, I endured the surgery and found a loyal babysitter to pick up the slack while I healed. She was a nanny for a local family, a big-boned, tall woman in her sixties, and I trusted her from the first time I returned from the grocery store and she greeted me totally relaxed in the foyer with one baby under each arm. A little quirky, she was exactly the help I needed while I prepared to have three babies under fifteen months old after another C-section. There were moments when I had a hard time keeping a straight face, like the time she let me know that she'd lost a fake fingernail somewhere on the main floor and denied leaving her Fixodent on our powder room sink, but she was so much better than a teen glued to her mobile phone. We embraced our own Mrs. Doubtfire with secret smirks.

It was the second week of May 2006 when I arrived back at Beaumont Hospital for my second hotel stay (the hospital was the closest I'd get to a vacation at that point). Tom and I happily welcomed our feisty little baby girl, Isabelle Maria. She weighed about seven pounds, and I was thrilled to experience the beauty of *one* newborn. I had a private, serene room with a view on the mommy/baby floor along with my favorite nurses, Darla and (the infamous) Gloria. I loved my nurses. I made it very clear that I needed to rest during my stay, leaving Tom and my mom to handle the babies on the home front. I was fully prepared for this delivery. During the last month of my pregnancy, I organized the house and wrote a one-inch thick handbook, "Taking Care of Twins for Dummies" style, which was received with a few eye rolls and secret gratitude that step-by-steps were in place for back up. This time around, I knew not to look at myself naked in the mirror for at least two months after delivery. I came prepared with my Kmart granny pants and accepted maternity clothes as part of my postpartum wardrobe for a few weeks. Isabelle completed our family. I got through the worst of my recovery, and I just needed to enjoy my babies and get back to my old self. Having three in less than fifteen months felt miraculous. God knew I wasn't a natural baby lover and therefore customized a fast-track plan. Growing up, I was the one who would politely decline the offer to "hold the baby" at family gatherings. Babies didn't feel natural; they were scary to me. Floor plans and sketches felt natural. Everyone thought I'd be the designer in the city, not a twin mom plus one, and they were humored yet impressed by my "organized design mom" style.

The first evening in my hospital room was quiet. I'd sent Isabelle to the nursery for a few hours so I could catch some sleep. After an hour of watching the news and a rerun of *Friends*, I decided to make the move to the bathroom to brush my teeth and wash my face. It took a few minutes to inch into the stark white bathroom due to post-op pain, and making it without help was a victory toward recovery. I looked in the mirror for the first time since leaving home that morning. I looked pretty good. I'd straightened my hair. My face was clean. I was going to get through this. I gently massaged my face with sensitive skin wash and bent over to splash clean. I patted my face with a rough, white, sterile smelling towel from the towel bar and grabbed the toothbrush from my toiletry bag.

What happened next was unfathomable. As I hunched over the sink brushing, I noticed that the foaming water was *falling* out of my mouth. *It's supposed to stay in there until I spit it out,* I thought. I emptied my mouth and grabbed a Dixie cup. The sip of water I took to swish around my mouth behaved like a cruel joke from an unknown source. I sipped and swished. The water simply poured out of my mouth again. I leaned closer to the mirror and touched my face. Everything *looked* normal. Maybe it was a weird reaction to all the drugs running through my body. Deciding not to panic, I pressed the red Help button for my nurse.

Within moments, Darla, the first nurse I'd met the previous year and the one I trusted most, was in the bathroom with me. She was in her early forties, petite with brown, shoulder-length hair, and she'd given me some of my favorite new mom tips, like never putting babies to sleep in a quiet home or they'd expect silence every time they napped. That suggestion had worked, and I was confident that her advice about this lazy lip action would work too.

"What's going on in here?" she asked with a sweet smile.

"I was brushing my teeth and the water started spilling out of my mouth. I have no control over it," I replied, assuming she'd have an answer. She didn't. She was calm and collected, but she didn't say anything.

"Let's get you back to bed and figure this out." She got me situated and looked at me with a little concern. "I'm going to get the MD on call to come and take a look at you."

I didn't know what to think. I still thought it was drug related. About ten minutes later, a nice female doctor in her late twenties stopped in to examine me. She tested my eyes, had me open and close my mouth and turn my head from side to side, and asked a couple of questions. She then said, "Well, we can't rule out stroke. I'm going to call in a neurologist."

A STROKE? A NEUROLOGIST? What did this hospital do to me?

Tears started rolling down my cheeks as the doctor left the room to make the call. Darla stayed by my side as I picked up the phone and called Tom. He was at home with my mom and the twins, and he was half asleep. It was after midnight. He was in the car within seconds.

"I've never seen anything like this on the mother/baby floor," the young on-call's voice rang in my ears, freaking me out. A few minutes later, a nice older gentleman came in to look at me.

"Classic case of Bell's Palsy," he diagnosed within the first minute. I hated the sound of "palsy" more than "stroke." It sounded like I had a serious medical condition I'd be living with forever. I pictured myself in a wheelchair surrounded by my three children. I'm not sure why a panic attack wasn't setting in. I attributed the lack of it to sheer shock as I looked at the doctor with tears in my eyes.

"Bell's Palsy is the inflammation of a nerve inside your left ear," he casually continued. "It's viral and can be onset by trauma, very much like shingles. It can appear after the body endures events such as car accidents or surgery." *This was not happening.* "Your symptoms will probably worsen within the next few days. Recovery takes a minimum of six to eight weeks, and in some cases, months." I had to be brave as I remembered my husband's "Dad's Dead" call and knew he'd give anything to have heard the term "Bell's Palsy" instead.

"What are the symptoms?" I quivered.

"The entire left side of your face is experiencing paralysis," *No, no, no… I can't do this or look like this…* "The severity ranges from case to case, but your eye may droop, and the left side of your face and mouth will lose muscle control. You may experience a general numbness on that side, and it's imperative that you use eye drops because your eyelid will not close on its own. This will prevent your retina from getting damaged. We can give you some steroids to help with the swelling. It has to run its course."

By that point, Tom was with me. I wanted to know the worst-case scenario. I wished I hadn't asked. Eighty percent of those affected make an almost complete recovery within the first four to six months. That meant that the other twenty percent looked like stroke victims forever. I was devastated. Tom let me bawl my eyes out. Darla left the room. He didn't have much to say in that moment, he just hugged me and tried to hide his fear. I wasn't sure how I was going to get through something so awful *and* heal from the C-section. And nurse a newborn. And take care of my two babies at home. *I can't do this.*

Every mom I know will tell you that she has stacks of photos of their first-born. I have at least two little albums of Noah and Emma that capture every waking and "unwaking" moment of the first two weeks of their lives. That practice came to a halt the minute we brought Isabelle home. There are a couple of newborn photos of her, and should I ever pull them from the moving boxes stashed deep in the basement, she will probably want to keep them but will never know that it pains me to remember any of it. I spent my second Mother's Day being wheeled out of Beaumont Hospital void of motherly love and filled with fear of what I was about to endure.

A photo of me sitting in our kitchen chair holding my newborn, my parents standing behind us, reveals solemn faces that look superimposed from a historical moment a hundred years earlier. Our minds were far from our new bundle of joy and instead worried about the fate of my face. We were happy to have a healthy baby, but the grim outlook for my days and months ahead felt like a death sentence. Just as the neurologist predicted, my symptoms worsened by the day. Tom had to pry my eyelid open to give me my drops, and I humbly allowed him to place a piece of scotch tape over my eyelid to keep it shut so I could sleep for two-hour increments through the night. Can you imagine lying down and closing your eyes, only to realize that the simple task your brain is asking of them is *out of order*? My right lid would close, but my left, until forced shut, remained open.

The left side of my face felt like I'd received enough Novocain to endure a double root canal. I'd wake up every morning and sneak to the bathroom sink to check the status of my palsy. Staring straight into the mirror, I'd touch my hand to my numb temple, cheek, and chin. Forcing a smile, I'd witness my split personality in abject horror. The right side was me—bright eye, wide smile, a tiny dimple in my right cheek. The left was paralyzed by one minuscule nerve deep within my ear that may or may not return to normal. I looked like a freak show, and my hospital diagnosis spun through my soul like a tornado of anxiety that was sucking me far away from all things good. Far from God. Far from Tom. Far from the twins. Far from my new baby. Far from ever being happy again.

What if I don't recover from this? They said there is no cure; what if I look like this forever? I would rather have a hundred pounds of pregnancy weight to lose than look like I had a stroke for the rest of my life! I am an attractive woman, used to feeling pretty; will I ever get over losing my looks? Am I vain? No! I'm not vain! I'm experiencing a REAL loss that may possibly destroy my self-esteem, my dignity, and the way the world sees me forever. I would rather have cancer than look like this. Tom would never forgive me if I said it aloud, but it's true. I know he watched his mom die a horrible death, but I would rather have someone tell me that I will be sick and experience hair loss for a few years if it meant the possibility of recovery. That doctor was so nonchalant about the whole thing. I KNOW it's not life threatening, but I would rather DIE right now...

Through my turmoil of tears, I pathetically stood at the sink, watching the confusing display of emotions, half of my face in distress, the other frozen in time. Unable to view myself any longer, I fumbled into the walk-in-closet and closed the door. Leaning against it, I sunk to the floor for an all-out meltdown. I was gripping for a reason to come out, but my fear continued its downward spiral as the reality of my stressors robbed me of any sense of control. Bell's Palsy. Twin toddlers. A colic-driven newborn. Healing from a C-section.

Raging hormones. Lactation. Painkillers. Steroids. Eye-drops. Old lady underpants. Post baby weight. Sleep deprivation. The house. The meals. Feeding the kids. The diapers. *The diapers alone will total more than two hundred a week, a grueling job in and of itself! Nobody can do this but me. I have to get over this for the day. They all need me.*

A flash of inspiration calmed my storm for a moment as I remembered the story of Jacqui, who captivated me during an episode of *Oprah* a couple of years earlier. The Venezuelan car crash and burn survivor was once vibrant, young, and stunningly gorgeous. Completely disfigured, she bravely told Oprah that she allows herself one five-minute pity party cry a day, then picks up and moves forward, her beautiful soul trapped inside an unrecognizable body without a face or hair, and with only stumps for hands. She was the bravest woman I'd ever seen, and in this lonely, dark moment of my morning ritual, I'd draw on her strength, scold myself for allowing my condition to destroy my day, and pray for the power to heal, care, and enjoy the beautiful baby I'd been gifted, along with her siblings. *There are always people out there who are worse off than me. I can. I will.*

I did. For fourteen long days, I carried on after my closed closet cry and survived each with hope that the next would bring a sign of progress that I might recover from Bell's Palsy. On the fifteenth day, my symptoms stopped progressing and stood still for a week. Then, miraculously, the horrible view in the mirror began to clear up ever so slowly each morning. Tom was there to help me every step of the way, and Noah and Emma, although a bit leery of their not-so-normal looking mom, were champion siblings. Isabelle on the other hand, was feisty inside and out. The pressure of her need for only me to hold her, walking her around the house until she fell asleep, was exhausting, and my plan to enjoy my "one baby" was tainted by the predicament of my health.

On the sixth week, my morning smile check revealed the most beautiful person I'd ever seen: *the real me.* My face was finally balanced, and the Bell's Palsy had disappeared into a tiny fear deep within that would haunt me for the rest of my life, knowing that it could possibly come back. In that moment, I embraced my reflection with the thankfulness that a survivor of any storm would appreciate. Even though it hadn't been even two months since giving birth, I broke my rule and took a look at the rest of me. For the first time in my life, I didn't focus on the extra five pounds or, in this case, the extra fifteen. I didn't care about the nursing bra or my blobby abdomen filled with stretch marks. The only thing I saw in my reflection that morning was my smile. My perfect, even smile. It brought a sunny ray of light into my soul. It hinted at my happy heart, my love for my family, and my desire to be a wonderful mom. I wasn't perfect or even beautiful by society's standards. I was naked of all things pretty. My body could be fixed. My face felt like a gift. I admired my straight-out-of-bed expression for a long moment without internal criticism. I remembered Tom confessing that he knew I was "the one" in those first seven seconds. I never believed him, but maybe he *did* know. Maybe he felt it all through my smile.

CHAPTER 6

MOTHERHOOD, MASS & THE TRIP FROM HELL

"Hello, I'm calling for Hollie," said a friendly voice.

"This is she," I replied, holding Isabelle on my hip while unloading the dishwasher. The rainbow of mismatched little plastic sippy cups, bottles, and bowls were piled in the top rack for the third time that day.

"Oh, hi. My name is Julie Anderson and I'm your local contact for our twin play group through Beaumont Hospital," she started. I knew exactly what she wanted. Since I'd had Noah and Emma, a nice parent would check in on me now and then to invite me to join their group. I declined in the early months because the thought of packing them up by myself (Tom worked late most nights) to go plop them on the floor with other twin babies who were unaware of their surroundings seemed like a waste of time. I politely told Julie that I appreciated her call and it sounded nice, however the logistics would not work for my family. And that was that when it came to support groups.

I was so busy from Day One keeping up the status quo that extra-curricular socialization was not an activity I considered. I was killing it at home since healing from the Bell's. Plus, I didn't just have twin toddlers. I had a newborn as well as the house, which I maintained to perfection possibly even more efficiently than I did before having kids. The adventures of life with three kids under two did not stop there. Tom and I lived exactly as we had before they came into the picture. We traveled luxury-style during the cold months and Foss-style throughout the summer. I grew up camping. My Dad grew up camping. Tom embraced camping simply because it reminded him of growing up on the canal and sleeping overnight on his boat. I gladly managed all travel expectations and powered through, knowing it was just a season, and I was done having babies.

I thrived on the challenge of keeping up with life. I was an overachiever, and for me, productivity defined my success. Days were filled with feeding, changing diapers (twenty-eight per day to be exact), scheduled naps, feeding, more diapers, more naps, making dinner, dishes, laundry, and the bedtime routine, which started promptly at 8PM. I'd squeeze in meal planning, workouts, errands, and outings with precision to ensure happy mom and happy babies. My late-night ritual was sitting in the library with Tom watching Jim Cramer's *Mad Money*. Every husband has his thing, whether it's sports, working out, or loving a hobby—building model airplanes, for example. My husband happens to be a die-hard stock market guy. Tom and Jim taught me about bulls, bears, and *Booyah* cheers when we'd make a quick $5,000 at the push of a button. I liked being part of his passion, and I liked the beat of our collective drum. It was all in a day's work. And it was good.

Social time for me, and for us as a couple, most often involved our Catholic friends Todd and Claudia. They were the first of our friends to start a family, so naturally I ran to Claudia for advice. She made it look easy. When I was pregnant with the twins I stopped by her cute little bungalow for lunch and registry ideas. I walked in as she had her one-year-old in a high chair, homemade chicken noodle soup on the stove, and brownies made from scratch. I couldn't believe she could do all that *and* take care of a baby! Besides being young, beautiful, and a great friend, she was amazing (and still is), and I decided to follow her mom style without a second thought.

So, as we had our babies, our two families found it fun and easy to spend time together, as we were also devoted Catholics in the sense that "we" considered weekly Mass a privilege, not an obligation. I emphasize "we" given my background—I was baptized in the church but raised Protestant and planned to stay that way. This didn't pose a problem when we got married. I agreed to Mass, and Tom agreed to attend my non-denominational church of choice once in a while, keeping us content on both sides. Since I always had a plan, on the God front it would be to convert my man from his lukewarm holy water ways, eventually landing our family in a church without so much ritual and obligation.

There was one thing that made it hard for me to be a *true* protester of Catholicism, and that was the fond memory of attending Mass with Grandma and Papa when I was a little girl. I would often stay overnight on Saturdays (bowling night for my parents, part of all things early eighties). Situated about two hundred yards from our house, Grandma and Papa lived in a cozy brick ranch decorated with Belgian keepsakes and her beautiful oil-on-canvas paintings that would be handed down to me and my children. Yes, she could sew *and* paint with her European elegance and style.

During those sleepovers she'd make popcorn over an open flame and we'd watch *Dance Fever*, *The Muppet Show*, and *The Love Boat* before my "blue room" tuck-in (the walls were covered in light blue floral mini print wallpaper with vertical stripes). The sheets were clean and crisp, and the painting hanging above the headboard featured a cobblestone street with Clydesdale horses pulling a carriage. I used to gaze at it and envision what it would be like to stand on that dusty ground at the turn of the century. She'd tuck me in, and with the pad of her finger, mark the sign of the cross on my forehead. I was asleep within minutes.

Sunday morning was an early rise. Grandma would help me get dressed and I was allowed to sit in Papa's chair at the head of the table to eat my fried egg and toast. He left early to set up coffee and donuts at St. Rita's, and I loved the smell of his aftershave lingering in the hall near his small bathroom. When Grandma and I would get to church, she'd sneak me into the basement kitchen so I could select my custard-filled donut covered with chocolate frosting. She'd set it aside, placing a white napkin over it as if it were hiding, ensuring that it was mine.

Then we'd go up to their usual pew, about six rows back on the left. A small balcony with an organ overlooked the sanctuary, and I loved turning around in my seat to spy on the organist playing the hymns. Like clockwork, the old man a few rows behind would wink at me, which frustrated me because I could never figure out how to wink back. The four-year-old me spent many 8AM Sunday services snuggled next to my grandma while enjoying the formalities and working on my wink. My early childhood memories of the Catholic Church were incredibly fond and precious, which made the idea of raising my children Catholic palatable, even if I didn't believe it all.

* * *

Isabelle was seven months old when Christmas rolled around that year, and since I'd been pregnant the two years prior, I assumed that adding babies to my old-school holiday prep was not only possible, it was essential. I couldn't give up my holiday traditions if I didn't have the "with child" condition.

I went full force with decorations, gifting, cooking, and making my famous chocolate walnut fudge, complete with samples packaged and sent across the country to friends who lived as far away as California. We took on the cumbersome task of going to see Santa, and I discovered that gift-wrapping dozens of baby toys was tedious, not to mention the removal of packaging and assembly. We also hosted Christmas Eve and Christmas Day dinners, went to Midnight Mass, and booked a trip to Phoenix, since leaving town the day after Christmas was Tom's family tradition. We recruited my parents to join us so we'd have help with the kids.

The day after Christmas, I found myself in a heap of toys, trash, dirty dishes, laundry, babies, and a husband off to work with the expectation that I'd have the family packed for his dream trip to Phoenix. For the first time since I'd married Tom, I felt like the task at hand was more than I could handle. I wasn't sure where to begin. Clean? Laundry? Make a list? I was overwhelmed, and the baby noise clouded my usually focused thinking. My mind went blank. Within minutes, my pulse was racing, and my face was tingling. *Bell's Palsy! What if this stress was the onset of another episode?* I ran into the powder room and flashed a smile check. I couldn't tell if it looked normal, but just the *thought* of it threw me into hyperventilation.

I jumped on the phone with my mom, who got out her mama bear claws and called Tom, then sent me to the family doctor. Poor Tom. He had no idea that I was suffering from "perfect-hostess-type-A-parent-syndrome." Meeting me in the exam room, we were relieved to find out that I was experiencing nothing more than a classic panic attack. I left in tears with my husband and prescriptions for heavy drugs to chillax for my travels.

Against my better judgment, we continued on to Phoenix the next day as planned. The trip was cursed from the moment we arrived. What was supposed to be a poolside vacation turned into a low fifties, jackets-required trip, and we spent three days going to local zoos. Noah ended up with the puke/diarrhea flu, and Emma followed shortly thereafter to round out our last couple of days there. We had sick kids who couldn't sleep, a seven-month-old who wanted to be continually held, puke-covered laundry that required a walk to the coin-operated machines, and a grandpa and grandma who made us promise never to ask them along on air travel trips as baby helpers.

A few days later, we found ourselves pushing our sick babies through the airport, eager to make it all end. Emma, my little eternal optimist and animal lover, was in the doublewide stroller next to her brother as we headed to our terminal. This creative and unique little girl of mine looked up at the ceiling, and was, I imagine, replaying one of her zoo visits in her head as she howled like a wolf. She then projectile vomited all over the place. When she was done, she looked at us as if nothing had happened. Thank God for Emma and her easygoing demeanor, which brought a second of comic relief as I figured out how to de-puke her ride. Tom held her on the plane. My parents sat one row in front of us with Isabelle on their laps, and I tried to comfort Noah. The poor kid was still sick. He really had it bad. It had moved from upper to lower-level flu, and all he could do was cry. Of course, we were on a four-hour red eye, and I had the honor of being *that* mom with *that* kid. He cried every single way he could to show his discomfort, and I tried every trick in the book to calm him down. Nothing worked. I decided to take him to the bathroom to check his diaper. Carrying a thirty-pound toddler on one hip and my twenty-five-pound diaper bag (Prada does turbulence) on the opposite shoulder, squeezing by irritated travelers to my Stall of Hell was one of my worst mom moments. People were mean. They were rolling their eyes and letting out sighs of irritation. I was used to being praised everywhere I went for my well-behaved babies, so this was breaking me. I crammed my kid, my Prada, and myself in the dirty little bathroom and discovered that my poor son was covered in a burning wet explosion and had made a mess of his entire outfit. By that point, my mom was outside the bi-fold door for backup, and we managed to find something dry for him to wear.

For a mom, *nothing* is worse than a crying baby you cannot comfort. Nothing, that is, except experiencing it in public, surrounded by strangers who want to sleep. I held him back in my middle row seat and suffered through the rest of the flight brewing with anger that I'd allowed this trip to happen in the first place. I found out later that morning, once I hauled my three to the pediatrician on zero sleep, that Noah had a double ear infection to top off his flu. God bless all future moms of crying babies at 30,000 feet. This trip marked a significant turning point for me. *I couldn't do it all.* I'd popped out my entire family in fifteen months instead of the six-year plan we'd dreamed of back when we were dating. Christmas couldn't remain the same. The most wonderful time of the year had been tainted by motherhood and that giant neon sign. I needed to figure out how to minimize my stress during the holidays. Travel had to change. I had to understand my boundaries and be realistic about what I could handle to ensure that I wouldn't have panic attacks. Moving forward, I stood my ground when it came to air travel, eliminating it from our life all together until we had kids who could walk themselves, their luggage, and their little butts to a bathroom to puke in the potty like pros.

CHAPTER 7

THE BIG HOUSE

"Are you driving by it? Does it look nice?" he prodded with excitement from his desk at work.

"It's not just nice," I replied, "It's enormous and way out of our budget. This neighborhood is nuts!" I was in the car with my mom and Tom had me drive by a house that had sparked his interest. It was mid-September and we'd just accepted an offer on the bachelor pad. A great offer. We took it as well as the condition that we had to be out in thirty days. During one of our trips to Florida that spring (I know I swore off air travel, but the chance to get away during the gloom of early spring was hard to pass up), we decided to list our house to see if we could get top dollar. It was a beautiful home, but the living space was too small for our family of five. The kitchen had zero prep area, and I moved our little round breakfast table to the foyer so we could squeeze a rectangular Parsons table in the nook, which barely sat six. The baby gear took up the rest of the space, and Noah and Emma had outgrown their gated play area. The floorplan was unsafe to let them have free rein with our high-end furnishings, steel railings, and man-cave taking up the lower level, complete with the Jacuzzi death trap. We hoped to find a traditional two story with bedrooms upstairs and more living space on the main floor.

Another driving factor was that our neighborhood fell just outside the Bloomfield Hills School district, the best in the state, and at that point we figured we should upgrade to a home within the boundaries so we would have the option of public or private schools. We listed in the spring, and I required a day's advance notice for house showings. We didn't have them often, but when we did, I created a beautiful illusion of the original design, minus the Baker dining furniture, which had been neatly placed in storage along with the baby gates. My presentation was perfect. It was clean, strategically staged, complete with fresh flowers on the kitchen table and Tom's favorite smooth jazz setting the mood through our built-in speakers. Maria Chirco, the ex-wife of one of Detroit's most prominent developers, entered our home and fell in love. She knew the architect, loved the design, and appreciated all the upgrades. It was perfect for her new beginning with her boys, and within days we accepted her offer.

The day after the drive-by phone call, I found myself at the front door of 34 Pine Gate Drive with Tom and our realtor. The house sat on a hill at the highest point of the neighborhood. The mailbox was a miniature of the estate, and the driveway led up to a paver circular front entrance. There was a four-car garage to the right, and the front yard was a hillside of meticulously landscaped tiers of enormous boulders, flowerbeds, perennials, groundcover, and small trees. A large terra cotta brick colonial estate with limestone surrounding the front entrance and windows, it looked much like a version of our starter home on steroids. The dark mahogany front door had sidelights and a palladium window above that exposed a three-tier brass chandelier. To the left of the entrance was a beautiful chimney flanked by two-story windows. To the right was a large bay window with a copper-plated roof, and a large arched bedroom window above. About eight feet behind the bay was another two-story window, assumed to be the laundry room, and finally the garage. The roof had high peaks and stone-gray shingles; it easily could have been a third floor if it were an older home, but I knew it was just an attic. It was about ten years old, and I couldn't wait to walk through it.

"Hello, I'm Joan, nice to meet you," a petite blonde realtor greeted us as she opened the door. We stepped onto a beautiful cream-colored marble foyer floor. The floating staircase to the left was very grand as it wound to the second floor. It also extended to a lower level with an open mahogany railing and white spindles. There was a handsome wood paneled library to the right; opposite was the formal living room, which opened up to the formal dining room. We started our tour on this side of the house. The double crown moldings and custom millwork were stunning. The west wall of the living room was a ten-foot bay window flanked by custom glass-shelved bookcases. The carpet under foot was thick and plush. I cringed at its light cream color and its run all the way through the formal dining room. It reminded me of the mid-century wall-to-wall carpet craze, when it was all the rage to cover hardwood floors. Very dated. Easy fix.

We moved into the formal dining room, which was filled with a large Queen Anne dining table, chairs, and three-piece china cabinet. The chandelier hung from a medallion surround and hosted hundreds of glistening crystals. Both rooms boasted layers of heavy chintz draperies. All floral. All 1985. All had to go. I must have been looking at $20,000 worth of special order, professionally installed draperies.

"Wow, these draperies are nice, right?" Tom whispered in my ear as we passed through the butler's pantry, walk-in pantry, and into the kitchen. I shot him my evil eye. *Are you nuts? This looks like the death wish of Laura Ashley, assuming she'd want to be surrounded by her own designs while laid out.* I glanced at the bay window adorned with closed sheers, chintz panels, swags, and layers of rosettes. Perfect for a casket. *If I end up here, these are getting cremated.*

The kitchen was spacious and traditional, with white cabinets that had beautiful fluted edges, dentil crown molding, and carved fruit above a double, matching paneled Sub-Zero refrigerator. The kitchen sink was nestled under a six-foot wide window with a nice view of the backyard and bluestone patio. Dark hunter green marble countertops covered the L-shaped workspace and gigantic island. I cringed a bit at the trademark 1990s selection (not such an easy fix), but quickly envisioned the kids sitting at the counter rolling cookie dough or doing homework. Past the island was a large breakfast room that made it easy to envision the five of us sitting together for dinner over the years. To the right was a beautiful arched doorway with heavy molding that passed into the foyer and a kitchen desk with upper cabinets, and to the left a twelve-foot wide set of traditional French doors opened to the patio. There would be no squeezing into the heart of this home. I was now standing on a beautiful dark oak floor, which spanned from the dining room all the way to the great room. Classic. Love. *Thank God they did the hardwood right.*

The breakfast area opened into the great room, which had a two-story, twenty-two-foot ceiling. It was magnificent! There was a large fireplace facing the backyard with custom white woodwork all the way to the ceiling, topped by a broken pediment. Two-story windows covered the rest of the walls, and I fell in love with the wide second staircase opening up to the second floor that was positioned straight ahead. There was a landing halfway up the staircase joined by a full-height palladium window, which was anchored by a bench that would be the perfect spot for a young girl to snuggle up with a book. The view showcased the lush green side yard next to the garage. The great room and landing also had a significant investment of deathbed window wear. Burgundy damask trimmed with hunter green and gold fruity floral. This time they'd gone circa 1992, which annoyed me since the home was built in 1998. *They either hired a designer who was selecting dated fabric or one who cared more about making the sale than the integrity of their work. Or, even more tragic, both parties had bad taste.* Clearly, this pained me.

"These draperies are nicer, right?" Tom snuck in as we checked out the expansive mudroom, walk-in closet, mud bath, and laundry room. *Yeah, nice enough to make play clothes for the children.*

"Just because they look expensive doesn't mean I *like* them," I snapped back in an expressive whisper. "But I LOVE THIS SPACE!" I mouthed without sound.

"Don't say anything out loud! Act like you don't like it!" he coached with an elbow to my shoulder.

We followed the petite realtor up the back stairs to a small loft area and large bedroom to the left, situated over the garage. To the right was a hallway featuring a nice bedroom that faced the backyard and opened to the main staircase. The large, open plan led us left to the front bedroom over the library and then straight ahead to the master. All the bedrooms were full suites and full of 4x4 mauve, green, and blue Corian tiles, which likely wouldn't be making it onto my already lengthy reno list for at least twenty years. The only consolation was the immaculate condition of it all. *The kids will trash it over the years anyway,* I thought.

We glided over the cream carpet, through the foyer below and into the master, again doused in (take a wild guess) heavy floral red and green drapery. Thick polyester sheers blocked the bay window's view and were flanked by layers of the now trademark chintz swags and panels. It reminded me of a funeral home. The Laura Ashley casket replaced the bed for a moment, and I shooed away the vision while secretly making the sign of the cross in my head. *Focus! This will not stay! The architecture is beautiful!* The front of the room featured another beautiful fireplace, tall narrow windows, and a set of plaid country French upholstered chairs with matching ottoman. The bedding matched the draperies, and the walls were covered in heavy, faded burgundy wallpaper. Classic Chippendale furniture filled the suite and screamed the suburban mom and dad taste from every 80s movie I'd seen growing up. The bathroom was covered in the same dark green marble as the kitchen (were they too naïve to know that the builder got a great deal on it because *it was outdated?*), a large shower, a jetted tub in the bay window, and double sinks that sat on white cabinetry. A short hall sported a vanity and his and hers walk-in closets. I did want my own closet.

We took the main staircase back down to the foyer and down to the basement, which was fully finished with a family room, workout room, playroom, full bath, billiard room open to a full kitchen/bar, and a long hallway with more storage rooms that led to the back staircase. It was amazing. This was play space for the kids. The lower-level carpet was also thick and plush, and of course, dark hunter green with a salmon and beige floral pattern that reminded me of a hotel conference room. *I really need a synonym for floral right about now.* The realtor had gone upstairs to give us some privacy. I looked at Tom, and he looked at me, and we were on the same page. I think.

"This is amazing, but out of budget," I started.

"Yeah, but it's been on the market for a year and the owners live out of state; they want to unload this," he plotted.

"It's huge. I can't even afford to clean the whole thing every week," my budget kicked in.

"But we need more space," he coaxed.

"It looks like someone puked flowers in every room! We'd have to remodel everything as the kids get older," I pushed back.

"Big deal; walls are easy. Even the master bath can be upgraded to what we're used to." He was working my downside design thoughts.

"True. The floor plan is perfect," I dreamed aloud.

"We can sell the condo, sell the plane, and with our investment properties in California, we'll be adding to our income. This is doable if they come down to our price," he said. "And it's move-in ready. That's worth it right there. This could be our forever home," he coaxed. I was staring at the busy, dated carpet and thinking about looking at it every day. Could I live in a dream house knowing we wouldn't remodel it for a long time? Yes. The kids would destroy anything new, so it would be natural to decorate by the room as they got older.

I digested his proposal of offsetting the cost by selling his hard-earned assets. The condo: a ski-in/ski-out dream retreat nestled at the bottom of one of the most desired ski resorts in the world, Whistler-Blackcomb in British Columbia. A prized purchase when we met, we had spent many family Christmases and summers there, the last just weeks before his father passed. Our little love nest had sat empty due to our new life as parents combined with the unrealistic cost of air travel and lodging for a family of four. Now five. I could live without Whistler. And the plane. Flying was my husband's passion. He was an amazing pilot with IFR certification and hours of schooling, private lessons, and test flights under his belt. It represented a time in his life when he needed to immerse himself into something as he grieved the loss of his mother. Sadly, as exciting as it was to have at our disposal while we were dating, his little four-seater Mooney was collecting dust and would continue to do so as Tom was needed on the home front and his flight certification was already outdated. The plane and the associated hangar rent were as much as the condo, and it would make for a nice down payment on our dream home. Worth it.

The investment properties in Mammoth, California included two under construction units at a new ski resort, and they were scheduled to close within the year. The rental income from those alone could pay for almost half of our new monthly mortgage, and even if it didn't, we could always cash out and recoup an enormous amount of cash. These were our wild cards, but either way, they made an offer on this house a sensible next step for our family and fast move predicament. Tom was always on target when it came to money.

I then thought about the added cost of a larger home. I could do a bit more of the cleaning myself. We'd have to spend much more on landscaping; every inch of the one-acre property was covered in manicured beds. But our future with the kids meant less travel, and that would beef up our home budget. I was sold.

"I think we should make a ridiculously low offer and see what happens," he interrupted my pro/con contemplation in a low voice.

"Let's do it." I was in.

Within minutes, we proceeded to the Coney Island across the street with our realtor and wrote our offer, $500,000 *less* than the asking price. They would never take it. My parents were at the house to watch the kids for our anniversary weekend getaway. We drove up north with butterflies in our stomachs, and later that night we received word that they'd dropped their price a little. They wanted to play the game. Over the next twenty-four hours, we played the sport otherwise known as "they didn't say no." Tom would get off the phone with our realtor and say, "They didn't accept our counter, but they didn't say no." On Saturday night, we got *the call*. After we inched up a little on our end, they dropped to our final offer and accepted it. We were going to move into the dream house! And we had two weeks to get it done.

Fourteen days later, we shipped the kids to my parents' house and began our two-day move. I single-handedly packed over 250 boxes; we had two college students pack the garage and basement. We were moving everything in storage that we'd kept from his dad's home, and it needed a room to rest in until Tom was ready to go through it. It took two full days, six movers, my directing, and Tom filling in wherever he was needed to get it done. It was so much more work than I anticipated; cleaning the old house once it had been vacated was crazy in and of itself. But we got it done.

I'll never forget Maria coming to the front door of her new home so we could officially hand her the keys. Tom opened the door, and I took one look at her beautiful Italian face and sweet smile and burst into tears. It all hit me at once. Seven years ago, we'd met and fallen in love in this home, and now I was leaving part of my life behind. So many good years, and *poof*, they became only memories. My eyes hurt like I'd been on a red-eye flight with screaming babies for five days. Maria grabbed me and we hugged; she had her own overwhelming stress of downsizing to fit into my home, her divorce, her ailing mother, and her four boys. We bonded on the front porch of the bachelor pad. Sometimes you connect with people in strange ways; Maria and I didn't know each other, but we understood one another as though we were best friends. All with a hug. And we have been friends ever since. She ended up loving that home so much that she redecorated and landscaped the backyard to look like a resort and told me she'd never move. She's always insisted that it is "our" home, open for Gyarmati visitors any time.

On the third day, my parents brought the kids to their big new house. It was the first week of October 2007. Noah and Emma were coming up on three and Isabelle on eighteen months. The kitchen and great room ended up needing seven baby gates to contain my little toddlers. The first week I was home alone with the kids was horrible. I was so drained from the physical labor, stress, and chaos of living amongst boxes that it overwhelmed me to tears every day. I couldn't take care of kids *and* settle into a house that was twice the size of my old home. Needless to say, I ended up back at the family doctor, who gently smiled and reminded, "You are working too hard. Remember: *you can't do it all.* You've put yourself into another panic attack state and can't catch your breath." I reluctantly walked out with another round of prescriptions and yet another lesson that nobody was watching out for me. That as a doer and a go-getter goal-setter, I was susceptible to taking on more than I should, and without self-made boundaries, I would continue this sequence at the cost of my health and the happiness I longed to have as a wife and mom.

CHAPTER 8

AND GOD LAUGHED

It took a couple of months to settle into our new home. We loved it. Thankfully, I only popped pills for a week before I chilled out and stashed them high up in the corner cabinet. The kids had plenty of space to run around, the kitchen was babyproofed, and I gated off the bottom of the basement staircase so I could put them down there to play, allowing me to sneak up to change a load of laundry or keep whatever household tasks I had moving.

The basement staircase was identical to its beautiful, expansive counterpart that led to the upstairs balcony. It was fabulous because it was open to the foyer and about six feet wide at the base, so the kids didn't seem so far away, and I could hear everything all the way from my bedroom. Plus, moms really *do* have eyes in the back of their heads; they're called ears. When you have three toddlers, your hearing becomes bionic. You know every sound, what's being explored, who's exploring it, if it's something that you can ignore or if you'll have yet another interrupted moment. One time, Isabelle was bawling her eyes out standing at the gate and I knew she wasn't hurt, but I had to see what was wrong. Poor baby; she was holding the white spindles to the gate in misery. Her brother had taken every matchbox car he owned and stuffed them down the front and back of her onesie!

The bottom five steps of the basement stairs became my office. I could fold clothes, make to-do lists and grocery lists and phone calls, and even use the laptop without little hands getting in the way. This new freedom allowed me to dip my little finger back into design, and for the first time in three years, I took on some small commercial jobs to satiate my passion.

Get-togethers with Todd and Claudia still topped our list of favorite pastimes. By that point, they had three boys. Once you hit the three-kid mark, you realize that your only option is to find people with just as much crazy as you have, and Claudia made it easy to co-exist as great mom friends. She'd been an elementary teacher before full-time motherhood, which was like winning a golden ticket when it came to keeping kids happy. The two of us were the perfect team; we loved the logistics of schedules, organized play, run-around time, feeding times, and backup plans just in case the weather got yucky. We'd shepherd the kids while our men sipped their craft beers and talked about life, church, and old-school days growing up in the 80s. Once the summer months came, Claudia and I purchased season passes to the Detroit Zoo, and we'd meet every Wednesday at 9AM with our strollers, toddlers, and runners for a two-hour self-tour (our secret was to start at the exit to avoid people traffic). We ended with picnic sack lunches, exiting before noon, which brilliantly ensured afternoon naps. Our standing Wednesday phone call those weeks was held live, and we had even more time to plot and plan how to save time, money, and keep our families happy.

I also had help from my mom at least once a week when she was in town. Grandma days were the best. My mom has always loved pre-school-aged kids; anything a four-year-old can come up with, she is game for, from making cookies, playing make-believe, Barbies, or exploring the yard for cool rocks and leaves. On these days, I'd take advantage and get my errands done, mostly grocery shopping and a trip to Costco, which was only five minutes from the house. One July afternoon, I was recouping from one of these busy trips with a cold drink at the kitchen table when the phone rang. It was Tom. The kids were off playing, and my mom was sitting across from me.

"How do you feel about a puppy?" he asked in his sparkly blue-eyed voice. I felt nothing. I was pretty happy with life the way it was and didn't feel like we were missing a thing.

"A puppy?"

"Well, there's a farm out in Metamora, and I'm looking at this ad in the paper of these cute English Springer Spaniels, and there's a black and white one that looks really cute."

"I don't know. Are the kids old enough?" Isabelle was just a tiny little snort, and I didn't know about a big dog. Tom is an animal lover. He had two different Springers growing up and was so in love with them that their name alone brought tears to his eyes. When we rented *Marley & Me*, he had to leave the room before Marley died; he refused to watch it. It was equivalent to any woman making it through the scene in *Steel Magnolias* when Sally Field is gripping the steering wheel after losing her daughter. I knew a puppy would steal his heart and his time, which was already spread thin.

"We always said we'd get a dog when the kids were big enough," he begged.

"Yeah, I guess; they'd love a puppy," I conceded. At this moment, my mom, who knew my husband and what was coming, scribbled a note on a piece of craft paper and held it up. DON'T DO IT. YOU WILL REGRET IT. This was obviously a warning of some sort, but I wasn't sure about what, exactly. We had a dog and a cat my whole life. I disregarded her signal.

"You should see this picture; he's *really* cute," Tom continued. He was in love. *Puppies ARE cute. Why should I deprive the kids of the life I had?* I caved and said yes. He thanked me and told me he was leaving work to drive out to see him—and would hopefully be bringing him home that night.

My mom's warning was like the neon motherhood-is-coming sign I wished I'd seen. A family dog was another mouth to feed, clean, and care for. "You know how much work a dog is? Everyone loves the dog, but guess who's always stuck taking care of him? The mom. You're going to be the one feeding him, walking him, taking him to the vet. Dogs are like having another kid. Do you *really* want more work around here?" she advised with visions of bathing our German Shepard in tomato juice and pulling burrs out of her fur after she chased skunks into the woods. That was a great dog. *I loved my dog.*

She had a valid point. But so did Tom. The kids should grow up with a dog. The timing felt right. We were settled in the house, I was done having babies, and a puppy was the next step to building the life we planned. Plus, it was summer—the perfect time of year to potty train him. I'd have to lay the ground rules that I was not going to be stuck doing all the work. I knew that wouldn't be the case, and my bigger concern was how much money the dog would eat into our tighter family budget. The new house was wonderful, but it took a bite out of expenses like babysitters, date nights, and little splurges like manicures and pedicures. Our vacation style had also scaled back. No more five-star hotels, but that came with the territory of toddlers anyway.

That evening, Tom proudly walked in with a white corrugated mail container, the kind you pick up from the post office after being out of town for a few weeks. In it sat the cutest little puppy I'd ever seen. He was six weeks old, black with white paws, tummy, and collar. He had soft, wavy ears and droopy little eyes that immediately called for an old-soul kind of name. He looked like he'd be mellow. Man's best friend. His little nose was spotted, and when Tom set him on the floor his paws looked like they belonged on a full-grown dog. The kids adored him, and so did I. Tom had done well, and that night after the kids were tucked in, we sat on the floor of our bathroom mulling over dog names. We both agreed that he needed a strong, European name, and we went to work thinking of old family names from Belgium and Hungary. Tom came up with his late Uncle Otto. One look at his little bear butt and sad eyes and we knew it was his. Little Otto was officially part of our family, and I was going to add "puppy trainer" to my resume.

Within the first week, I determined that puppy training was not easy. The little guy was wild and under foot at any given moment. I don't know how many times I accidentally stepped on him, but it must have been comparable to the number of puddles I had to clean up. It was like having that toddler running around who required a helicopter parent, which I clearly was not. So I decided to go back to the basics. If I could take care of multiple babies at once, then a puppy must be similar. Goal: potty train and keep him alive. And off the cream carpet. And away from my toddler. And not waste a minute because I was already punching in seventy-hour workweeks as a stay-at-home mom. I set a Pack-n-play up in the kitchen and plopped him in there when I needed him contained. I took him out to get his business done every couple of hours, and to everyone's amazement, I tucked him in for his afternoon nap in a crate in our bedroom. 1PM is naptime if you are under the age of five at my house. Tom thought I was nuts. I closed the blinds, gave him a little pat, said, "Take your nap, puppy" in a gentle voice, and closed the door behind me. What baby doesn't need a nap?

A few weeks later, I was off to Chicago with my sister-in-law for my very first mom getaway. We drove over and had a leisurely three days touring the city, shopping, and dining out. I bought my first pair of jeans that actually smoothed over my new-mom muffin top, and the word "sexy" nudged its way back into my wardrobe. I'd worked really hard that year and was close to my pre-baby weight, but the twin pregnancy did a number on my middle. To celebrate my jean victory and our last night in the city, we settled in for a casual bite on a nice patio at Navy Pier. By that point, we'd exhausted any form of conversation, and I was content with people watching. I missed the kids. Two nights would have been perfect; three was the breaking point.

"I don't want French fries!" a two-year-old screamed at her mother. This young family was sitting next to us, and they had a baby in a stroller. The mom was beautiful and blonde; her husband handsome enough and a little stressed at the public outburst. *Didn't they know that kids are crabby and tired at 7PM and should be in bed?* I caught myself in this pathetic moment of judgment and gave them the travel pass. Schedules are next to impossible if you're traveling. The dad took over coaxing his daughter with milk, nuggets, whatever he could find as she continued the constant whining. The mom now had the baby on her shoulder, and I knew they would not get to enjoy their meal. Holding babies and fighting toddlers is not only exhausting, it makes you sweaty. It's a wonder I hadn't lost more than my extra baby weight given all the grueling travel and church moments. I thought about my potty-trained twins who no longer needed a stroller. And cute little Isabelle with her copper hair and big blue eyes. My life was perfect. I had my mom break, new jeans for a date night, and a wonderful husband at home proudly taking care of the family. *Three kids, three and under! We were amazing! I was a supermom. I was designing again, and we had a dog. Model All-American dream life.* I crossed my legs and sat up straight in my chair in my proud moment, taking a delicate sip of my Pinot Grigio.

"You couldn't *pay* me to be pregnant right now," I announced in a low voice to my sister-in-law, who was also watching the sweaty young couple grappling with their kids. She smiled. We drove home the next morning, back to my perfect, upscale, suburban life in Detroit.

The following evening, I got the kids tucked in and my Chicago bags unpacked. Strangely, I felt hung-over. I told Tom I was calling it a night and crawled under the sheets to watch TV. In the morning I still felt queasy.

"Do you think you're pregnant?" Tom asked as he was brushing his teeth.

"No. I don't think so. I guess it's always possible. Maybe I could be, but I'd be shocked."

And that was all it took. The man who will spend an hour getting ready for work, showering, shaving, grooming, and wouldn't consider running out in public before had slipped into a T-shirt and shorts and was off to the "corner of happy and healthy" a few blocks north on Woodward Avenue. I didn't like this one bit. He was wasting his money. Within ten minutes I was in the kitchen, and the kids were at the table having bowls of cereal.

"Here. Go. Test," he instructed with as much anxiousness as the proposal moment in Maui. I reluctantly grabbed the test and moped into the mudroom. I locked the door, peed on the stick, stuck the clear plastic cover over the saturated end, and sat on the floor watching the pale yellow bleed into the magic fortuneteller window. Tom and I had just reluctantly discussed another baby. Not ready to call it quits, I thought it'd be nice to have one more once everyone was in school. Maybe. I never had the chance to enjoy *a baby*. Tom hated that plan. He said he was too old at forty-two, which I thought was silly; he wasn't the one destroying his body or killing himself taking care of them and a gigantic house. He was thinking about graduation day. And how old he'd be if he had a baby after the age of forty-five. We agreed to disagree. Coincidentally, just weeks before I'd been on my Wednesday Claudia call and casually mentioned that I was trying a new pill from my OB.

"Ohmigosh, have you started taking it?" she probed with caution in her voice.

"No, I just have a couple months of samples right now."

"Well, I wouldn't take it. My sister has a friend who started taking it and she just had a stroke a couple of months ago. Isn't that horrible?"

"It IS horrible! Is she okay?" I asked, second-guessing my pill switch.

"She is, but it gave us all a scare. The pill is really bad for you, especially if you're over thirty-five." (I was thirty-three) "You might want to consider natural family planning. It's reliable if you do it right."

My super Catholic friend then went on to sell me on all the benefits of her method. I had decided to give it a try; the stroke risk that came with birth control pills freaked me out. I knew firsthand what it felt like to look like I had a stroke, and I didn't need to experience it again. I looked down at my white stick. Two solid light blue lines. *You've GOT to be kidding me! Damn Claudia and her holy rhythms. I can't go through another pregnancy right now! I've just recovered from the last!* Any woman who's held the positive stick understands that this is a serious life-changing moment. For me, it meant the miserable nine months of growing a human. It meant sacrificing more time and exhaustion to my role as mom. It meant not being able to be the fun mom for the three I was content with. It meant that I had to figure out how to pay for another person. It meant that I begrudged Tom for talking me into a dog. It meant that there would be no rest for a very long time. It meant baby gear. Again. I hated baby gear. And, most of all, it meant that I fully understood that the little Gyarmati inside me was going to be just as amazing as the three I had and that the love I had in this that moment was already unconditional for the little soul. I just wished it wasn't happening right then. I walked into the kitchen, holding the test in my hand.

"Well?" Tom asked with a giant grin on his face. I handed it to him in silence. Then I looked at Noah, Emma, and Isabelle, who were making their way through bowls of Special K with Berries. Strapped into her booster, Isabelle was dumping her milky cereal bites onto the table instead of into her mouth. *Copper headed and stubborn. Bell's and colic.* Tears started rolling down my cheeks.

"I can't do THAT again," I blubbered as I pointed to her cute little face. The kids had no idea what I was talking about. The rest of that moment was a blur. *I can't handle four kids under the age of four! I am not one of those moms! I'm a designer. I wanted a family, not a daycare.* Thoughts whirled in my head as Tom embraced me in a blissful hug and moved on with his morning. *I just want a simple life like the one I had growing up. My mom was never frazzled and stressed. I've never even been around families with more than three kids. This big house with the new big family is cramping my style.* As I stood at the kitchen sink that hot August morning, I looked down at my bare feet. *I am barefoot and pregnant. Maternity is not my style.*

When Tom left for work, I got the kids out to the driveway for bike riding, sidewalk chalk, and play structure time. I called my mom and dished the news. She mourned the loss of the "life is good" plan I had going, but within minutes was encouraging me and reminding me of how wonderful my three were, which helped me envision life beyond another round of nursing and diapers. I thought about my "hoity-toity" comment at the Pier. Embarrassed and humbled, I pondered the fact that I was *not* in control of my life. "You couldn't *pay* me to be pregnant right now," echoed in my soul like a little chuckle from Heaven. God had a sense of humor, and He hadn't even gotten to the punch line.

By the end of September, I was scheduled for a routine ultrasound to determine my due date. I was a month into my Coke and Saltine diet to keep morning sickness at bay, napping with the kids to sustain enough energy to get through the day, and slowly coming to terms with destiny's child growing within my womb. My mom came to babysit the morning of our appointment. It was our tradition to schedule late morning hospital appointments followed by lunch at the Red Coat Tavern for the best burgers in town.

"Hollie Gyarmati?" a nice, middle-aged technician called as she opened the heavy door of the waiting area. Tom and I got up and followed her like professional ultrasounders to the exam-sized room, which was dimly lit with the exception of a small window covered by blinds. She instructed me to empty my bladder, remove my shoes, and get situated on the table.

"So, you already have children?" she asked as she sat in her swivel chair to my right. Tom was in the guest chair to my left, but she told him he could pull it closer for a better view.

"Yes, we have boy/girl twins who are three and a two-year-old daughter," I responded proudly. "This is our surprise baby," I added.

The tech pulled up my shirt, and I folded down the elastic panel on my pants. I cringed at the recognition that I was already in maternity wear. I thought for a moment about all the work I'd done finding the perfect pair of jeans in Chicago, which I later returned to Gap. She squirted cold, clear jelly on my tummy, and I looked at Tom with excitement to get the first glance at our new little Gyarmati baby. She then grabbed the wand and plunked it on my abdomen, moving the mess around until she settled on her first view. I was watching her, not our overhead monitor. I always like to see the tech's initial reaction first. She burst into a big grin.

"Does any of this look familiar to you," she asked, completely amused. I looked at the overhead. It was black and white, not 3D, but very clear. *Oh, I know exactly what I'm looking at. Two little heartbeats thumping away, side by side! I am carrying another set of TWINS! This is not happening. This is not happening. This is not happening...*

The color in my face faded and my limbs went limp. It's a good thing I was lying down. Otherwise, I would have passed out. Tom grabbed my hand with joy. I gripped his with fear. *How in the world will I take care of five kids? I'm not that mom! I'm just a designer who wanted a nice little family that could live the normal All-American lifestyle. How will I get through a twin pregnancy while taking care of my exhausting three and that little animal my husband brought home a couple of months ago?* The future of our finances flashed through my mind. There was *no way* I could do this alone; I'd need real help. The kind I despised. I'd have to hire help. I'd need to hire Alice from the Brady Bunch. *I can't afford Alice.* Whatever the case, the visual was one of our bank account hemorrhaging combined with the control

I'd lose over…everything. I was in a whirlwind of future freak-outs. Vacations: done. How do you travel with five kids, ages four and under? I was going to be a slave to my grocery list, Kroger, Costco, and my kitchen sink for the next few years. I would not be able to enroll Noah and Emma into extra-curricular activities—dance, gymnastics, soccer, pre-school. I already felt shafted in terms of missing precious mom moments with every one of my babies because I had too many to dote over from Day One. Designer: gone forever. *Is God punishing me?* Everyone around me will be telling me how blessed I am while I'll feel like it's a life sentence of work instead of motherhood. *I cannot do this.*

Tom was still holding my hand as I felt the jelly being wiped from my tummy. Gazing at the small window, I clung to the tiny beams of late morning light sneaking through the metal horizontal blinds. Their brilliance reminded me that God was in control. I had no idea what was coming, but I knew I had to reel it in before they strapped me to that bed and admitted me to the mental health floor.

We walked out of the hospital, hand in hand, shocked with our news tucked into my handbag—little black and white photos of our new babies, already created with little personalities of Foss/Gyarmati genes. Sitting at the Red Coat, I got a grip and Tom assured me that we'd figure it out, which reminded me that he was my partner and would help me get through. It would be okay. Just like when I had my meltdown over baby number four—at this point, one more was not going to kill me. We'd already accepted that life would be different with four. It would be one more different with five. As we focused on thick, greasy onion rings, we had a chuckle over Isabelle, who'd been pushing her "strow" (stroller) stuffed with two dolls in it around the kitchen telling me she thought I should have *two* babies. My little Snort had placed her order. The joke was on me. And God was most assuredly laughing.

CHAPTER 9

DONNIE: PART 1

"Mom! That is the most beautiful sign I've ever seen!" Emma exclaimed as I held up my newest piece. It was a half sheet of white poster board with hand drawn block letters across the front that said "Donnie" (the "o" was a perfectly drawn heart), and underneath in quarter scale read, "Since 1989." All the letters were colored in with black sharpie and the heart with red. I layered black glitter over the black letters and red glitter over the heart with such precision that it looked like it had been professionally screen printed. It really was over-the-top stunning and almost a shame to take it to the concert knowing it would get trashed. I'd spent a couple of hours making it.

Preparing for one of the greatest moments of my life was the perfect antidote for baby stress. I was a little perturbed that I'd be meeting Donnie Wahlberg four months into a twin pregnancy. I decided to embrace my "glow" and the expertise of my stylist, concert co-conspirator, and owner of our bachelor pad, Maria Chirco. When the concert news broke in April, before the puppy and more babies, it was a given that I was not going to just "go" to the concert. None of this balcony or thirtieth row floor seat nonsense. This was serious business, and if I was going, I was going all the way with VIP seats. Not cheap, but worth it to get two minutes of face time with the band and guaranteed seats within the first ten rows.

Our call went something like this:

"Hollie, hi honey, how are you?" said my sweet Maria.

"Maria! HI… OMG, I have a wildly bold favor to ask, but don't worry, it's super fun. I was IN LOVE with New Kids On The Block when I was fourteen. Concert tickets are on sale now. I want the VIP seats. Are you in?"

"Say no more. I was in love with Prince. I totally get it. I'd love to go with you!"

And just like that, I had found the perfect date. What's funny is that Maria and I didn't hang out or even talk regularly. But I knew that we'd be loyal friends forever, the kind you could see every couple of years and just pick up where you left off. Tom secured our package through Amex, very much in the dark about my teen dream Donnie obsession, and Maria took me to Somerset to scour sale racks for the perfect pregnancy camo outfit. I was determined not to wear maternity clothes for as long as possible, and in the frumpy stage of a twin pregnancy, I was about the size of a typical woman at five months pregnant. My mom converted my favorite pair of jeans into transitionals with an elastic front panel from a pair of tummy control panties I snagged at TJMaxx. They worked like a charm and eliminated the annoying baggy crotch you get with maternity jeans. I had them on for my big shopping trip, and Maria and I plotted to find a flashy sundress to layer over my jeans that would accentuate my assets and hide my bump.

Maria was the perfect stylist. Italian glam from head to toe, she would confidently dress me with the right bling to stand out in the crowd, which I needed since I'm typically a T-shirt and jeans concert goer. We agreed that I had to step out of my J.Crew comfort zone and move into sexier lines. We walked through the Bebe store. At a comfy size eight, I don't think I could have fit one boob into their XL dresses. No go. We then tried BCBG, one of my favorites from my design days working at Marshall Field's. I tried on a few dresses without much luck. We then wandered into Nordstrom. As a spoiled former department store employee and discount junkie, I of course beelined to a sale rack of dresses. When I worked in the studio, I took on the role of personal shopper for my less enthused co-workers. I could put together a $1,000 outfit for under $100 with my savvy sale rack steals. We found an armful of possible contenders and headed to the dressing rooms.

About three dresses in, we found it. It was perfect; I can't even remember the brand, but it was a $300 number significantly discounted from a summer collection. Bright, multi-color, almost Pucci-like pattern with a halter-top and beautiful gold metal leaves strung under the chest. It hung about ten inches above my knee and completely hid my babies. And it was comfortable. I felt fabulous. Maria gushed over me as I twirled in front of the three-way mirror. My double bump was completely hidden. Next, we hit up the Laura Mercier counter where I scheduled an appointment for concert day to complete my look.

At home I dug out my NKOTB keepsakes that had sat boxed in my parents' barn for almost twenty years. The box was filled with concert tickets, programs, and hundreds of photos that had been cut out of *Bop* magazine and carefully trimmed to fit the wallpaper collage in my ninth-grade bedroom. There were drawings I'd made of Donnie, Jordan, and Joe and a couple of concert T-shirts. To see it all again brought a flutter to my tummy like it was yesterday. I was obsessively in love with Donnie Wahlberg. I was convinced that I was the girl in his song, that he was dancing for me, and that one day he'd open my fan mail and call. Or, better yet, spot me at a concert and pull me on stage, sing like he did to the cute little girls at his concerts, except he would kiss me in front of the entire stadium of screaming fans and then secretly make me his girlfriend. The End. (I've always been a big dreamer, so why stop at the stage serenade?) Unfortunately, while I lived in my big dream world, the people around me could hardly understand my infatuation, which felt very alienating. The only person in the world who understood me was my dear friend, Crystal Star

Lowe. Now a French teacher and tennis coach on the other side of the state, if you asked this woman how in the world a fourteen-year-old girl could be convinced she was in love with a celebrity, she'd vehemently tell you it's very possible.

It all started the summer of 1989. Crystal and I shared the same circle of friends in junior high. She called one hot August afternoon and asked if I'd like to drive to the state fair to see New Kids, who were on tour with Tiffany. I had a hunch I wasn't her first call, but we'd always had fun together, so I jumped at the chance to see the boy band that had every teenaged girl in the country glued to MTV. The next morning, my mom drove me to her house, and we rode in the backseat of her parents' Bonneville the two plus hours to Ionia, which is situated about an hour east of Lake Michigan in the middle of Michigan farmland. Nothing scenic except for the fairgrounds, which were in full swing with carnival rides, games, and junk-food vendors at every corner. Crystal's parents spoiled us with plenty of ride tickets and let us loose for a couple of hours. We discussed Jordan, Jonathon, Donnie, Danny, and Joey in detail while we whipped and turned on every ride we could find. Crystal was a Jordan follower and I was all about Donnie, so it was nice that there'd be no competition between the two of us. We could see the stage set up in the middle of a field, and from the top of the Ferris wheel, a tour bus that had us giddy at just the thought of being within a hundred yards of these superstars.

This tour was right before they hit it big. They were with Tiffany, who had been washed up for at least a year, playing only small venues. Crystal and I didn't know it, but this detail would serve as the reason we would leave as "Blockhead" converts that evening. Our lives were about to change. We'd finished the rides, checked in with her parents, and redeemed our concert tickets at a gate that led us into a field filled with sweaty teenaged girls donning big hair, acid-washed jeans, and neon T-shirts. The good news, we discovered, was that it was standing room only, and if you wanted to get close to the stage you had to create your own destiny. The bad news was that we had two hours before the show started, and the field was filling up fast. The ground was nothing but dirt and the air thick, humid, and filled with dust. It had to be ninety degrees.

Crystal and I made a pact to get to the front of the crowd no matter how hard we had to fight because we were determined to get close enough to see the sweat dripping from their temples while they sang "The Right Stuff," "Please Don't Go Girl," and "Hangin' Tough." We spent the next two hours working our way through a hostile environment of sweaty, mean girls thanks to the chart-topping levels of estrogen running through our bodies. We were like superheroes, unstoppable. Sometimes we'd bust through a crowd really fast, and others it was a sneaky step or two here or there. The closer to the front we got, the tighter the crowd became. At times, we had to put our hands over our heads to keep moving. I felt as though I would pass out from heatstroke, and girls were becoming grumpier by the minute. Finally, we landed in a tight group about ten feet from the front left of the stage. The sun was setting behind the field, and suddenly the lights turned on and Tiffany came bouncing out onto the stage in her denim overall shorts, auburn hair, and black brimmed hat. We were thrilled! I reminisced my earlier years of seventh and eighth grade with all of her songs and could feel the push of the massive crowd behind us throughout her entire performance.

After her last song, the stage went dark. The sun had set, and we waited, dripping in salty sweat, make-up, and sticky hairspray for the men of our dreams to appear. Finally, after what seemed like another two hours, the announcer rolled his voice in excitement for the starring act. And then, in the most magical moment of my fourteen years, five young men came dancing onto the stage just like I'd seen on MTV all summer long. They were even *better* in person; they were angelic compared to the boys at Sherman Middle School we'd been exposed to over the years. They were tall and beautiful and wore matching acid-washed jeans and either black or white T-shirts. Joey McIntyre wore his famous black hat. Their hair looked like they'd jumped out of a spread from *Seventeen* magazine, and they danced perfectly in sync with every step. They were like the bad boys you wanted to run with gone good—so good that you'd envision your parents giving you their blessing to run off and live happily ever after at first sight.

Within seconds, Crystal and I morphed into screaming, teary-eyed, crazy girls just like the ones in the "Hangin' Tough" video. There was something magical about that moment as well as the next one hundred moments of our lives. We felt unstoppable, like we were on top of the world. And even though we looked and sounded like every girl around us, this group had a way of making us each feel like we were THE ONE. It was a phenomenon, and the only thing like it until that time was Beatle Mania. We were experiencing the All-American path of the celeb-crazed teenaged girl. We fell into this sweet little age gap of being too old to be little girls and too young to roll with the older girls. Too young for real boyfriends and making out in cars. Too young for real love. But at the perfect age for celebrity love. And that's how we fell.

We screamed for two hours only five feet from the stage that night, raging with monoamines (falling-in-love hormones) that would have surpassed the legal limit if there were such a thing. If you could have seen us in the back of the Bonneville driving home, I'm sure we had an angelic glow hovering over our heads as though we'd experienced a religious conversion of some sort. When we woke the next morning, we felt the same connection to each other and to our new reason for living. It was as if our hearts would explode if we didn't devote every moment we had to Jordan and Donnie. *This* is what it felt like to be in love.

A few weeks later, we started ninth grade, and for the entire first semester of school we were inseparable. Our friends quickly found our new exclusive friendship ridiculous and annoying. Our lockers were smothered in Jordan and Donnie pictures from *Bop* magazine and any other publication we could find. We had their stats listed and memorized. I could give you Donnie's birthday, height, weight, mother's name, favorite color, favorite TV show, and favorite food faster than I could sing our high-school fight song. (And I was a cheerleader). Crystal and I would get home from school every day, pop in our NKOTB "Hangin' Tough" VHS and documentary, and lay on our backs in front of the screen, phones nestled on our shoulders to discuss these men that we would someday meet, marry, and procreate with (a concept which, at fourteen, still grossed us out, but we envisioned the full dream with these men).

We saved every babysitting dollar for more concert tickets and fan-club dues, and we wrote our future husbands love letters every week. Our milk money purchased the latest issues of *Bop* instead of Little Debbie snacks. We'd rip out our beloved NKOTB pictures, tossing the rest of the publication and its Kirk or Cory newcomer or more mature Johnny Depp and lucky-to-be-there Wil Wheaton in the trash. My bedroom quickly became a Donnie shrine, and my family, *God Love Them*, endured the "Hangin' Tough" cassette tape blasting from my Sony double cassette player day-in and day-out. They knew the words to the A-side *and* the B-side. The madness lasted through January—five long, lovesick months.

The dream of a returned letter finally dissipated as two concerts at the Palace Basketball Arena proved that having seats forty and fifty rows from the stage was like piercing daggers into our hearts. *Nothing* would compare to the sweaty crowd at the Ionia State Fair. Nothing. And nobody would ever understand our NKOTB experience.

And as fate would have it, as the snow thawed and we both turned fifteen in March, Crystal and I ended our relationships with Jordan and Donnie and decided it was time to communicate with real-life boys, the stinky junior high guys going through puberty just like us. The ones who wore Levi's and Chicago Bulls sweatshirts and smelled like Old Spice after gym class. We decided that they would have to do. At least they were real and happy, and we could hang with them without NKOTB being part of the conversation. I think there was a quiet, unspoken celebration amongst our friends when we came back to our senses. The photos in our lockers were replaced with real prints of our latest sleepovers and sporting events and the mention of NKOTB no longer sent us into daydreams. We closed this chapter of our lives, and I stashed it neatly into an old winter boot box, where it would eventually be relocated from the top shelf of my closet to the basement storage, and finally, to the loft of the barn. For almost twenty years.

CHAPTER 10

DONNIE: PART 2

"Have fun!" my mom yelled as I backed my minivan into the turnaround. An overnight with Grandpa and Grandma was not new to my kids, and it was a *must* so I could have the day to primp. Waving out the window, I turned onto my beloved Hensell Road and headed toward the paved road and expressway. Pressing Play, the newly released NKOTB CD blasted threw my empty mom ride, and I felt free for the first time in months. *Alone* free. The CD was not my "adult Hollie" genre, but I needed to know it to enjoy the concert in full. It was sexy-pop-dance-club-meets-the-bedroom music. Only one song was okay for the kids to listen to. They'd been through my 1989 New Kid's music daily for lunch cleanup for the last month as I waited for the new release. Gone were the days of record store lines of crazed teen girls eager to purchase it. These new "kids" on the cover were now pushing forty and looking a little less "boy band," but seeing their faces together again made me happy, and I pushed my way through every track wondering if they'd ever consider making some great classic jazz music in the future. The thirty-three-year-old me had turned into an old lady. Curiously enough, and true to fashion trends, my music of choice was all things 1940s, 60s, 80s, and 2000s. I skipped decades in twenty-year increments just like the runways of New York and Paris.

My afternoon at home that day was the first time as a mom that I had an empty house to myself. Otto was the only one home, and I guiltlessly left him gated in the kitchen. I took my time getting showered and blowing out my hair, then drove to Somerset for my make-up session. I couldn't wait to get my glam on. I missed the good old days at Marshall Field's, stopping to visit my friends at the Chanel counter to get my makeup done when I had an important client coming in. On this day, I was seeing the Laura Mercier rep and was happy she knew her stuff. She looked great, not "made up." My hair and makeup rule of thumb has always been to never let anyone cut, color, or apply if you don't like the way they look. This woman seemed like she could pull off my Chanel look. I told her about my big night, and she got to work.

Forty minutes later, she spun me around as she unclipped my hair from my temples. After all that work, I expected runway beauty, but instead I looked much like myself, just "enhanced" with light plum and neutral eye color; long, luxurious lashes; perfectly glowing skin; and neutral lips that had been glazed with cotton-candy-tasting gloss. My hair had blond highlights and long layers that fell just below my shoulders, and it was thick and full thanks to my extra twins-made strands. I felt even more beautiful than I did on my wedding day yet craved the opportunity to ditch my girl-next-door beauty for stop-in-your-tracks glam and knew that once I slipped into my VIP look, my confidence would skyrocket. I needed that to balance the nerves running through my gut. By the time I parked in front of my old house, I was so psyched up I felt like I could go for my old six-mile run around the lake. I rang the doorbell and took pause to admire the entrance to my old home. The heavy solid Mahogany door that had been custom made in Canada was just as beautiful as the day it was installed. Tom had great taste. Within a few seconds, Maria swung open the masterpiece and I instantly felt like I had an entire cheerleading squad at my disposal.

"HOLLIE! Ohmigosh, you are a *bombshell!*" she squealed, very proud of her makeover on the girl next door. My plunging neckline pushed the envelope enough to know that it was a good idea to be gone before Tom got home from work. I smashed my lips together and felt the splurge of my new $30 gloss. I embraced her in a big, loving hug as I stepped onto our old Tibetan wool rug in the foyer. Maria purchased our rugs with the house. I felt a little, well, a *lot* sad about transitioning from the bachelor pad to the house of traditional vomit.

"I'm almost ready, honey, come see the what I've done to the master suite," she said as I followed her through the great room and into my old bedroom. She had decked it out with every shade of cream imaginable. Tom's old sage wave textured carpet had been replaced with soft wool, and Maria's king-sized bed boasted luxurious silks and a giant fabric headboard. She'd painted the entire bathroom, including the sage green marble detail on the shower floor, cream. It sparkled like a department store. The closet was California style, complete with a chandelier and poofy ottoman in the middle. I loved it. Tom would have cried. His bachelor fantasy suite had gone girly. The only thing that remained was the glass-paneled fireplace that ran between the bedroom and the Jacuzzi tub, on the edge of which I took a seat as Maria finished her prep.

"Ok, I brought a fourteen-year-old version of my typical fan mail love letter, want to hear it?" I asked as Maria finished her black ensemble in the closet.

"Of course! You are so cute!"

I whipped out my white envelope and read her the handwritten love letter I had carefully crafted over the last couple of weeks. It wasn't really a love letter, just my story and the hope that after the hundreds I'd sent eighteen years earlier he might accept this final chapter, redeeming my broken junior high heart. If he took my envelope, my mission would be complete.

"I love it; it's perfect and sweet," she complimented with a twinkle in her eye. "Let's go!"

As we walked through my old house, I tried not to reminisce all the wonderful memories of my old life. My two-story, tone-on-tone, raw silk, plaid draperies hung proudly in the great room and dining room. I'd selected that fabric at the design center years before, and I loved it just as much now as I did then. The six-burner Viking oven in the kitchen was going to kill me. I decided not to look. Too painful. This house had spoiled me. We made our way into the garage and slid into the leather interior of her white Cadillac SUV.

"Are you ready for this?" she glanced at me with a smirk.

I unrolled my glittered sign: DONNIE SINCE 1989.

"I'm going to be the girl with the right stuff tonight," I said, cheesy pun intended.

"He is going to flip *out* over you," she beamed, with the pride of the older sister I'd never had.

We chatted our way to the Palace, home of the Detroit Pistons basketball team. It was the last place I'd seen him on stage, and I was so far away that he was the size of my thumb. On this night, I was guaranteed a seat in the first ten rows. I remembered the sticky night with Crystal screaming at the larger-than-life young men sliding in unison, all with sweet voices that melted our teen hearts every time they crooned the word "gggiiiiirrrrllll," which seemed to be the topic of every song. Maurice Starr had his marketing plan down to a science. Gone were the 1960s and 70s filled with Glorias, Brandys, and Jennys; these boys sang to us "girls," guaranteeing undying love from millions of babysitters in global proportions. The man was *brilliant.* "*Girl.*" That's all it took. Along with some shredded jeans; black leather jackets; a loose, white shirt with "HOMEBOY" screen-printed across the front; and big hair to match our Rave3 hair-sprayed to perfection 1989 trend. If we were old enough to hold up cigarette lighters, our toxic bangs would have lit up the arena within seconds.

Maria took a Michigan left into the parking lot, and we immediately spotted two large tour buses parked sitting side by side on the south lot. That was it. They were here. This was it. *After eighteen years, I was about to experience something I'd dreamed of for years.*

"EEEEEE!!" I screamed, as if my fairy godmother had waved her magic wand and transformed me into Hollie from Holly. Small-town almost ninth grader who'd kissed a boy in the parking lot after a school dance and who believed with every fiber of her naïve youth that she was in love with Donnie Wahlberg. Maria busted into enthusiastic laughter and was purely amused by my glass slipper moment. She had shared with me her infatuation with Prince and the way he singled her out during a concert and pulled her on stage. My pulse raced at the thought of just being within an arm's reach of my crush. Suddenly, the two little people who were growing inside me disappeared. My family was non-existent, and I was the girl in the front row. The one he sang to in the "Hangin' Tough" video while dripping in twenty-year-old celeb sweat and making millions of dollars.

I was sure there would be thousands of thirty-somethings like me sneaking out for the night, leaving their husbands at home to take care of tuck-ins, ready to relive the dream. We parked and made our way in with our VIP passes. I strutted through the parking lot next to my sexy Italian diva, and we swung through the revolving doors into the lower lobby of the arena. We entered a long line of fellow VIPs from all walks of life. I was thoroughly amused by the crowd. We were all in our late twenties and thirties. Maria and I were like luxury cars crammed into a sea of city traffic. For a moment, I felt a little out of place and foolish about my mission. We patiently waited in line, focused on what was to come. Maria proudly took my photo holding my couture Donnie. She had to jump almost a decade into my world but did so with a camaraderie that no one else could have given me. I was truly grateful. Within minutes we were checked in and gifted our

NKOTB coffee mugs, fleece blankets, and VIP passes. I didn't care about fleece; I just wanted my tickets for the floor! When we got to the front of the line at the next window, a nice elderly woman handed me ours, and I fumbled with them to get a view of our row and seat numbers. Holding them about eight inches from my eyes, I grabbed Maria's arm with excitement.

"We are in the sixth row, center stage," I squealed. *SIXTH ROW!* This was already a dream come true. Unbelievable! We were led down a long, gloomy hallway with charcoal painted walls and tired commercial carpet still sporting bright pink, blue, and yellow graphics. Maria grabbed my arm as we gushed over our seat assignments. After what seemed like four or five different turns, the older gentleman leading us opened his hand into a large conference room deep within the underground Palace infrastructure.

"Welcome to the VIP lounge ladies. Enjoy the show," he smiled as we politely thanked him. Rounding the corner of the charcoal steel doors, we entered an entire parking lot, metaphorically speaking, overflowing with economy cars, SUVs, minivans, and a few luxury cars all waiting to cross over to the other side. About two hundred people in total, all sitting at round tables nibbling cups of popcorn and sipping cocktails that had been mixed from a long, dark bar that ran the length of the back wall. A nice woman awarded us with two drink tickets each to enjoy our lounge experience. Maria worked her way through the crowd to grab us a couple of cokes, and I navigated to two seats next to some black curtains in the far-right corner of the room. I felt like I was at a bowling alley. The entire room had obviously not been updated since the Palace had opened in the mid 80s. The dark walls were marked with table and chair abuse, and the bright carpet *screamed* soiled. *This was 1989.* I embraced the vibe, channeling my teen Hollie. My heart was pounding faster than I thought possible.

Our secured seats were the last two available at our table, and I politely smiled at my fellow classmates, most of whom were giving me the once over and fake "I hate you" smiles. A couple of them were wearing their vintage concert shirts and still had their stiff bangs and bleached, permed, long blond hair that hung past their bra-straps. These girls never packed away their New Kid treasures like I had. I wondered if they still had a shrine in their bedrooms and if their boyfriends or husbands cared. Maybe they were so die-hard that they never "broke-up" with Donnie, Jordan, Joey, Danny, and Jonathon. I smirked with a little judgmental guilt as I quietly stashed my handbag in my lap.

On the other side of the room, my dear Maria was stuck in a line at the bar, which was really a waste since neither of us planned on having a real drink. I noticed a nice luxury car at my table and started up a conversation. She was exactly my age, a mom of three, and she drove to the concert with her sister from Ohio. Donnie lover. We bonded. I shared my stats and we both agreed that thirteen or fourteen was the most lethal age to fall for a celeb. Maria made her way through the lot and snuggled in next to me with a couple little plates of popcorn, white cocktail napkins, and clear plastic cups of Coke. My baby mama needs reached my stomach, and I scarfed down the pathetic VIP snack in a fit of survival and nervous energy. As my mouth filled with stale popcorn, an older gentleman grabbed a mic at the back right corner of the room.

"Goooood Evening Ladies..." the room fell into the most excited silence I'd ever witnessed. This guy had a radio voice and looked like he'd been with the group for years. I think he was their manager, or one of them anyway. He proceeded to debrief us on how we would meet the group. There was a roped off line from where Mr. Manager was standing that created a corridor straight over to the black curtained off area, which was about a 15X15 square "room," if you will. The guys would be hangin' in there with a photographer and bodyguards while we would be let loose for two minutes in groups of ten. We were not allowed to bring anything with us, no cameras or autographs allowed. This was considered "face time," which meant that hugging was okay as long as they were comfortable with it.

Women started getting gushy and giggly at the thought of touching their muses. Maria and I quickly started plotting.

"I want to give him my letter, what should I do?" I probed.

"Bring it. We'll sneak it in." Maria rocked. I was such a rule follower. If security took it, it wasn't the end of the world. Maybe they'd even pass it along to him later. The dream was being close enough to whip a letter onto the stage in hopes of him taking it, reading it, and writing me back. (That was the second-string dream if pulling me on stage didn't work out.) Our host was rallying the ladies for the entrance of the guys. I could just catch a glimpse of one of their shoulders standing in the hall ready to walk out. I wasn't sure what to expect, but I joined in with my fellow traffic, honking my horn and wooting for our men. At this point, I don't remember exactly how he sounded, but the seasoned old man rolled out his introduction in his deep voice just like I'd heard almost twenty years earlier.

And out they came, stage pros, walking single file in their street clothes along the roped off area toward the black curtained room. We screamed. They politely waved with gracious smiles that screamed back, "We love you, and will love you forever!" These guys, my guys, were…older. Smaller. Different from who they were in 1989, when I was fourteen and they were larger than life and more beautiful than any human beings I'd ever laid my eyes on. I guess that's what MTV will do to you. The reality of what they really looked like was tainted by amazing film production. And teenage lenses of naivety. Tonight, they looked like average good-looking guys. And while they were older, I have to say that if I passed any of them on the street and they were not NKOTB, I might not look twice. With the exception of Matthew McConaughey, *only* in *A Time to Kill*, I don't think I noticed anyone besides Tom. At this point in my life, I was so busy keeping people alive that Matthew would have to be sitting at my kitchen table fighting with my kids to get a rise out of me!

As they waved their hands in the air and disappeared behind the curtain it dawned on me that the proximity between The New Kids and me was only about thirty feet! One folding round table, an old black polyester curtain hanging from a metal rolling rack, and a couple of big body guards. I quickly pondered all the dollars I'd spent on these men, and all for what? To go to sleep every night wishing and praying that maybe tomorrow there would be a handwritten letter waiting in the mailbox from Donnie? What was it all for? I wasted six months of real life in a la la land of "Please Don't Go Girl" and "I'll Be Loving You Forever" when I could have been scribbling and receiving sweet love notes from real boys and using all that money to buy clothes from Express and The Limited at the mall. In that moment, I morphed back into lovesick teen dream queen and decided not to look back. All those wasted moments were amazing back then, and I could never regret them. What Crystal and I had was something more than celeb crush. Later, I would learn that we were, with the other transits, referred to as "Blockheads." And as I harnessed all those feelings of love, loss, and hopeless heartache, I determined that I would be redeemed "Tonight" (the name of one of my favorite songs).

The first few rounds of hot mamas made their way behind the curtain. They had them lined up like a slow-moving exit ramp. Maria and I calculated that we would be stuck in the jam for at least forty minutes. As I watched the women exit one table over, I noticed that one of the curtains kept sticking, and there was a continual gap of about eighteen inches through which I had a direct line of sight to everything going on. There were lots of hugs and photos and vehicles walking out with their boxy T-shirts, smiles, and utilitarian four doors. Then it hit me. What was I *thinking*? Why was I not taking action? The New Kids On The Block had a beeline view of a luxury vehicle, and I was sitting back like I was wearing a dustcover! I was a *BMW. Baby Making Woman*. I could do *anything*. I should be *in* the showroom! I quickly shifted in my chair, sat up straight, and shot a glance as the next group walked out into the room, immediately catching Danny's eye. I flashed a Christly Brinkley driving-next-to-Chevy-Chase-in-*Vacation*-smile and a flirtatious wave. (I have never flirted so with such physical obviousness in my life, my style is much more conversational, but I was willing to do what was necessary to make this work.) He waved back with a flattered grin. *Game. On.* I nudged Maria, and she joined in. She was like having a bright red Ferrari parked behind me. We waved, smiled, and flirted with every single band member as if *they* were the lucky ones. We were insanely confident that night. It was a sense of empowerment that I had never before felt. By the time our table was excused, the energy and excitement were almost too much to bear.

About fifteen minutes into our road test, we were actually standing in line with our group of ten. I was literally flipping out. My palms were sweaty. My pulse was racing. Maria was worried I might even faint. I started to focus on my breath as she calmly stated our plan.

"This is what we are going to do: we are not walking, we are *running* to Donnie. I'll nestle up to him on his right, you to his left, and we will monopolize the full two minutes with him." I just nodded and kept breathing. I had never been so nervous in my entire life.

"I can do this," I confirmed.

"You can do this! You are beautiful! You are amazing! He is going to go crazy over you."

I can do this. I am beautiful. I am amazing. BMW. My engine was revved.

We were the next group to go in. I watched the calculated flashes of the cameras and composed myself for the performance of a lifetime. It was happening. I would have given anything for Crystal to be standing next to me so she could run to Jordan like we'd dreamed of so many times. A young security guard standing at the curtain entrance saw the white envelope in my hand.

"Excuse me, miss, but you can't take that in; no autographs," he said with as much authority as an insecure mall cop.

"I just want to give it to Donnie; totally harmless. I've been waiting for almost twenty years," I pleaded, as if I were begging for just one more slumber party with my girlfriends and skipping church the next morning. Easily won over, he smiled and signaled me to sneak it in like he hadn't seen a thing.

In that moment, Maria and I were standing at the curtain entrance, and they signaled us to come in for our two minutes of glory. I can't tell you what any of them looked like. They were no longer larger than life like they'd been all those years ago. They were just normal, fit, well-dressed guys. The kind you might see strolling the mall with their wife and kids or in line at Starbucks. I don't think any of them were taller than five-foot-eleven or weighed over 170 pounds. They were dressed in dark shades of gray and black. Maybe there was a white T-shirt in there somewhere; I couldn't tell you. The only man I saw was Donald Edmond Wahlberg. Born on August 17, 1969. Five feet ten inches tall. 165 pounds. Has eight brothers and sisters, his mother's name is Alma, and she makes his favorite chicken dinner. The man I was running to was the twenty-year-old sweaty Donnie with his big dishwater blonde hair, white *homeboy* shirt with oversized sleeves and shredded jeans. He was the Donnie I'd screamed, cried, and dreamed about for 180 days of my precious teen life. *I could do this.*

And this is exactly how it went down, with Maria as my witness, should anyone ever doubt my story.

We rushed as gracefully yet swiftly as possible up to him. He was grinning from ear to ear and wearing a black baseball cap pulled down tight to his brows, a chunky black and white hounds-tooth wool scarf, a black shirt and ebony rinsed jeans. Very "Boston boy meets Michael Kors." I couldn't believe it was really *him* and he was smiling at my arrival to his left. Just as she planned, Maria flanked him on the other side, and he must have said "hello" or something. It was a blur. A complete blur! I was on an autopilot of endorphins, teen dreams, and BMW hormones. All I remember is blurting out, "I've been in love with you for eighteen years, and I have a set of twins who are three, a two-year-old at home, and I just found out that I'm expecting *another* set of twins and this is my last night out. *EVER!*"

He smiled the sexiest smile I'd ever seen and without voicing his reply and without missing a beat, his lips were on mine like he'd been waiting his entire life to kiss me! *Donnie Wahlberg was kissing me, and I was fourteen and had been dreaming of this moment every day for six months!* His lips were soft and gentle, and they locked onto my cotton candy Laura Mercier gloss like we were meant to experience this Mississippi second for almost two decades. It was absolutely the greatest, most coveted, lusted after, surprising moment of my entire life. It was redeeming all I'd sacrificed *and* making my wildest dreams come true! In a moment of shock, he pulled back, and I saw the look of amazement on Maria's face. Even she was blown away by the instant chemistry we had.

"And she'll name one of the babies after you if she has a boy!" she squealed in a tizzy.

Then, the *unthinkable* happened: Donnie Wahlberg gave me a smirk that was even *sexier* than the one he gave to the front-row blonde in the "Hangin' Tough" video. He was so caught in the moment—as if the first wasn't enough—that he leaned in for another, in which I nearly passed out and reciprocated with as much enthusiasm as I did the first. It was a complete out-of-body experience that I will never, ever forget. There I was, lips locked for a *second time* with Donnie Wahlberg. We were perfectly embraced like a rehearsed movie kiss; innocent and sweet, not gross but irresistibly sexy, sexy, sexy. Then, without warning, we were interrupted by the photographer's voice, instructing, "Okay, everyone turn to me and smile!" He pulled away and wrapped his arms around Maria and I just as the cameras flashed.

There were two photographs taken that night. Both group shots of five men and ten women. In the first, Donnie is shooting a grin toward his bodyguard to the left of the curtain. In the second, he was looking at the camera. Now I don't know exactly what transpired in that moment, but it was obvious that the "lip-to-lip" was *NOT* a regular occurrence and only Maria would ever understand how magical it was. After the flashes, I handed him my fan mail and he slid it into the back pocket of his jeans. This was first *and* second-string dreams come true! I also threw in my seat location and gave a descriptive detail of my hand-made sign. He agreed to find me. And just like that, the bodyguards ushered us out of the exit. I sauntered past Jordan, Joe, Jonathon, and Danny with casual elegance. They seemed curious and confused, as I hadn't even bothered to gush over them. "Hi, nice to meet you," I teased with a justified sexy smile that I knew would only be mine, like a true Cinderella story, for the night.

The hours that followed my epic double feature were just as amazing as the first. Our seats were front and center, six rows back. I snuck my glittered sign by security and shot it high above my head in-between every song or if I caught a cameraman pointed in my direction. Later, Crystal, who was there with another friend from high school, told me she'd seen it on the big screen. Mission complete. That night, I was the girl from the "Hangin' Tough" video. No, it was better than that. I had a man who'd leaned in and kissed me, not once but twice, pointing and winking at me throughout an entire concert. I wasn't the naïve teen who'd sent over a hundred sappy letters to the fan club. I was experiencing front-and-center attention that millions of girls around the world would have killed to have. About halfway through, the sign was confiscated by a grumpy security woman who obviously had no appreciation for mad-teen love or classy Sharpie work. I secretly hoped she was a closet Donnie fan and hung my piece over her bed. *I had to hope.*

While my experience that night was one in a million, something else had been ignited at the Palace and around the world between our beloved boyband and their fans. When we were young, these boys gave us hope. They sparked our dreams. They made us feel accepted and loved, in the awkward stage of growing up that we were in, and for that, us "Blockheads" are grateful. To be reunited with the greatest, most loyal fans in music history was clearly remarkable for the group. Donnie, Jordan, Joe, Danny, and Jon were, without a doubt, reliving the greatest days of their lives. And so were we. There were tears flowing from both sides, and it was then that I realized that the draw, the feeling, the love we had for each other was greater than a dream or infatuation or, for them, millions of dollars. It was that we felt like we were on top of the world, and our being there made these five boys from Boston feel the same. Together we were invincible, overflowing with what would later become Donnie's favorite hashtag, #loveeternal.

On the way home, I realized that A, I had to call my husband, and B, I had to somehow tell him that I allowed another man to kiss me. When he answered, he obviously inquired about my evening and whether it met all of my expectations. He wanted to make sure the Amex charge was worth a girls' night out, which was something I'd neglected since forever. I casually told him about our encounter, leaving out most details that I knew he could care less about. In the months leading up to the concert he was pretty much annoyed with Donnie and Crystal stories, and I think the only thing that got a rouse out of him was when I told him how the ninth-grade boys at school referred to them as "New Kids on My *ock." So middle school, yet fascinating that my forty-one-year-old husband thought it was funny.

I led into my kiss moment, and he was silent for a second.

"You *KISSED* him?" he questioned in shock.

"Well, *yes* but *no*. He kissed *ME*. It was a complete surprise," I stammered.

"Two times," Maria chimed in from the driver's seat. She couldn't help it...

"TWO TIMES?" he was obviously not happy. I quickly held my finger to my lips as Maria smiled the biggest Italian diva grin I'd ever seen. Then she winked.

From there it was damage control, and I decided that since he didn't know me when I was fourteen, hadn't lived with my crazy antics, and had never had to listen to the "Hangin' Tough" cassette tape, sides A *and* B, over and over, he'd just have to get over it. I had no guilt. I was growing two more of his little people inside me and was in for five more months of incubation, toddler care, and puppy training in the big house. After I hung up, Maria and I stopped for a late-night bite, and we relived the entire evening just to make sure that I hadn't missed one detail of the historic event.

A few nights later I was nudged awake by Tom and his Waterford Crystal nightstand light.

"We have to talk," he insisted with spousal authority. I sat up and glanced at his clock. It was 2AM.

"Are you kidding? It's two in the morning," I complained, feeling like I was in the middle of an *Everybody Loves Raymond* episode, only it was usually Debra rousing her husband to "talk."

"I want to settle this kissing thing once and for all."

"There's nothing to settle," I said combatively, irritated yet a little amused by his jealousy.

"I want to know everything. Were you backstage alone with him?" He had obviously decided to omit my earlier details of the mass crowd of women and the fact that I only had two minutes to greet the New Kids. I think he had a vision of Eddie Van Halen entertaining women with VIP passes after a sweaty concert. It was almost comical.

"I told you exactly how it happened."

"And he kissed you but nobody else," he interrogated.

"Yes. But Maria was on the other side of him, and we didn't let him have much of a chance to talk to anyone," I stated for the record, leading him to believe that it could have happened to anyone in that room. Channeling the Raymond vibe, I decided to get defensive.

"Besides, I can't believe you woke me up for this!" I complained. "You should be flattered that a celebrity heart-throb kissed me. And you can look at it this way: you're that much closer to Mark Wahlberg now." I was *not* going to feel guilty. Even my mom had cheered me on with excitement when I called her, locked in the laundry room the morning after. He just glared at me. I sighed. "Okay, who did you have a crush on when you were fourteen?" I countered.

"Farrah Fawcett," he stated without hesitation.

"Fine. If you had the chance to meet Farrah Fawcett and she kissed you, I would be happy for you. And flattered that she thought my husband was worth a lip lock!" He said nothing. He really had nothing to talk about; this was the awkward thing about the light on in the middle of the night role reversal. He wanted to "talk," but had no idea how to express his feelings. He should have let me sleep.

"Tom, seriously, what do you think is going to happen? Do you think that Donnie and the New Kids on the Block are going to drive the tour bus up the driveway and whisk your pregnant wife off to tour the world?" I knew I was pushing my limits, but I was clearly winning this argument. He still had nothing to say. I don't remember how it all ended, but I refused to apologize or take a scarlet letter for my encounter. I agreed not to discuss it in front of him or watch Donnie's new TV show, *Blue Bloods,* to ensure that I would not relive my moment while giving him hand tickles on the sofa.

Within a year, my concert coffee mug had moved to the top shelf, and Tom actually offered to buy me tickets to see them on tour with the Backstreet Boys. I wholeheartedly declined. Nothing would ever compare to my VIP encounter. And a few years later, Donnie had also found his true love with the ever-talented actress, model, television host, author, and screenwriter, Jenny McCarthy, which I found to be ironic, because they'd each brought some much-needed confidence to me during each of my twin pregnancies. Word.

CHAPTER 11

FIVE UNDER FOUR

While I was living my teen dream during the fall of 2008, the rest of the country, and especially Detroit, was entering an economic crisis of epic proportions. After tuck-ins, our evenings were spent lying in bed watching presidential candidates debating, the stock market plummeting, the housing bubble bursting, and talk of the big automotive bailout. The financial portfolio my husband had strategically worked to build his entire adult life was being hit from all directions. We had lost a large percentage of our diversified funds, from the stock market to real-estate investments, both of which we were banking on for extra income. When we moved into the house, we had planned on maybe one of these unfortunate losses just to be safe, but sadly, we had to face the fact that our "cushion" was being ripped out from underneath us, and we, along with millions of others around the country, took massive hits.

The dealership also took a huge blow when their main creditor for all leased vehicles went under. Because of this, their car sales went from upwards of two hundred a month to well under a hundred. Tom and I would lie there, watching our flat screen, silently digesting the uncertainty of the future. Our giant upgrade in living suddenly became a giant headache as our income decreased by a third within a matter of weeks. Thankfully, we'd sold the Whistler condo and bachelor airplane before the move, but those Mammoth condos? The builders were looking to schedule a closing, and we'd been wiped out of the funds to do so without a moment's notice. Not only would we not be able to close on them, we would not have the funds to pay the mortgage on them or count on their rental income to help pay for our big house.

It was a tragedy we kept to ourselves, as it was unsuitable to discuss with anyone in our circle. We were the well-off couple. So while those around us were lamenting their own losses, it would have been thoughtless and insensitive to bring up our misfortune as we sat in our mansion in the heart of Bloomfield Hills. We kept silent. And we kept our near future foreclosures and the complete loss of all of our financial assets locked in our spousal vault, for fear of the misunderstanding and judgement we might receive from our peers.

Within just a matter of weeks, we lost everything except for our home and Tom's job, and even that had been diminished in the process. And yet here we were, bringing two more babies into the world. It should have been enough to have us both frazzled. Instead, we accepted our financial demise and focused on what we were thankful for. We had a home. We had healthy kids. We could pay our bills (for the moment). We had health insurance. We had each other. We would figure it all out.

The holidays came and went, and by the new year I was close to finishing up my second trimester. We'd found out around Thanksgiving that we were having two girls, and just as I had with Noah and Emma, I'd gone from a nice little baby bump to the twin discomfort I experienced only three years earlier. My parents were in Florida, and I spent the entire month of January nesting while I still had mobility and energy. One morning I grabbed my legal pad and wrote the longest "to do" list I'd ever concocted in my life. Our house had over twenty rooms including the 2,000-plus square feet of finished basement. I would pick one room a day, get the kids into a morning play routine, then declutter and organize with my morning cup of coffee. *Yes, I drank coffee while pregnant.* I was completely confident that I was growing healthy babies and was a rule breaker on all levels. I didn't drink alcohol, but aside from that, I ate and drank what I wanted because it was about survival. I was already doing what most moms found exhausting *without* carrying twins. I worked hard all morning, napped with the kids, made dinner, and got through the bedtime routine before settling in for a night of restless sleep. I'd been notorious for having bouts of insomnia, and the babies made it extra hard to get good rest. As soon as I'd lie down, they'd wake up ready to play, kicking me every which way and bringing me to what was my saddest design moment in history: the purchase of an oversized brown leather recliner.

"We just got our Costco rebate," Tom said one evening as he was going through the mail pile on the kitchen island. We are weekly shoppers, so the rebate was like a nice tax refund.

"That's great. I have a pregnant lady request." I had his full attention. And a request of the rebate meant a purchase, and if Tom got to shop, he was always in. "I want you to take that refund, go to the warehouse, and bring me home the biggest, ugliest brown leather recliner you've ever seen. I want it to look like a mattress when it's opened. If they have the ones with the little refrigerators and remote control holders built into the side, that's even better." My husband looked at me as though I'd gone off the deep end yet seemed to be turned on by my request for the kryptonite of an interior designer. Not only did I want the one thing I refused to sell to my clients, I was entrusting him to be my hero and pick it out all by himself. There was nothing to discuss; this was a winning wife encounter that he could only have dreamed of.

My sleep issues brought me to the feet of my OB, who ended up writing me a prescription for Ambien. We discussed it in full detail, and while it wasn't the healthiest choice, we both knew that I wouldn't make it without at least six hours of sleep at night. The babies were into their last couple of months, and the drug wouldn't harm them since they were fully developed. I decided not to stress about it and believed that this little white pill of wonder was my friend. For the first time in weeks I began waking up with energy I hadn't felt in a very long time. I had my recliner, a remote, and drugs. I was ready to hunker down for the last two months.

By February, my energy levels were down, and I spent most of the day in the lower level in our cozy family room with the fireplace, TV on, and baby gated doorways that ensured I could park my pregnant butt in the Lazy Boy all day. The house was trashed with toys, and I'd gotten really good at bribing Noah and Emma with Swedish Fish to make trips upstairs. The baby name books were marked and highlighted like an old textbook that had lived through years of different backpacks. Everyone was getting along pretty well, except for the animal my husband had brought home in the box just weeks before I found out about the additional people on the way. The crazy puppy had been the thorn in my side the entire fall season and had me stressed out and in tears begging Tom to take him back to the farm or I was going to quit. The springer was the cutest thing ever but being the dog trainer had me livid daily. He was chewing everything, eating things like flashlights and sippy cups, and thought the giant lady waddling through the kitchen was an open invitation to charge and tackle by wrapping his giant furry paws around her ankles and gnaw at her calves. I was constantly yelling at him to stop jumping on the kids, and every time I'd place a grievance with my spouse his reaction was always the same: "He's just a baby puppy..." This reaction was his payback for the Donnie kiss, as he knew it pushed my buttons more than anything. Miserable, knocked-up wife carrying twins scored lower on the empathy list than his dumb fur ball.

One evening, he came home from work with a brochure for dog obedience school and announced that we would, for six weeks, go as an entire family every Tuesday night to learn how to dissolve my canine despise. Great; he was being proactive. Could he have thought about this before I was carrying fifty-five pounds of baby weight? I now had to get three kids loaded in the car not once (Mass) but *twice* a week. In the middle of freezing Michigan winter. *Blech.*

The first night of class, we marched into the small gymnasium in downtown Birmingham and proved to twelve other dog owners that "Yes, I was busy," "Yes, my small children could sit quietly on the floor for an hour" (again, Mass benefit), "Yes, my dog was, compared to most, a *really* good dog, capable of learning how to be nice," and "Okay, I'll take the attention, because yes, I *was* the cutest thirty-two-weeks-pregnant twin baby mama ever." The combination of really awesome dog trainers and everyone doting on my condition was enough to keep me motivated to attend every class. In the end, I agreed to start referring to the animal as Otto or The Dog. Tom negotiated for The Puppy, but I reserved the right to relegate all baby references to those residing in my uterus until I decided that I really loved our pet.

With the dog situation under control, I thought I was covered for the last seven weeks. By this time, Tom was on grocery duty and my cleaning lady was around every Tuesday to take care of our heaviest-hit rooms. I was under house arrest, and any venture into public at this point was a chore. I was dealing with massive personal space invasion from all sides. Inside (babies kicking), outside (kids smothering me), and bending over even to put on my shoes was next to impossible. I surrendered to my varicose veins because I wasn't strong enough to stretch my knee-high support socks around even an ankle let alone a blood-filled calf. The days were getting longer, and I could have used some help. The kids had cabin fever, and I can't remember even a glimpse of how I kept them busy during those last few weeks, but one week I will *not* forget is the one when we got the puke flu.

I can't recall who got it first, but in short, I had three kids vomiting from the middle of the night into the morning, my full arsenal of beach towels on the floor, three sunbathers stretched out on them, all with puke buckets next to their heads ready for the next round. Their sippy cups were filled with iced-down Coke and they had an endless supply of Saltines. Tom had gone to work, I was using every last drop of endurance I had to keep up with laundry and the infirmary, and I wasn't feeling so great myself. I was nauseous and wishing I had my mom to help me. When you're queasy, the last thing you want is water. When you're pregnant, *very* pregnant with more than one person, and you aren't drinking enough water, you get dehydrated, fast. When you're dehydrated and in your thirty-third week of a twin pregnancy, you are grateful that you are not on bed-rest, and flu-like symptoms will send you into a series of Braxton Hicks contractions that will throw you into panic-filled pre-term labor.

I didn't have anyone to call and Tom was busy at work. The only two people on the planet who would venture into a vomit castle with a crazy sick mom on the throne are the spouse and the mother of the queen. One was in far-removed work land, the other was kayaking the alligator-infested rivers of Florida with my adventure-clad father and their snowbird friends. I made the dreaded call to my OB. I knew exactly what they'd tell me. Calling any doctor with a question that involved any level of uncertainty always resulted in the same answer: "We really can't do anything over the phone; to be sure, you really need to come into the office." In this case, it was, "You need to get to the ER right away." Damn. *Damn, Damn, Damn the puke flu.* I called Tom.

"I have to go to the ER, like, right now. Whatever is going on at work is over; you need to come home," I informed him with what was probably the meanest crabby pregnant voice he'd heard yet. Within twenty-five minutes, my husband, who loves me more than anything, walked into the kitchen with the fear of God in his eyes. Not because he thought I was going to deliver babies on the kitchen floor, but because I was leaving him in charge of two three-year-olds and a two-year-old who could, at any moment, create the biggest mess he'd ever have to clean.

By then, I was a regular at Beaumont Hospital in Royal Oak, a straight shot down Woodward Avenue that took, at most, fifteen minutes to get to from the house. Of course, I martyred myself by parking on the deck and trucking over the crosswalk, holding my bulging, tightened abdomen while praying and cursing in the same breath. By the time I made it to the delivery floor, I was ready to pass out. The ladies working at the desk took one look at me, and before I could count to ten, I was stretched onto a bed in triage with an IV pushed into my veins, filling me with fluid. My dear Dr. Ann Rehm was on call and stopped by to check my stats. The babies were fine. She could have sent me home, but with a wink decided that my husband should really brave the night alone with the kids and I should stay overnight. I didn't argue. My IV and I got carted into a quiet, sterile-smelling room that made me remember the night I discovered the Bell's Palsy. Ugh. That was one thing I didn't want to worry about this time around. Note to self: I needed to go see the family doctor for preventative care before my C-section.

While hoping to get a little bit of rest, my overnight check-in resulted in nothing more than nurses bobbing in every hour to check my and the babies' vitals and me driving myself home in the morning, rid of the nausea but fearing the work I'd face when I got there. Surprisingly, Tom had managed everything like a pro, and life was back to normal—or at least as normal as it was going to be for the next couple of weeks.

"Hollie?" my Aunt Ginny asked as I answered the phone while stepping into my office (aka the pantry). I always knew my Aunt Ginny's voice. She was sugary sweet and always called me "honey" or "sweetie" and it had made me smile ever since I could remember.

"I don't want to alarm you, but Grandma's had a stroke and is in the hospital. She's alive, but we are not sure what damage has been done, and we are calling your parents right now; we wanted you to know." My heart sank. I loved my Grandma Foss more than anyone. Yes, of course I loved my mom, but my personality was an equal split of my grandmas. My Grandma VanPachtenbeke had been stolen from me before I'd had a chance to spend time with her as an adult. She was everything I wanted to be: the perfect European housewife that oozed easy elegance like the finest Belgian linen. When I lost her, I vowed to spend every sacred moment with my three remaining grandparents as if they were each my last. I invested a lot of time with each of them, and it was one of the most rewarding decisions of my life. Papa and I formed a bond that I never would have had if we hadn't lost Grandma so early, and my Grandma Foss and I spent many "girls only" evenings sipping Pinot Grigio and talking about life.

When you're a kid, you really don't pay much attention to your grandparents or how they impact your lives, but after losing my first, this grandma was the holy grail of grandmas to me. She was all I had, filled with seventy-five years of life lessons and experience that I wanted to know in full detail. And she shared it all with me the year following my grandpa's passing during a trip to Florida to visit Great Aunt Mary and her daughter, Pat.

Patricia was an interior designer in Sarasota, and my long weekend with these women was the perfect coming-of-age getaway for me. During our long walks on this trip, Grandma shared her darkest secrets about growing up during the depression in our small hometown. The heartache she experienced early in life shed much light on why she loved us so much and acquired a "tough as nails" persona. She lost two brothers, her high school sweetheart (and first husband), mother, and best friend before she was thirty-five.

That weekend we had cocktails, told stories, laughed until we cried, and toured show houses until we were sick of Florida-style floor plans and their negative basements with screened in lanais and in-ground pools. By the time we came home, Grandma was convinced that, while trying on my 34C, my aunt had stolen her cardigan out of the guest bedroom. The stubborn old ladies, who had been friends since they were in their twenties, decided to hold a grudge against each other over it and never spoke again. This memory made me want to talk to my Grandma.

After I hung up the phone, I sat in the pantry with the door closed for a few minutes before returning to the kids. The next day, Tom stayed home in the morning so I could go visit her, even though the drive was in the opposite direction of my hospital. I didn't care; I just wanted to see her. The good news was that she was alive and would possibly make a full physical recovery after a few months of therapy. The bad news was that she'd lost her speech. Mentally, she was pretty much there, but she could only nod her head in either direction. My grandma was awesome. Here she was, trapped in her body, sharing a hospital room, and she smiled at me when I walked in as if she were greeting me on her screened-in porch back on Clarence Street when I was a kid. She had an infectious smile, always sincere with cute little dimples at the corners of her grin. She was honest about everything, whether you wanted to hear it or not. And a fake smile was not in her repertoire, ever. I just wish I could again hear her say, "Oh shit!" during a heated discussion or a game of cards.

The stroke brought my parents home from Florida about a month early, which was a huge blessing to us because those last few weeks I really needed my mom. She put my dad on grandma duty and came over at least three times a week until the end. I was still driving to the hospital for non-stress tests and ultrasounds and leaving my mom with the kids meant peaceful alone time during those outings.

"Thomas Patrick Gyarmati!" I scolded while standing at the mudroom door. No answer. Just his happy voice enjoying a fun, casual morning conversation with his father-in-law, who was sitting on a barstool at the kitchen island. He loved to be the host. My mom stood next to him, holding the cup of decaf he'd brewed for her, and the kids were in the lower level running around. I'd already kissed them goodbye at least fifteen minutes earlier.

"Tom," my mom interrupted the car talk. "Your wife wants you." His wife was standing at the door with her hospital bag, car keys, and nearly sixty pounds of thirty-nine-week babies ready to introduce themselves to the world. Unfortunately, the event of a twin delivery at the Gyarmati house had become about as common as a dental cleaning. Routine. I was scheduled to be checking in within thirty minutes.

I'd waited on this man on nearly every Christmas Eve, family BBQ, date night, and practically every event that required his on-time presence. I'd learned almost ten years ago to pad the time and pray for grace to keep my cool anytime we were leaving. I'd pouted and given him the silent treatment on numerous occasions while driving out to my parents' house. He'd then rebel by driving ten miles *under* the speed limit on Davisburg Road, the long, two-lane drive that wound through the tree-covered rolling hills to our dirt road destination. I'd battle myself during my sulk, and in the end, I knew I couldn't control him, and my tactics were failing miserably. I'd always resolve to keep my temper under wraps and not let the extra fifteen or twenty minutes get to me. But I *hated* being late; I was woven not only from the on-time cloth but from the get-there-five-minutes-early one as well. By the time we'd turn onto Hensell Road, he'd have his hand open in my lap as a white flag, and I'd shoot him a brown-eyed glare while consoling his palm with the little pinches that signaled my forgiveness.

"I love you, even though you make me crazy," he'd say. I'd roll my eyes, continuing my tickles as a sign of acceptance. This morning, this very important morning, I knew praying for grace would *not* deliver an angry wife or her twin daughters.

"Tom! If you don't get your butt out here right now, I'm driving myself to the hospital! I want these people out of me! NOW!" Only my mom shared my anxiety, and she pushed him through the kitchen, sending us on our way with well wishes and love. I could see my dad's smirk through the doorway, thoroughly amused at my tantrum and Tom's leisurely approach, ignoring the Hollie hormones as he put on his coat. When I was only his designer, I remember Tom telling me I was cute when I was mad during one of our many phone conversations. Back then, I was secretly flattered, a little embarrassed, and the context of my huff was over paint colors and leather samples. Today, it was major surgery. Keeping true to my ways, I pouted all the way to Beaumont. I waddled through the parking structure and refused the wheelchair from the nice, elderly volunteer at the front entrance just to prove my point. Nothing urgent, here—just a mom ready to pop out her second set of twins. By the time we reached the front desk on the second floor, I was standing with my arms crossed over my chest to prove my point. Tom ignored my efforts entirely.

Within an hour, we were in a semi-private room in pre-op. I was in my gown and hooked up to an IV that must have had a direct route to my bladder because all I could think about was emptying it, which, for the record is *not* easy to maneuver in that condition, nor is pulling a bag of fluids on wheels with you. Dr. Beals was operating and had just broken the news that I'd been bumped from the OR for a triplet delivery. I groaned in misery, and he promised to see what he could do to round up a team to move things faster.

Tom handed me the latest issue of *People* magazine to help me chillax while my bladder filled up again. I looked at the cover. Jennifer Aniston was still pregnant; she'd been expecting for years. Tom sat in the guest chair against the wall just behind me. He casually grabbed his phone from his pocket and opened up Safari.

"Well, since we're waiting here for a while, I guess I should give you my baby name ideas," he stated, looking to get a rise out of me.

"I already have the names picked out, Tom. You just need to go with it; they're perfect." Baby A was Kate Theresa and Baby B was Natalie Brooke. End of story. Except the man would not commit to these names until he actually saw the girls. And every time I'd whip out my textbook-ish name book, he'd make up an excuse to be non-committal to anything until they were born. He was also really good at shooting down all my favorite names. He hated Audrey. Stella was a beer. Abigail was an old spinster. He'd offered his coveted "Lisa, Kim, or Kelly" back when we were selecting Isabelle's name. All hot girls from his graduating class of 1985. As a result, the girls went to their dad on Christmas Day to receive a baby doll name. Lisa, Kim, and Kelly live happily amongst the American Girl collection in Emma and Isabelle's room.

"I'll just start scrolling at the beginning of the alphabet. Let's come up with cool, matchy names, like…Cindy and Windy."

"Are you NUTS? You are joking, right? I refuse to name my kids 1970s names!"

He kept his cool, knowing he had me right where he wanted me; I was like an angry raccoon stuck in an animal trap. He decided to really mess with me.

"I'm in the C's… What do you think about Capri?"

"HIDEOUS! That sounds like bad mom pants! You'd seriously name your daughter after bad mom pants?" I snapped.

"No, it's after the Island of Capri. I like it. It's very tropical," he replied with a straight face. This man was either going to bring on full labor, or he knew that I wouldn't last two minutes with that *People* Magazine and had to engage me in something to take my mind off my beach ball belly, my bladder, the double baby monitors taped to my abdomen making me itchy, and the IV, which made me queasy just thinking about the needle they'd inserted into my vein.

In that moment, a very excited Dr. Beals popped back behind our curtain and announced that he had an OR prepped and had rallied a wonderful team of doctors for my C-section. It was time to roll!

CHAPTER 12

HOW WE GOT OUTTA DODGE

Round three. I'd been prepared for the worst, but God gave me a break this time around. Bringing Natalie and Kate home from the hospital into our already crazy family of five plus a dog was the most peaceful time I can remember. I don't know if it was because I knew what to expect, was healthy, was free of scary post-surgery palsies, had tremendous support at home, or was simply filled with nice post-partum hormones that happy moms tell you about. Regardless, for the first time post-delivery, I was calm and relaxed. One look at my little angel babies had me wondering what I would have done without them. They were just under six pounds each. Natalie, the official baby of the family outweighed her older sister by five ounces. They were different from Noah and Emma. I was different. My mood was consistently even-keeled, and I'm certain my babies took my lead and were easy, happy little people because of it.

Tom and my mom took over the "Big Three," the official nickname for the older siblings (and very Motor City), and I was responsible for keeping our newbies alive. It was a cakewalk. Twenty-four hours a day, I fed my babies every three hours. Eat, keep them awake for thirty minutes, and put them down for a nap. Routine. They were little champs, so easy that I could manage all the nighttime feeding on my own with my newfound, super Zen-like persona. Noah and Emma had no interest in babies or feeding and seemed pretty happy to be rid of Isabelle, who was glued to my side as personal assistant. She'd line all of her babies up around us and was completely enamored with the fact that she had two *real* babies who were girls and the same size as Lisa, Kim, and Kelly.

After the first five days, Tom went back to work, and my mom came three days a week to help out. This was the beginning of life with five kids under four years old. I was Mom. My only mission was to take care of kids. I took a mental leave from design work, crabbing about the ugly wallpaper and draperies hanging in my house, and accepted the kid clutter without a twitch. I was resting in the comfort and joy of baby land and wanted to enjoy this newfound happiness while it lasted. I missed it with Noah and Emma because I was a stressed-out new mom. I was a hot mess with Isabelle because of the Bell's. I didn't want to miss out on snuggle time with Natalie and Kate. These two were *my* babies. They looked like me. With three blue-eyed Hungarians dominating the gene pool, I finally had two little mini-me's who were so identical that even I had a hard time telling them apart. I loved swaddling them up and nestling them in their crib at the end of my bed. I'd wrap another thin, cotton blanket around them both so they looked like little peas in a pod, and they'd look up at me with big, sparkling hazel-brown eyes. "Good night, babies. I love you," I'd whisper in my sweetest mom voice. And they'd look up at me, smile, then peacefully fall asleep. All this was happening, of course, with Noah, Emma, and Isabelle running through the rest of the house causing as much ruckus as ever, but I'd learned to focus on my little surprise babies and soak up the love. Life was good.

It is a rare occasion that I should remember an exact date, but when I do it's because it holds life-changing significance. The day was May 14, 2009. It was a Thursday, and I was sitting crossed legged on an oversized, purple upholstered chair that came with the house in our "fancy living room" feeding my six-week-old girls when the phone rang. I reached over and saw that it was Tom calling from his cell phone. It was around lunchtime, and I assumed he was in the car on the way to a restaurant or running an errand. I balanced the phone on my shoulder while holding a bottle in one hand and a nursing baby in the other.

"Hi," I answered.

"Life as we know it is over," he announced in a dry, calm voice that I'd only remembered hearing after the tragic death of his father. I had no idea what he was about to tell me.

"What's wrong?" I asked, also unaware that his opening statement would become a sentence we'd be quoting for years to come. I could tell that he was sitting in his office with the door closed as he lowered his voice.

"I've just been delivered an official letter via UPS. They are 'eliminating' the dealership." My heart sank. The potential of this had been a source of gossip for a few months, but Tom thought they were safe due to their high sales volumes.

"What does this mean exactly?" I asked, wanting to further digest my husband's future.

"We are no longer a Dodge dealer. They are taking Dodge away from us and handing it to the Chrysler dealer across the street. No compensation, no offset, no alternate replacement location. *Nothing*. We have two weeks to sell all of our cars and salable assets. *Two weeks*. Can you believe it?"

I could believe it. Very little after our year of financial losses could shock me. What I couldn't believe was that he'd received a break-up letter. Nothing in person, just the sterile "it's not you, it's us" letter. They deserved a more formal announcement and a lot more notice. Only a year before, Tom told me that his brother could have sold his franchise to the same guy across the street for a profit he could retire with (at an upper-class standard), and now it was gone. They'd been dumped by letter. I thought about the eighty-plus employees who worked there and their families. Good, hardworking people who might be losing their jobs and receiving their news from Tom. Tom was the backbone of the dealership. He did the hiring, the firing, the banking, the marketing, the ordering, and acted as the Human Resource department. He had a full staff who spent their days working off decisions he'd made to keep the dealership in motion and the profits coming in. He was the one who'd handle the tough customer service issues or internal squabbles. No matter what came his way, he kept his calm demeanor and resolved problems with fairness and integrity. He knew this was the secret to retaining long-term customers and employees in an industry largely devoid of loyalty. I wondered what would become of these employees more than I wondered what would become of us.

The remaining minutes of our call consisted of whatever words of encouragement we could muster to give each other, and then I went back to feeding angels. I sat in the big, ugly chair immobilized by the news. I could have started worrying about all the "what ifs," but at this point it was too early to do so. When you have two perfect little ten-pound babies resting in your arms, it's pretty hard to freak out about anything. I remembered a conversation we'd had while we were dating when he asked if I'd be happy if there came a time when his income placed us in the "middle class." My firm answer was that I might love him *more* because I grew up with modest means yet had the kind of childhood I only dreamed of giving my children. I envisioned Tom finding another job at a dealership; he'd be a catch for anyone. Maybe we could move out of Michigan before the kids started school. Live in a warmer state. I was partial to North Carolina. We could buy a nice, normal-sized Colonial home and start over. I would leave it all behind in a heartbeat. Michigan native, yes. Cold, long, winters, no thanks. My parents would follow us in their camper wherever we lived, as long as they could drive there. I would have no problem packing up my family and starting from scratch. It would all be okay.

For us, we were digesting this loss from a very personal perspective, but what was unfathomable was that we were joining the ranks of elimination with almost eight hundred other Chrysler dealers that day. Dealers across the country, from Fuller Jeep in Rockland, Maine to Island Dodge in Hawaii, were delivered their fateful letters due to the historical automotive bailout and federal bankruptcy that had given Chrysler a "unique opportunity to trump the tough and restrictive state franchise law that otherwise governed agreements with their dealers" (as later presented by Neil Barofsky, author of *Bailout: How Washington Abandoned Main Street While Rescuing Wall Street*). This "delivering of the letter" would ultimately result in the loss of almost 100,000 jobs for Chrysler alone nationwide in the coming months, all of which we, or at least I, was protected from as I sat in my big, ugly purple chair feeding babies. But what did I know? I was focused on keeping babies alive. And it's a good thing, because to think of all the families facing hardship such as job loss would have been a burden I couldn't bear. So I kept my head down and nursed the wounds of my family in the best way I could.

Within a few short weeks of the break, the Five Star accredited Mt. Clemens Dodge would go from its highest point as one of the nation's top grossing standalone dealers to non-existent. And in the coming months and even year, the landscape of the Motor City would change in ways never before seen. The bailout and elimination had been the final blow to our already declining economy, and what was left could only be described as a ghost town. So many people were out of work, from executives to parts suppliers and engineers, and the devastation permeated into everyone who supported the once booming economy. Retailers, restaurants, dry-cleaners. The hurt could be felt all the way into the small towns. It was so bad that the freeways were devoid of traffic during rush hour. Friday afternoon traffic jams headed up north for the weekend subsided along with the American dream most middle-class citizens had worked hard to achieve. Anyone and everyone without reason to stay was leaving the state to pursue new work. And we couldn't blame them.

As big as the blow was for us, it was even bigger for Tom's brother and his family, so the plan to move forward was painful but necessary, a one-foot-in-front-of-the-other proposition. The rebound plan was to become a used car dealership while new automotive franchises were pursued. I knew there was a plan underway, and Tom was busy with all the nuts and bolts of dissolving the business and making contacts to help him move forward. Maybe this was not a bad thing at all; maybe we'd come out ahead. I rested on that "what if" and continued on with my life as The Mom. The only thing I tweaked was my grocery budget. Everything else had already been cut. I went from an unlimited budget with Noah and Emma to feeding a family of seven on about $200 a week. One quarter of that was allocated to diapers and formula. All of my babies ended up on formula and breast milk since my breast was *not* best when it was on double duty. I gave up organic milk for the kids and my fancy powdered formula brand for Costco's Kirkland formula. It was a tough pill to swallow, but I had no choice. I even called the manufacturer to make sure it was made in the US to BandAid my guilt. My budget cut was the best I could pull off to help our ever-diminishing salary, and Tom appreciated my weekly diligence.

That summer, life went on in the Gyarmati house as normally as it could. In July, we took our camper up north for a trip with my parents. I wasn't thrilled about doing this with newborns and preschoolers, but I packed a good attitude along with all the baby gear, food, diapers, Pack 'n Plays, strollers, and tricycles. If my mom hadn't been a campsite over, I'd have said no to the whole thing, but she, along with Tom and my dad, were on call if I needed them. We stayed at a beautiful state park in the northern lower peninsula that was situated next to a large inland lake; it had to be a couple of miles long. When we pulled into our campsite, I got out of the van to assess the set-up plan. State parks in Michigan are stunning. They commonly have nice wooded sites covered with grass and a cement pad. We had a giant outdoor rug that we'd position under our canopy with the picnic table centered on it, and if the grass were less than desirable, we'd move the kid area to the rug. The site I was standing on was void of grass entirely; it was covered in black dirt. Not nice, dark sand but real dirt; pig-pen-style dirt. My good attitude had already unpacked itself and was standing at the exit hailing a taxi to go home. I reeled it back in and put a smile on as I motioned for Tom to back in. I envisioned what this dirt site would translate to with the kids, and before I could complete my thought Emma had jumped out of the van and thrown her sweaty little body and strawberry blonde curls into the middle of the site where she started making a snow angel, smearing black dirt onto her clothes, under her nails, and into her scalp.

The air filled with dust as she pumped her arms and legs back and forth with four-year-old excitement. All cute for those not responsible for washing those little arms and legs. In that moment, as Tom unloaded the rest of the kids and set Natalie and Kate, snug in their car seats, on the picnic table, I made the executive decision that this would be the last time I'd agree to a camping trip with anyone who couldn't clean their own cracks and crevasses. What followed was an exhausting week of feeding, cleaning, pumping in my tiny camper bathroom stall, schlepping dirty bottles to my mom's camper to hand wash them three times a day, and campfires that warmed my bobbing head as I fell asleep during the only adult interaction I'd have throughout the day. I made my announcement on the way home, and Tom agreed that the attempt really was crazy. We sold the camper the next month and never looked back.

Fall soon approached, and most kids Noah and Emma's age were in pre-school full-time. Not mine. I looked into pre-school and discovered that it would cost $6,000 (which I didn't have) to send them both for the year, and it would take at least three hours out of my schedule to get them there and pick them up, all with five-month-old babies and a three-year-old in tow. Just loading five kids into the van, each with a car seat, was a ten-minute process. I nixed pre-school all together and prayed that they wouldn't miss out on anything too important. I viewed it as going Greek in college. Not required, but expensive to be social. I didn't pay to have friends at the university, and I wouldn't be doing it for my kids. We had enough social activity under our own roof, free of charge. Thus began another method of streamlining my life.

I also stopped nursing around this time, and as my double Ds returned to their original size, my happy hormones dried up, and I was left with my very first round of postpartum depression. I couldn't figure it out or even understand it, but everything I did threw me into a state of panic or extreme sadness. My mom Zen was gone, and I woke up one morning to discover that I lived in a mansion with five little people whose combined needs could keep the staff of an entire college football program busy should they be responsible for feeding, cleaning, bathing, disciplining, scheduling, shopping, laundering, and nurturing them to become well-rounded people. And there was just one me. I was lonely. Everyday tasks like driving to the grocery store had me paralyzed. Just one year earlier, I was beautiful and canoodling with celebrities, and now I was looking in the mirror at a thirty-four-year-old frumpy woman who'd lost her body, style, smile, and soul to be a mom. *I hated my life.*

I talked to my OB extensively, and she assured me that I'd return to my old self. She may have given me some drugs. I honestly can't recall. I just remember that by Thanksgiving I had bounced back from the darkness and had my mom game back on. I was cleaning up Round One of dinner, and Tom walked into the kitchen with his mail pile and coat under one arm as the kids smothered him with conversation and hugs. He looked at me with a smirk.

"I've just made your Thanksgiving dinner much easier," he knew I was fretting about cooking a giant raw bird for my family while carrying on with baby feedings. Worried that he'd gone and done something crazy like downloading Martha Stewart's step-by-step cooking guide for the perfect turkey, fixings, and pumpkin pies from scratch, I replied with a hesitant, "What?"

"I am picking up the entire dinner at 2PM on Thanksgiving Day from Kruse & Muer, and you don't have to shop or cook a thing." *I married the greatest man on the planet!* He understood that there is a time for sacrifice and a time to splurge. Kruse & Muer was one of our favorite restaurants, and just the thought of their poppy seed encrusted buttered bread made my mouth water. A turkey would be amazing! I smiled at him in awe of his attentiveness to my needs.

"How much?"

"Get this; the whole thing, complete with pumpkin pie was $250, and it'll feed us all."

It wasn't a splurge, it was a steal! This was the greatest gift he'd ever given me, hands down. Make my life easier and you are my hero forever. Forget diamonds!

That Thanksgiving I decided to go all out and boycott tradition by serving our restaurant meal buffet style. Grandma and Papa were with us, as were my parents, my brother and his wife, and my aunt Kathy. Get-togethers with my side of the family are usually very loud. We took our plates full of succulent turkey, mashed potatoes, roasted vegetables, and bread to the formal dining room, and there, under Noreen's giant crystal chandelier, which I'd spent two hours cleaning earlier in the week, we enjoyed the best Thanksgiving Dinner ever in almost complete silence. The only sounds were the constant *Mmmmmms* and *Ohhhhs* combined with the clanking of our forks and knives on the china. I felt incredibly blessed to have two seven-month old babies and three beautiful kids who I got to spend the day with, watching the Macy's parade on TV and sipping hot chocolate instead of sticking my hand in a dead bird with the fear of letting my family down with a meal I didn't enjoy cooking. That year, we shamelessly made Kruse & Muer our new Thanksgiving tradition, deciding to save our home-cooked meals for Christmas Eve, cold winter soups in my Dutch oven, and Tom's famous filet and shrimp skewers during the summer months. All done raw bird. All done.

We brought 2009 to a close with continued gratitude for a job, health, and successfully entering into the official Big Family category. Tom and his brother were setting up as a Kia and Hyundai dealer, which had Tom working hard and focusing on big success for the new year. On the home front, I was still on wife and mom duty. I managed to sneak in workouts during naptime and had a grip on running the money pit with as much enthusiasm as possible. Noreen's dingy floral wallpaper and heavy draperies were suffocating me, so I set my sights on somehow removing some ugly over the next year so I could start making the house feel a little more "us." I missed the bachelor pad and secretly wished we had stayed, even though it would have been tight. I adopted Tom's positive outlook for our future success but hoped that we could one day move from the big house back into a normal neighborhood so we could have our life back. I wanted to feed and clothe my kids stress-free and hire a sitter once in a while for a date night. Simple, small town girl stuck in the executive home on top of the hill. I kept my faith and hope and believed that we would come back bigger than ever, in a way that would make us thankful for the break-up letter. 2010 would be our year.

CHAPTER 13

SMOKING HOT

"Okay, honey, lie all the way back on the table, and let's take a look," my family doctor instructed as I stretched out with a twinge of excitement and a bit of dread. I lifted my shirt so he could examine my abdomen. He felt my lower area and told me I definitely had a small hernia. Then he took his right hand, turned it sideways with his thumb pointed toward the ceiling and slowly pressed it into the middle of my tummy. Once he touched my skin his hand quickly sunk into my abdomen like it was a bowl full of pudding. *This is so gross*, I thought to myself.

"Just as I suspected, your abdominal muscles have ripped apart from top to bottom. They are floating around in there, and the only way to fix them is reconstructive surgery," he diagnosed. After housing Natalie and Kate, I knew I didn't have a chance at returning to any state of normal after they were born. They ripped my abdomen apart. Nice.

"Can this be covered by my insurance?" I thought of all the obese people who go through extreme weight loss and then receive help to remove excess skin. Growing humans should rank up there with binge eating. If they deserved to look normal, so did I.

"You could try, but honestly, the easiest way is to just go see Dr. Mitchell; he's the best." Funny, a family friend who was a surgeon also recommended him. I couldn't wait to make an appointment. I'd been plotting this since I had Nat and Kate but was waiting for the right time. My body had returned to its pre-pregnancy state and what I was left with was a droopy spare tire around my middle that was filled with stretch marks and loose skin. My old belly button was hanging in there somewhere, stretched to the size of a silver dollar. I felt ugly. My battle wounds had left me scarred and my usual high self-esteem had withered away with the old Hollie. Designer Hollie. Fit Hollie. Walk through the store in high fashion to the studio on the third floor Hollie. She was gone. Selling my husband on this surgery was Step One to reclaiming my identity. I left the office and imagined how my conversation with him would go while I drove home.

Later that night, I brought Tom into our master bathroom and sat him on the marble step of the tub. He was on guard because I'd removed him from the sofa and had announced that we "needed to talk." I was nervous that he'd shoot me down, tell me that we couldn't afford it, that I could die on the table all in the name of vanity, or that he loved me just the way I was. I'd counter with selling my engagement ring to cover the cost, that I'd be with the best surgeon in the state, and that I had to love myself more than he loved me because without that, I'd be good for "shet" (the way his dad used to pronounce "shit" in his Hungarian accent.)

"I want to schedule an appointment to see Dr. Mitchell. He's a plastic surgeon. I want him to fix my muscles and remove *this*." I stood in front of him and lifted up my long-sleeved T-shirt over my bra. He took one look at me and winced. I don't think he ever paid attention to what I looked like post twins! I pulled my soft, wrinkly skin away from my body by the handful to give him a full visual.

"Stop! It's disgusting, you're right. Schedule the appointment, and we'll figure out how to pay for it. I'll sell some stuff on eBay." I was shocked. I lowered my shirt and gave him a big hug, and by the next morning I'd booked my consult.

Three weeks later Tom and I were sitting in the exam room of Dr. Edward Mitchell. The nurse had already logged my stats, conducted her interview, and taken before photos for my file. She was in her late forties, petite, blonde, and had shown off her own tummy tuck to us, selling me on how wonderful it was to have it done. Tom sat in silence, pretending to be bored, but I think he was secretly checking her out and imagining my transformation back to his flat-tummied wife. Within a few minutes Dr. Mitchell walked in, and I was immediately infatuated with him. He was on the shorter side, maybe fifty years old, with dark hair and chiseled features; he was a good-looking man. My infatuation stemmed from the fact that before me stood the man who would give me my life back. People were always gushing over all the kids, the two sets of twins, and would praise me on how wonderful I looked. What they didn't see was that I was *really* good at camouflaging the darkness that I carried every day.

I knew I was sitting in this office for the right reasons. I was not being vain. I wanted to fix what had been broken, and it wasn't about wanting a bikini body; it was about wanting to pull on a pair of jeans without excess flab drooping over the waistband. It was about being able to wear a fitted T-shirt. It was about cranking out serious workouts and seeing results instead of my floating abdominals. It was about claiming my happy back. And I would not feel guilty about that. My hero gave me a thorough examination, confirming that my muscles were ripped apart and that he would need to fix my hernia, stitch my muscles from my sternum down to my pubic bone, remove at least ten inches of loose skin from side to side—including my belly button—and create a new belly button. This was going to be the ultimate complete reconstructive surgery. I was thrilled. Tom continued to look at the floor while he sat in the side chair as the doctor described the procedure.

Then, Dr. Mitchell said the greatest thing, something Tom and I both needed to hear. He told me that I was the perfect and most deserving candidate for this surgery. I was healthy and physically fit, didn't have to lose any weight, and was his favorite type of case to work on because we are hard-working moms who deserve to feel great. I imagined his wife, friends, and colleagues who were all walking around with perfect midsections. I would be happy to jump into that tribe. After our consult, he sent us to meet with the blonde nurse who walked us through the procedure and went over all medical details, recovery, and billing. We scheduled the surgery for the end of April, just after the twins' first birthday.

Prepping for my big day was just like planning another baby delivery. I made meals to stock the freezer for a month and got the house organized to survive an off-duty mom for at least two weeks. My mom would stay with us for the first week and then I'd be on my own, in pain, taking care of my brood. Natalie and Kate were in full motion crawling around, and the Big Three needed their routine to keep from uttering the words, "I'm boooooored." I spent my evenings reading every internet tummy tuck story ever posted, which was a big mistake. Who posts stories unless they had a horrible experience? After reading at least a hundred "My doctor destroyed my body" posts, I logged off for good.

My biggest fear was the pain factor. I'd been warned that it would be painful. I would power through the pain with drugs just as I had everything else over the last couple of years. And the six to eight weeks of "Don't lift anything heavier than a gallon of milk" were always unrealistic, so I'd just have to take it day by day and figure it out. I was as ready as I was going to be, and I couldn't wait to rid myself of my pregnancy leftovers.

On the day of the surgery, I was checked in and taken back to pre-op. Tom stayed in the waiting room. My operation would take about four hours. Lying on the gurney this time was exciting. I welcomed the IV as it was plunged into my veins, and I was wearing my favorite pair of low-rise bikinis so Dr. Mitchell would know where to make his incisions. I wasn't afraid as long as I didn't envision what they were going to do to me on that table. The videos I'd previewed were not for the faint of heart. I was going to look like one of those plastic mannequins with the removable organs used in medical school. These people were going to slice me from hip to hip, and my entire abdominal cavity would be exposed to the world. A flash from *Silence of the Lambs* invaded my thoughts, but I fought back with my Jenny-McCarthy-hot-in-her-bikini-after-Weight-Watchers photo that I'd pasted in my food journal. My pulse was racing. I needed a Valium. I wondered if I should ask for drugs.

Before I could blurt out a sign of fear, a couple of nurses gathered around me and opened my gown. Dr. Mitchell stood between them with his handsome smile and remarkably naturally aging face (not a sign of Botox) and whipped out a black Sharpie. Ironic, since the black Sharpie is the only brand of marker I'd used for twenty years on every design project, poster, and even to-do list I'd ever made. Tom hated my Sharpie addiction because using it on paper sucked the ink out faster, but I insisted that the line quality couldn't be beaten. My doctor then started marking my body up just like I'd seen done on reality TV shows. Thank God it wasn't my face or boobs. I'm happy to age gracefully from here on out in those areas. I slightly lifted my head just enough to see the giant line drawn from hip to hip, a few marks noting where my new belly button would be placed, and some lines along my sides. I looked like a voodoo doll waiting to be poked with vengeful pins, and my pulse quickened even more. Thankfully, as I plopped my head back on the flat sterile pillow, I heard one of the team members tell me to relax as they gently placed a mask over my nose and instructed me to count backward, lulling me into my deep surgical sleep.

I'd had plenty of surgeries over the last few years, and just in case you're wondering, you don't dream while you're under. At least I don't. I had no sense of time passing, and what seemed like moments later I was coming to in recovery, hopefully with a face to greet me that I was happy to see. In this case it was Tom. And we were happy to see each other.

"How are you feeling?" he asked.

"I don't know. It's too early to figure it out."

"Your surgery took more than four and a half hours. I was getting worried, but Dr. Mitchell came out to talk to me and said he took extra long because he wanted to give you a really nice belly button." Tom smiled. I knew this extra attention made him feel like he was getting his money's worth, and he always appreciates that. A nice belly button! I couldn't wait to see my belly button. I tried to look down, but as soon as I shifted my head, I immediately felt nauseous. Me plus surgical drugs equals miserable nausea. Every time. After every C-section and my appendectomy, I was plagued with nausea that lasted for hours. Ugh. I slowly took my hands and felt my tummy. I was tightly wrapped like a burrito with layers of bandages. I wouldn't be seeing anything for days. Instead, I grabbed Tom's hand and pleaded for some Coke. He knew exactly what to do and quietly excused himself from post-op. By the time I was situated in my room, my husband had snuck out to the parking garage, zipped a couple of blocks to McDonald's, and brought me back a large Coke and chicken McNuggets—the two things sure to cure my nausea spell and bring the color back to my face. I sipped the syrup and nibbled the processed, deep-fried miracle cure over the next hour until I could incline my bed enough to watch TV. Recovering from cosmetic surgery was not glamorous. The nurses weren't sweet and friendly like they were on the mother/baby floor. No Darla or Gloria here. These nurses were heavyset and a little grumpy. I was feeling a little judged by them, and I wanted to blurt my story out, but they didn't care. They just took my vitals and knew that I'd be outta there in the morning, when the next round would arrive with wrapped torsos, lipo'd hips, breast implants, and face-lifts. I hated being lumped into this recovery group and couldn't wait to get home.

As was the case when reading up on caring for twins, the guru advice for massive abdominal surgery was realistic for someone *without* kids, who had a relaxing environment and a full-time nurse for the first six weeks; it was a joke. I scuffled into my family circus pumped full of Vicodin and lived on the sofa for the first five days. Miraculously, I was able to tune out the noise and my mom and Tom were superstar caretakers. I've never felt as helpless as I did that first week. I walked like I was halfway to a toe touch because it was excruciating to stand up straight. They both did a wonderful job keeping the kids busy and giving me lots of space. The hardest part was not picking up the babies. I wanted to hold them more than anything. Their little chubby cheeks, hands, and thighs were unbearably sweet. I needed more than TV to take my mind off the pain and my immobility.

Enter Bella, Edward, and Jake. What better time to read the *Twilight* series? Sadly, I hadn't read a novel in years. Too frugal to buy the books, I had my mom check out the first from her library, and I devoured it faster than a vampire did a teenage girl. Motherhood had me so busy that I'd forgotten what it was like to get lost in a fantasy, and this easy adolescent read was exactly what I needed. I was suddenly grumbling about a seventeen-year-old with the saddest personality I'd ever known, wondering why this beautiful old soul vampire couldn't go find himself someone who would make him laugh or handle the sight of blood. And the wolves. They *really* ripped through all those jeans every day? Life on muscle relaxers and flat on my back was suddenly not so bad.

One evening that first week, Tom was working late, and I was situated on the leather sofa in the great room surrounded by icepacks, pillows, and the kids, who were watching a Disney movie on the flat-screen in the built-in cabinet by Noah's staircase. It was after dinner, and the sun was setting on the other side of the house. My mom had finished the dishes and plopped into her favorite armchair with matching ottoman, another Noreen leftover but one we'd grown quite fond of. The two-story room was still boasting her heavy burgundy draperies with giant brass lion head tieback holders. The matching upholstered dining chairs sat across from each other at the game table near the fireplace. We had another upholstered rocking chair—my custom order from Marshall Field's when I was pregnant with Noah and Emma—and some occasional pieces. The floor had a cream wool area rug that was about fourteen by sixteen feet in size, stained with muddy dog prints, sippy cups drips, and at the moment, blanketed with every toy on the main floor. The seven baby gates were locked, and the lights were dimmed. We were all pretty mellow, and I was half asleep in my drugged state of mind. Then it happened.

"Do you smell that?" my mom perked up her head.

"Smell what?" I mumbled.

"I smell smoke," she replied, wide awake and on high alert. I of course propped myself up and sniffed the air. I've got a great nose. I blame it on my cigarette sensitivity, acquired in college when I made the mistake of living with a smoker. I lived (not for long) with a roommate who greeted me in the kitchen while I was eating my cereal with a Marlboro Light dangling from her lips, and I found the butts sprinkled everywhere from the TV top to the edge of the bathtub. From that point on, I could smell any kind of smoke as well as Smoky the Bear. If I was driving in traffic, I could get a whiff of a cigarette and within seconds figure out which car it was coming from. I smelled smoke, too. I quickly looked around the room, and within a second the smell was escalating. It was burning. Then I saw it. The expansive staircase had a landing at its midpoint with a beautiful palladium window and a built-in seat—the one that I thought would be perfect for a little girl curled up to read on a rainy Sunday. Of course, Noreen had matching burgundy draperies with a rosette securing the giant swags right at the top of the window. And that ugly rosette was smoking like bacon in the broiler.

"The draperies are catching fire!" I yelled in a panic, grimacing in pain. "Call 911!" My mom ran to the kitchen, and within seconds was on the cordless phone. Thank goodness we lived just a couple of blocks from the police department and paid taxes high enough to support a family of four. Within less than a minute we had three firefighters burst in through the garage door, and in seconds they had their extinguishers aimed at the smoking drapery. We stood in awe of their masculinity in full uniform and heroic action, clearly saving us women and children from our demise. The kids were cheering. My mom and I embraced the babies, both thinking of what could have been if we were in another part of the house when the drapery started to smoke.

"These draperies were about thirty seconds away from full flames, Mrs. Gyarmati. You're very lucky you called us when you did. This can light is way too close to all this fabric," the dark haired thirty-something officer indicated.

"Those horrid things came with the house," I said in disgust, wanting no association with selections that were not only ugly but not up to code. "While you're up there can you just remove them? And unscrew the light bulb?"

"I think that's a great idea. No problem. Guys, go grab a ladder and let's get this fabric down." *Could it get any better?* Not only did I get to watch Noreen's draperies almost combust out of their ugliness, I had three men in uniform removing them from my sight as if I were a beautiful damsel in distress who might faint if she had them to view them for one more day. As I stood there enjoying my ridiculous daydream, I carefully set my baby down and felt the rip of pain in my abs as I stood back into my old lady, hunched over stance. *Oh crap!* With all the commotion, I'd forgotten what I looked like, which was as bad as the old, weathered woman on the front of a Shoebox greeting card. I was a sight! I was wearing baggy, flannel pajama bottoms and an oversized long-sleeved T-shirt that covered up my bandages and wrap. My socks were mismatched, and I hadn't showered in at least a couple of days. I was grimy from head to toe, no make-up, yet I was smiling as though I looked like a million bucks thanks to my deceptive friend, Vicodin.

The officers removed the bundles of fabric—one with a hole through the white lining rimmed with black ash—and threw them in a heap in the garage. They politely smiled at me, I'm sure wondering if I was the same mom they'd met on numerous occasions since we'd moved in. I stood up straight even though I felt like I was ripping apart every stitch just to regain a little bit of dignity. I was so loopy I don't even think my face was able to flush pink with embarrassment. I knew they were wondering what was going on with me but were too polite to ask. When my friendly chatter came to a halt, my mom caught on and profusely thanked our firemen as they walked out the garage. That night, I flushed my pills down the toilet and called my doctor the next day, asking for something that would bring my brain cells back to life while keeping the pain at bay.

By the time my mom went home after first week, I had a pretty good idea as to what my results looked like. Though I was quite swollen and had lots of bruising, my scar was in the exact location of my three C-section incisions but much cleaner and wider. My skin was tight and still covered in tiny stretch marks through the middle (my Noah and Emma tattoo), and I had the cutest belly button I'd ever seen, perfectly placed. It looked real. It felt real. It was a little "innie" about the size of a dime. I didn't plan to ever show it off, and it would be years before it would see the sun—five years to be exact. I was thrilled with my new tummy and surprised by the pain. It was worse than I expected. It was a constant burning, throbbing, deep muscular pain that penetrated my entire torso. And now I was on my own with the kids to continue the healing process to the best of my ability.

The next several weeks were grueling. I can't compare it to taking care of three while carrying twins. This was different. The pain was severe, but I was motivated to move as much as possible and keep focused on the finish line, which was *not* sad, post-baby body but instead my restored "before childbirth" body. In the end, I had to rely on painkillers for over two months to get through the days. I hung out at home, wore my super tight Velcro bandage, and made sure my peeps stayed alive. Thankfully, the weather was nice, and we were able to spend hours outside on the play structure and riding bikes on the driveway. I even cruised through the rest of the *Twilight* series, deciding that I was Team Edward and that should he and his vamp family should fly back to Europe, I would live in their modern glass house in the Seattle mountainside alone. Bella could love the dog because he *is* man's best friend and he would cheer her up on her down days.

CHAPTER 14

THE DEVIL WEARS A DIAPER BAG

I opened my eyes to find myself face to face with my five-year-old son. His big, smoky blues looked like they'd been watching me for hours.

"Mom, does God love the Devil?" I groaned inside as my mental gears screeched from Sleep to Wikipedia. Noah shoots rapid-fire questions at me from the moment he wakes up until he negotiates his last sip of water during tuck-in. I wasn't ready for high gear, but I didn't have a choice. I thoughtfully considered my answer because whatever I was about to say may be used against me by my future lawyer, who was patiently waiting as we lay in his bed. The August morning sun was shining through his window. *How did I end up in here?* Oh yes, my 3AM wake-up: the snoring spouse. Noah's bedroom was furthest from mine (volume control), and he had a queen-sized bed (space). I decided to be vague in my response.

"That is a *great* question, honey. I don't have an exact answer, but it's a great one to ask Father Michael after Mass." He was happy with that. I rolled onto my back and listened for it. And there it was. Natalie and Kate were just waking up, and their twin chatter filled the hall with the sweet voices of morning bliss. At fifteen months old, they could hang out in their cribs for at least fifteen minutes before they'd start to get antsy. They'd babble back and forth in their unique twin language that only moms, dads, brothers, and sisters could understand. Isabelle would enter the scene momentarily to torment them. "Osbah," they called her. I could hear her swinging their door open and acting like Mommy. The screaming began. She was such an instigator! I'm not sure if it was the copper hair, the age of four, or being sandwiched between two sets of twins, but this kid made it her mission to have the attention of anyone, willing to scream it, punch it, tattle on it, or give it a talking to. Thank God Emma was still asleep in her top bunk. Poor Emma, after five years she was still trying to get a good night's rest without being roused. I rolled out of Noah's bed, leaving him with his deep thoughts and brewing energy that would run through the house as soon as he'd filed away my response.

I snuck through their hall into the foyer balcony, graced with its massive three-tiered brass chandelier that had been collecting dust since the day we moved in, and into our master bedroom to get dressed. As the floor squeaked, Otto stretched out of his dog bed and Tom rolled over out of his deep, peaceful slumber. "What are you doing?" he mumbled as he entered a second round of snoozing in his bed fit for a king. I didn't answer. *What do you think I'm doing? I'm taking care of our kids.* I don't sleep in (not that I would if given the option, but it would be nice to have it on occasion). Instead, I tried not to start my day blaming him for my exhaustion. He had no idea that I'd been sleeping in different bedrooms and sometimes on multiple sofas throughout the night or that my whirlwind life of noise and endless responsibilities had swarmed my mind to a point of perpetual motion. It stopped only if slowed into a drug-induced coma, and even then, was at risk of a baby, toddler, kindergartener, snorer, or puking dog giving it a spin.

When I woke up angry and irritated, I knew that I needed to refresh my attitude and forgive my innocent spouse to get through another day. For better or worse. I fumbled through my row of T-shirts hanging on their black, velvet-lined hangers in my closet and began a silent plea for a day filled with supernatural energy and love. Love that I found hard to give in the midst of the noise. Love that had slowly begun to dry up in my well of motherhood. Life was nothing like I'd imagined when Tom and I moved our family to this house. If someone had whispered in my ear my fate as the CEO of this life, I would have worried myself into an institution. I would never have believed that in just three years I would double my workload with extra square footage, wiped out funds, a dog, and another set of twins. I prayed for extra hours in the day to get it all done. I didn't have a crazy standard for my life; I just needed the bare minimums to be met throughout the day. I'd become a survivalist.

As I brushed my teeth and washed my face, I thought about my recent cuts. I'd moved my cleaning help to every other week to save money. This meant that the bathrooms were sanitized, and I was on my own for the rest of the house. Papa was now in his late eighties and required at-home care. He needed my mom more than I did, and we both agreed that she would only come over when I was really in a bind. This meant bumping my one and only time out of the house alone to weekends or evenings, both of which I despised as I envisioned walking the aisles of the busy grocery store or dimly-lit parking lot. I was performing the tasks of three full-time jobs, and something had to give, but I couldn't imagine what.

I sat at my vanity, turned on my late mother-in-law's backlit vanity mirror and pulled open my make-up drawer filled with a mishmash of bargain brands that I'd accumulated over the last couple of years. I missed my department store powder. I looked at my sad reflection and dug deep down for peace. I was the backbone of this family. Their mood hinged on my breakfast presentation. I dusted my shiny skin and applied a coat of mascara and gloss.

I took another look before running my brush through my mousy brown hair. I gave thanks for the day ahead and felt love lifting me from the depths of my sorrow. Renewed with a sense of gratitude and joy for my husband and my kids, I would *not* be defeated by the overwhelming tasks of my day. I would be cheerful and kind and take it one hour at a time. I would outsmart my littles by remaining one step ahead of their hunger, energy, and unique personas, just like Ben Stiller in *Night at the Museum*, which was the most relatable analogy I'd seen for my everyday life. I understand scary, unpredictable animal behavior over sweet and endearing movies on the Hallmark channel. I would not stoop to a five-year-old's mentality and argue with Noah when he blew up over a time out. I would compose complete thoughts through the noise. I would smile and mean it when Tom scurried through the kitchen in a late-for-work panic asking for assistance finding his keys, cell phone, or the sticky note he left on the corner of the island, expecting it to stay put in the control center of my kid zone. I would be beautiful inside and out and would have a great day. Amen. Transformed.

I popped into Natalie's and Kate's room. Their chubby little smiles erased my morning fret, and I found myself happily zipping through a round of kissing their cheeks, changing their diapers, getting them dressed, and guiding them backwards down the stairs and into the kitchen with the Big Three trailing behind on both sides. Our kitchen and great room had a total of seven baby gates that had to stay locked and secure at all times to ensure that Natalie and Kate did not escape into unsafe areas of the house. Getting from point A to point B, whether in or out of the home, was one of the hardest parts my job. One gate left open or one un-held hand could be deadly. Feeding them took up half of my day. By this point, I'd eliminated any choice of entrée for the big kids and focused on the basics: protein, starch, and fruit. If I could get them fed without something spilled or dumped across the table, I considered it a success. Natalie and Kate would sit through our meals in their highchairs next to the island, content with nibbling on their soft, bite-sized breakfast. I'd learned to give them only a couple pieces at a time and was humored as they discussed their treasures, passed them from one tray to the other, or dropped much of it into their laps. If they saw me cutting up a new round of food, they'd quickly slide whatever they were working on off their tray and onto the floor in the excitement of getting something better.

It was at this point that I finally found the love for Otto I'd neglected to nurture over his first two years. He was my right-hand man in the kitchen and saved me hours of cleanup every day. He'd start under the table and scarf down the big kid leftovers. Then, he'd make his way to the high chairs as I worked my kitchen triangle. Actually, he was the "Bermuda" in my triangle. Whatever ventured into it disappeared into his stocky Springer Spaniel tummy. Once he'd licked the floor clean, he'd stand between the twins waiting for morsels to miss their mouths and land on their chunky little thighs. He'd swiftly and gently nuzzle his fat nose in between their legs into what I referred to as the "crotch buffet." The summer heat left them barelegged and wiping them down with a soapy washcloth was fine with me. I'd even stoop to giving my four-legged Dyson the go ahead to lick their seats clean after they were gone to prep the surface for my disinfecting wipe down. My mom was disgusted the first time she witnessed this act, but quickly adopted it the first time she was on her own to serve lunch. I remember hauling groceries in from the garage one day to find Otto licking the high-chair liner. "Mom! I thought you said this was gross!" I teased as she stood at the sink rinsing plates. "What can I say, I give up," she declared, admitting to the unlikely convenience.

Feeding, cleaning, feeding, cleaning. The kitchen had become my office. Once I'd get through breakfast, I'd hustle everyone into clothes and shoes in order to be out the door by 10AM. With my stocked diaper bag slung over my shoulder and double stroller ready to roll, we were off either to run errands, play at the park, or meet Claudia at the zoo. Sometimes we went to the "country" to visit my parents, Papa, or Great Grandma Foss in town. This August was the first time I'd be caught up in the back-to-school hoopla. Noah and Emma would be starting afternoon kindergarten at our public school in a few weeks. I'd never had to purchase them clothes or new shoes by a specific deadline, and without my mom I found myself taking on ventures only a superhero would brave. I did it all with two fives, one very stubborn four, and two busy toddlers who could reach every shoebox in the Stride Rite store from the seats of their stroller. I fought my way through the mall, the big box stores, grocery stores, and Costco with supernatural composure (answered prayers) that had fellow shoppers curious about my story.

"Are these ALL your kids?" *Yes. I proudly smiled.*

"You look great! How on earth do you do it?" *With a lot of prayer.*

"You must have a lot of help." *Actually, no. If I did, I wouldn't be holding a grocery list, pushing this stroller* and *pulling a shopping cart, or ordering my walkers to STAY BEHIND THE CART!*

"You must have twins in this mix!" *Two sets.*

"Two sets of twins! And only one boy! How does he survive that?" *How does* he *survive? How about asking how* I *survive.*

"Well, you have your hands full." *Yes, how about holding the door for me or leaving me alone so I can go home and make lunch.*

"I know someone who had twins. They are now thirty." *Just kill me already.*

"Where does the red hair come from?" *What is it with the red hair? Why do you care?*

"Are they identical?" *No. But they look it. For you, the answer is yes.*

"How old are they? They are all so young!" *All five and under. I am starving. Why am I still in this conversation?*

"You are either Catholic or a sex maniac!" *And* you *are a dirty old man who should not be allowed to run errands with your wife. Also, I don't have time for sex.*

On it went just like this from old, young, male, female, gay, straight, and everyone in between. There was no discrimination when it came to the general public giving open commentary on my family. Just making it through a store was a challenge. The check-out was torture between the tight space, eye-level candy, grumpy kids who'd already emptied through my bag of tricks to keep them occupied, and the turn belt, which, at mouth level, is a parasitic breeding ground gross enough to make the me twitch just thinking about it. My constant smile and calm demeanor had everyone fooled. While they'd comment on how well I handled my kids and how great I was, the truth was that I was a wreck inside. The responsibility of getting it done *with* my babies *and* keeping everyone happy and alive was callusing me from the inside out. I was exhausted and overstimulated by the chaos. *There was no time not to hurry. Why was I in a hurry?* Oh yes, because I had hours of chores to get done and people to feed and keep on schedule or I'd be cycling through overtired tantrums and spats, and I certainly didn't have time for *that*. I was in high gear. All day, every day.

Once, I was moving so fast with my over-stacked grocery cart that I crashed into the automatic sliding door on the way out of the store, taking it completely off its track. The old me would have stopped to ensure that the right hands knew to take care of it. High-speed Hollie acted like she never saw it and scurried to her car with her crew to begin the ten minutes of loading the groceries, buckling the kids and babies, and returning the cart. At least I corralled my cart, and even that took careful calculation. The only time I slowed down was in the Costco lot. There was always some jerk of a driver who would follow me to my parking spot and wait impatiently for me to drive away. No stress, really. Did they not see that I had five kids who needed loading assistance before I could even consider unloading my groceries into the trunk? Without missing a beat, I strategically guided my preschoolers into the back row, climbing in to secure and buckle them. Then I'd heave-ho out the babies, one by one, strapping them in their five-point harnesses on either side of the car. The waiting driver would roll her eyes or shoot me a glare that penetrated her inconvenience right through her windshield and into my soul. I'd secretly use a smile to deflect their negativity. Next came the cumbersome task of unloading my cart of oversized toiletries, drinks, snacks, and produce, all while talking to or singing to the kids to keep them happy and engaged. During this process, when feeling like I was in a fishbowl, unable to help but wish for a helping hand or a smile of empathy from a passerby, I'd slow down the pace. Just to normal speed. It's one thing to rush to keep my people happy, but a complete stranger? Forget it. I'd glance over every trip back to my trunk and politely give my rude waiter a smile. I think about all the time they'd wasted on me, and how a normal person could have parked, entered the store, and had at least two or three samples of hummus on pita chips by now. Once my trunk was locked and my empty cart was in hand, I could hear them shift into drive. And with near diabolical motive, I would take complete pleasure in slowly strutting the two hundred yards to return my cart. *Take that, meanie.* This little act of rebellion satisfied my hunger for some control. I did *not* have to serve every request from every human every minute of the day.

Besides getting life done every day, I was, believe it or not, still passionate about making sure we were having fun. I was determined not to let the work override the enjoyment of motherhood. And I found that the trick was to embrace the little things in the simplest of ways. In the car, I'd roll with their urge to be loud and giggle over silly things like the word "fart" or "poop." So, I'd announce five free minutes to be as loud as they wanted (when we were off the main roads) or a pass to discuss "gas" without my mom mute button. I learned that bribery would get me anything, and I'd save it for the extra tough days that required more good behavior than a little army of under-fives should have to give. I learned quickly that kids are pretty awesome if you just give them ten minutes of time and let them have their fun. Let them have a can of shaving cream outside. Let them stay in a swimsuit all day. Let them eat ice cream for dinner. My kids giggling through the simple things in life was what kept me going during these long, fatigue-filled days.

For many, Sunday morning is supposed to be "easy" (according to Lionel Richie anyway). In our house, after my week of high-speed living and twenty-four-hour servitude, this "day of rest" was my reminder that I'd unwillingly become the martyr of my soul. We, as we had every Sunday since we married, we went to church. Even though I wasn't a practicing Catholic, confession was something I fully embraced at the beginning of Mass. If I couldn't think of a handful of sins before Sunday morning, I had plenty by the time we zipped out of our driveway in our church clothes, because I'd cursed my spouse at least four times in my head that morning. It was a struggle to get the kids out of the house any morning on time, but Mass was non-negotiable when it came to late arrival. Not even five minutes. We would arrive on time, even if it meant going forty mph in a twenty-five to get there.

As Tom would squeal into a parking spot, I'd be deep breathing away my frustration and anger. The morning would start off fine. We'd eat breakfast, the kids would go play, and I'd clean the kitchen while Tom read through a week's worth of mail piled up on the island (another part of my kitchen Bermuda triangle). As I was wiping down the countertops, I'd tell him when he needed to be ready to help me with the kids/walk out. He'd nod his head and I'd be off to find matching outfits, direct big kids, and wrestle toddlers into Sunday best. "Best" in our house did not mean frilly dresses with tights and dress shirts with ties. It meant an overall color coordinated palette (my best defense for not owning the formal wear), hair that was styled, and clean shoes. Getting this done would be cake if I had five little people who listened the first time, or second time, or could follow directions without losing focus or fighting with their siblings. It *never* happened this way. Claudia said it best: we are herding cats. They are all doing their own thing without a care as to what is going on around them. While disciplining and breaking into a sweat, I'd glance at the clock to see that, as usual, my husband was also taking the feline route and doing his own thing.

"TOOOOMMMM! You need to get in the shower! NOW!" I'd yell down as he wrapped up whatever had his interest. He was at least ten minutes late to the shower. I was irritated because he casually took his time to get ready, while I was stuck throwing on an outfit, slicking my hair into a ponytail, and carting my makeup mirror/bag to the kitchen so I could pull it together while watching the kids, who had already smashed their hair into seat cushions, calling for a re-do, or pulled off their socks (the babies). A poopy diaper usually appeared in the last ten-minutes as well. At least I wasn't in my bathroom; if I was up there while Tom was getting ready, he was either chatty (don't mess with me while I'm on a mission) or decided that he couldn't select a shirt without my input (I do not do menswear, and I am not a footman).

I'd glance at the kitchen clock and know that we would be late if I waited for him to come help with the kids. I got them into their shoes and whatever outerwear they might need. In the winter months, it was hats, scarves, and mittens. By the time my husband made his way to the kitchen, clean and looking fabulous in a nice button-down shirt and khaki pants, I was seething, as I had single-handedly done everything I needed help with *and* buckled the last seatbelt, all before he remembered to fill out the weekly church envelope. I was a hot mess, hence the bad parking lot attitude.

But it didn't end there. Marching our pack through the lot and into the building had its own challenges. We had to get the doublewide stroller out of the trunk and load it without the Big Three running ahead. There are old lady drivers and puddles to watch out for. Parents are always yelling at kids to stop running. Put them in a church parking lot and it will guarantee a leisurely stroll. Perfect for discussing the scenery, shuffling feet, or walking in the mulch. The two sets of heavy oak doors posed their own threat, the possible pinching of little chubby fingers, one of my top-rated mom fears of the Point A to Point B travel routine. As my five walked over the threshold of our beautiful church, they took a moment to stop and look around, a phenomenon I've yet to figure out. We'd hold the one-hundred-pound doors open with a crowd forming behind us as my offspring acted like they had no idea that they were supposed to keep moving into the church. They casually stared up at the ceiling and at the people around them. "Keep moving," I coached, assuming that they must be experiencing the mystery of their faith.

Once inside the sanctuary and past the baptismal font, which they had full access not to dip only the tip of their finger into but an entire arm (and sometimes a mitten when it was cold), I was the first into our usual third or fourth row pew. Always on the left. While still frazzled and guiding them into place, the stroller parked in the aisle, Tom settled into prayer on his kneeler, oblivious to the near-catastrophic hurdles we'd just overcome. I carefully pulled my kneeler down, fully aware of little toes as the heavy padded oak base made contact with the floor. As Natalie and Kate began to squirm in their stopped ride and Emma and Isabelle fought for my side, I'd glance over at Tom, who was still embraced in his holy moment of solitude. I squeezed in between my redheads and signaled them to get on their knees. Clasping my hands, I bowed my head and pretended to be happy to be there. I looked up at the cross and giant stained-glass atrium above the altar. My prayer was desperate and brief.

"Dear Heavenly Father, rescue me. I love them, but I don't know how much longer I can endure. Please. Help." (Sign of the cross)

As the opening hymn began, I started to sing, keeping an eye on the babies. They would last all of about ten minutes before grabbing each other's faces or screaming to get out and play, at which point I would push them into the foyer where I would remain to entertain them in hope of hearing just a portion of the homily, the closest thing to my Protestant upbringing I'd get, and far from our marriage agreement of sharing churches.

By the end of communion, I'd make my way back to my pew and prepare for the small crowd of grandparents who would surround us with compliments and questions as we made our way out. It was in these moments that God would send one angel to rescue my lonely soul.

"Honey, your children are the most well-behaved kids I've ever seen. I can't believe they sit through Mass at such a young age. You are a saint," a seasoned eighty-something mother of six and grandmother of twenty-five would tell me. *You are a saint. She said it, not me.* I'd look up at Tom to see him grinning from ear to ear with a proud husband smile that would smash all of my earlier "husband bashing" into a pile of dust. I knew I was doing the right thing. That it would all pay off and that this was just a season. And then I'd think about the after-church hustle of getting hands washed, outfits off and back into the closet for another use, lunches made, babies down for naps, and big kids out to play. The cycle was endless, but for this brief moment I would bask in the admiration of the stranger who had given me the strength to push through for seven more days.

After all those sweaty Sundays, hours of school shopping, and weeks of running solo with the kids, Tom surprised me with a date night to see David Gray at Meadowbrook Music Hall. An outdoor concert on a beautiful night—it was the perfect way to bring summer to a close. I hired a sitter, a rare but necessary event, and glammed up for my night out. Tom and I arrived with plenty of time to have a couple of cocktails and settle into our seats, which were center stage, about thirty rows back. We were excited to be out, and within minutes I'd forgotten about time-outs, Scrubbing Bubbles, Tide and Downy, and grocery lists, and actually felt like the old me for the first time in months. The amphitheater was about half full, and the opening artist, Ray LaMontagne, took the stage. We were seated far enough away to catch a glimpse of his weathered clothes and cap and hear his Van Morrison folk-style song. It set the stage for a comfortable night of romance. In full catch-up mode from our busy lives away from each other, I was finally at rest. I felt a little guilty about all my grumpiness but took comfort in date night and decided to just let it all go. It was just us, Ray, and a perfect sunset in the August sky. That's when I heard a woman's voice to my left.

"Excuse Me!" I ignored it. Someone probably trying to get to a seat.

"Excuse Me!" Again. *Who could be annoyed on such a beautiful evening?* I continued my conversation. Then I felt a tap on my shoulder.

"EXCUSE ME!" I turn to my left to find an average-looking thirty-something guy and a woman leaning over his lap with a distraught look on her face. *Did she drop something? What did she need?*

"Could you PLEASE be QUIET? I happen to be on a DATE," she scowled, giving me the once over from head to toe. I was wearing a grey J. Crew denim mini with a black T-shirt topped with a cute micro fleece vest. I looked at her in shock. The last time I'd been verbally assaulted was when I was a senior in high school by the mean girls. *Was I talking THAT loudly?* I was embarrassed and politely apologized, then turned back in my seat as if I'd been falsely accused of making a ruckus at the dinner table and denied dessert.

Shocked, I sat for a second replaying the scene. *She's on a DATE? Who does this girl think she is?* I shot a peak at her again through the corner of my eye. *SHE'S on a date?* There she was, sitting smugly in her chair with her arms crossed over her zipped up hoodie. She was miserable. *A date?* A date indicated that she was single and possibly pursuing a romance with this poor man sitting next to me. *Would it kill her to put on some lip-gloss or try to look nice for him?* She looked like she'd just rolled out of bed at noon on a Saturday morning. She was a bully, and I didn't like it. If we were in a quiet restaurant or at the opera it would be one thing, but an outdoor concert? Everyone else around us was talking; this was no different than being in any other outdoor event. And *I* was on a date. *Why was HER date more important than MINE?* I was always overly polite to everyone in public. I was passive to a fault. If you were in a bind at Costco, I would let you go first, even if I had kids with me. If you cut me off on the road, I'd thank God that I didn't get in an accident. I might even give you a wave. If I were on the sidewalk and passed you, I'd smile or even say hi if we were alone or made eye contact. I was a nice person. This girl was mean. And I didn't deserve it. And then, without hesitation, I did something I had never done and may never again do. I turned and leaned over to her date.

"Excuse me, would you get her," I pointed to his date. He tapped her on the shoulder, taking her away from crooning Ray and back to my annoying face. He acted like one of my kids when they know their sibling is going to get in trouble. He pulled back into his seat so as not to get in my way. I was the boss of this conversation. The mean girl looked at me as if expecting a complimentary beverage ticket or signed concert T-shirt for her inconvenience.

"You know what? I happen to be on a *date*, too," I announced loudly with a smile. This poor woman had no idea what was coming, and neither did I. For the next thirty seconds, I unleashed my pent-up anger on her poor, wretched soul.

"I'm on a *date* with my husband, who I haven't had a conversation with in months. I'm a stay-at-home mom with five kids who are under the age of five. I have two sets of twins and one in-between, and I happen to be paying a sitter $25 an hour so I can be on my *date*, so no, I will *not* be quiet!" She said nothing. She was in shock. So was I. Her mouth was hanging open like a stunned Daffy Duck in a Looney Tunes cartoon. Without retort, she sat back in her seat, and her boyfriend relaxed without comment, I think very much in support of my retaliation and probably plotting his break-up. I leaned back in my chair with an adrenaline high that I'd only felt after running six miles. *I couldn't believe what I'd just said!* The crowd started a round of applause, and Ray took a bow before exiting the stage. *Tom! I forgot about Tom!* Still relishing in glory, I turned to my spouse to find him wearing a smile even bigger than the one he wore in church. He was impressed beyond normal impressed. He was always rolling his eyes at my wimpy public behavior, but now he was admiring me as if I had taken my CEO status public. Like I was the girl boss. And if he was good, he might get to accompany me in my limo for the ride home. I shot him a big smile back and embraced the appreciation from the man I loved.

"Shit. I'm impressed," he praised. Then we stood up and joined the crowd, screaming and whooping as loud as we could, savoring our evening glory, and happy to be far from our own household of noise, which was sound asleep, charging up for another day.

CHAPTER 15

HELL'S ANGELS

Monday, October 4

I love school. Noah and Emma love school. I have the morning with them, everyone is happy playing, we eat lunch, I load everyone into the car, I drop off my fives, and I have two full hours alone with Isabelle while Natalie and Kate take their nap. It's the first time that I've had relief in the day to take a breather. I could workout in peace, I could make dinner without burning something, or I could eat Nutella on green apples with "Osba" while thanking God for Jamie Goldschmidt, our kindergarten teacher. Whatever it was, I could do it without kid static, and that took the edge off. On most days. *Except today…*

6:30AM: Noah wakes me up because he wants breakfast. He is hacking like a two-pack-a-day-er. I wonder if I ignore it if it'll go away. He continues to stand by my head until I get up. *Note*: I am the *worst* mom of sick kids.

8:30AM: Tom takes Noah to the doctor. I selfishly decide to squeeze in a workout downstairs. I'd recently switched from the Jillian Michaels 30-Minute Shred to old-school, heavy free-weights. In a desperate attempt to personalize my gym, I wallpapered one entire wall from floor to ceiling with beautiful pages from *Vogue*, *Marie Claire*, and *Allure*. It's like mall walking meets Pinterest, and gets rave reviews from my mom friends. For me, it's art. An outlet. And motivation to sweat out the stress. On this particular morning, it takes me forty-five minutes to get through three exercises because my eighteen-month-olds are fighting in their "zone." I hear the door chime; Tom and Noah are home. I abort the workout and spend the rest of the day in my sports bra, feeling anything but sporty.

9:15AM: Noah has pneumonia. With it a fever, a pharmacy bag of meds, care instructions, and the determination to eliminate all swallowing of food and liquids because it hurts his throat. He will not be going to school. I mentally prepare for the day ahead by making another cup of coffee with French-vanilla creamer.

10AM: Morning naps. I get Nat and Kate tucked in and set Noah up in his room with a sippy cup of Gatorade and a movie. I instruct him to rest with a kiss on his forehead.

11AM: I make lunch. This is the full round with high chairs, a sink full of dishes, faces and hands to wipe, and the complete kitchen cleanup. I am grateful they don't eat the crust; grilled cheese crust is the best mom lunch. Noah dumps his apple juice down the sink and lies to me about it. I am frustrated that he is making it impossible to care for him and worry he will dehydrate. Emma gets dressed for school; I put her hair in braids.

12:30PM: I get all five dressed and buckled in the minivan. We take Emma to school.

1PM: Once home, I unload Natalie and Kate, get coats and shoes off, and supervise the washing of hands. While Noah and Isabelle fight over the soap in the mudroom, I change over the laundry. The kids watch TV while I make beef stew in my Dutch oven. *It was supposed to be a relaxing fall day.* I give Noah a new sippy cup of Gatorade. He still refuses to swallow.

2PM: After an hour of nagging, I cave in and give Noah a Popsicle, even though the deal was that he had to drink his entire cup beforehand.

2:05PM: As I clean up the beef stew mess, I look over to find Noah feeding his red *twin* pop to his *twin* sisters in the great room. (He is not supposed to feed them because they are like bears; once they get a taste of real food, they will not eat their own or have food in the great room—especially red popsicle, which is now dripping all over my cream wool rug.)

2:06PM: I have a complete meltdown over the mess/lack of listening skills and scream at my sick son, sending him to his room for a nap.

2:10-3PM: Isabelle colors at the kitchen table while Natalie and Kate explore the kitchen and great room. I pick up baby toys and vacuum the kitchen and great room to regroup. Noah migrates down the staircase every five minutes. I firmly send him back up to bed, telling him to "take a sip" and "close your eyes!" Meanwhile, my little bears have explored their way into the mudroom and ripped open a kitchen bag of trash I had left by the door to go outside. I am inspired while crawling on Noreen's ugly white- and teal-tiled floor to take an empty garbage bag and bag up all of Noah's bedroom toys as a consequence for not listening to me.

3:10PM: Natalie and Kate take their afternoon nap. After tucking them in, I give Noah and Isabelle a banana and go through another round of dishes and laundry.

4:15PM: Exhausted after ten hours of hard work, I lie on the sofa to catch a ten-minute catnap before the bus comes. I drift into a peaceful sleep almost immediately.

4:16PM: Noah sneaks over to me and wakes me up, exclaiming that he hears the bus coming! I frantically jump up, worried that Emma will be trekking alone up the hill, only to discover that I'd been *tricked!* I try really hard to remember that he is sick.

4:30PM: With naps still in session, I get Isabelle's coat and shoes on her and take her to the mailbox to wait for the bus. She decides to test me by standing eighteen inches into the street. I threaten her multiple times within five minutes and remember 4:30PM martinis at

Grandpa and Grandma Foss's house on Clarence Street. I decide that the 1950s housewife started Happy Hour because the husbands had started during lunch, just like Don Draper in *Mad Men*.

4:45PM: Russell, our bus driver, pulls up to our driveway and opens the bus door. He is listening to Van Halen and is thoroughly entertained by Emma's front seat weekend review of our anniversary overnight date to Ann Arbor. I blush at the thought of her belting out our romantic endeavors to our retired UAW transportation hero.

4:46PM: Isabelle stubbornly shuffles up the driveway; Emma and I go inside.

4:47PM: Isabelle is screaming and crying in the garage because she can't open the door and thinks she is locked out for the night. I let her in.

5PM: I bring Natalie and Kate down after a diaper change and strap them in their high chairs. I slice my beef stew into bite-sized pieces on three kid plates and two baby trays. The big kids get wild. Isabelle belts out Noah's name. He apparently hit her on her back.

5:05PM: I put Noah in a time out in the corner and pour three cups of milk into our Ikea kid cups.

5:10PM: Isabelle, hard-wired to get wild after 5PM, grabs her yellow blanket and starts swinging it around in the kitchen.

5:11PM: As I scold her, the blanket whips over the kitchen table, knocking over an entire cup of milk (which is why they only get half cups at a time), saturating about thirty pieces of pink construction paper left on the kitchen table from afternoon crafts.

5:11and 1/2 PM: I march over, yank the blanket from her hands, open the French door to the patio, and throw it outside. I then park my little copperhead in the corner, opposite her brother.

5:12: I halt all food service to throw soggy construction paper away and wipe pink-stained milk off the table. Isabelle is screaming in her time out.

5:13: Dinner is finally served. Mine is three bites of stew as I stand between the high chairs. When I am lying in bed at 11PM and my mouth waters when a cat food commercial comes on TV, this is why.

5:25: I send the kids off and resume yet another round of kitchen cleanup.

6PM: I take everyone upstairs, let the girls play in their rooms, and set Noah up in his bathroom with the doctor-recommended steam shower. I despise his heavy frameless shower door and am convinced he will accidentally smash his finger in it. I tell him to stand there and not move while I go change diapers.

6:05PM: My informant (Isabelle), finds me and tells me that Noah is out of the shower. I am feeling hopeless as a nurturing mother of a pneumonia-stricken child. How hard is it to lay around and drink Gatorade all day?

6:06PM: I march into Noah's room with the phone, call Tom, have him say goodnight to the boy, tuck him in, then threaten to send him to an orphanage.

6:15PM: I get all four girls ready for bed. Vitamins, Pajamas, Teeth. We migrate back to the great room to read a story.

6:30PM: I grab a Bernstein Bear book and begin reading. Emma is sitting on the sofa, resting her toe on the edge of Kate's Pack 'n Play. Kate bites the toe.

6:32PM: Emma stops screaming.

7PM: It's finally, for the first time all day, just me and the babies. I let Otto outside and change diapers.

7:15PM: I get Natalie and Kate into their cribs and grab the Brainy Baby board book. As I am holding it up, going through the alphabet, Kate takes her cute chubby little finger and points to the "T-For Turtle." She looks at me and says "turtle" for the first time in her life.

7:16PM: I am still smiling.

7:30PM: I give my little angels their bedtime bottles and tuck them in.

7:36PM: When I go back down to the great room, I realize that there is only one rolled-up dirty diaper in the trash instead of two. Crap. One is missing. At least it was just a number one.

7:39PM: I park myself in my swivel rocker in front of the TV. *Dancing With The Stars* is on, and I'm too tired to look for something else. I stare blankly at the flat screen.

"Mom," I hear just inches from my left ear. I scream out loud and turn to find Emma standing next to me. "Otto is in my room and I can't sleep."

"Thanks. Go back to bed. I love you." I kiss her on the top of the head and follow her up to retrieve my springer. I wish he could fold a load of laundry.

7:45PM: I grab my journal and record the events of this day, thinking, "This is one for the book."

8PM: The door chimes. Tom is home. The house is picked up and quiet, I get up to greet him. Otto gets to him first, his black furry rear end wagging with excitement.

"Hi," I greeted him with a weak smile.

"Hi," he responds as I give him a hug. "How was your day? It smells good in here; what's for dinner?" he politely asks.

"Pot roast." I can tell he's had a long day. I decide to keep this one for "the book." And I did.

* * *

Tuesday, October 5

I am unloading the dishwasher after lunch (again) and slide open my utensil drawer to put away my wooden spoon. Nestled in the front corner is a nice, tightly wound ball of a dirty diaper, just the right size for a busy toddler hand to toss in while nobody's looking.

CHAPTER 16

TRANSFORMATION

Long days turned into long weeks, weeks turned into months, and before I knew it, I had two first graders, one kindergartener, and a set of twins who, at two-and-a-half would keep any mom busy, but I felt almost childless. I always knew that God had given me Natalie and Kate as a bonus round, but they were like winning a trip to Maui on the parenting spectrum. They were sweet, happy, healthy, and could entertain themselves for hours if they had to. I could actually start getting projects done around the house. Mostly cleaning out closets and storage areas. Nothing exciting, but it made me feel productive to have something to show for my hard work.

Tom continued to plug away, working toward turning a profit at both dealerships without luck. He was driving to Jackson, an hour and a half away, a couple times a week overseeing two skeleton crews. More than two years after the bail-out, Michigan's economy was still weak, and those who'd lost dealership careers had moved on, many out of state. I felt like we were the only ones at this point trying to push through, and Tom's future with the family business was uncertain. We discussed a change on many occasions, but he felt he needed to see it through until the end, as his commitment to his brother's business had been life-long. He was a team player and refused to give up the hope of rebounding his twenty-seven-year career running a successful dealership.

Finances continued to put a strain on everything, but we managed to always squeeze by. With hope in one of the dealerships picking up speed, we felt it best to stay put in our big house with its big utilities, big yard, and big ugly draperies. I religiously kept to my $200 grocery budget and had become shopping savvy. The grocery store was still my only trip out of the house and one I came to dread with each turn into my driveway and up the hill of my paver-clad brick mansion. It made my stomach churn. This house was not mine. It was Dave's and Noreen's. Filled with their dark green marble countertops, gold fixtures, dated wallpaper, and left-behind 1980s cherry Queen Anne furniture, nothing about it was Designer Hollie. Four years earlier, I envisioned a home here. Now I wanted to run from it and the financial failures it represented.

And as it turned out, while I was running the vacuum, my husband was running to church. Todd, God Bless his Catholic soul, had inspired Tom (over craft beers), to consider attending morning Mass. Todd had become Tom's only friend in whom he could confide his financial *and* faith portfolio thoughts over the years, and it made me happy yet jealous. I was frustrated that he enjoyed two mornings of peace in the chapel every week while I ran the mom race without a finish line in sight. He would rush out the door at 8:15AM twice a week, oblivious to my daily burdens. I'd clean the kitchen, rush through chores, and continually create new ways to keep my head above water. But, the reality, no matter how "together" I was on the outside, was that I had lost my joy for life. I was working so hard to do it all and do it successfully that I had no time to consider my own needs.

Not only did my jealousy extend to the newly added weekday solitude, it extended into Sunday Mass and my lonely walks pushing toddlers in the corridor. It was not fair that my faith needs had gotten squashed out of our life by default. I was doing all the work and giving more than I ever had; forgiveness was running on the low side. I'd stew over my hard work on Sundays and the new commitment of Religious Ed every Monday after school. Hauling my five to church after they'd had a full school day was like being forced to run the twenty-sixth mile of a marathon when you'd left everything you had at mile twenty. I had to walk all of them through a windy parking lot, through double doors, and up three half-flights of stairs to drop them off. Then I'd fight my little three back to the car and try to come up with something to do for forty minutes. And then we'd do it all over again at pick-up. It was cumbersome, and my kids were tired, hungry, and ready for bed by the time we got home at 6:30. I know hate is a strong word, but I *hated* Mondays. However, I knew it was the right thing to do. Another sacrifice from the mom. *Double blech.*

One Saturday late that fall, I let Noah have a friend from school over. This was a rare occasion, but since he was not in extra-curricular activities I tried to keep to status quo in every budget-friendly way possible. An extra kid or two (or even three) was always fine with me, as long as the extras blended in with my own. If they needed "special" attention or I found them wandering around my house because they were "bored," they were off the list. I couldn't imagine being bored with two sets of twins and a middle one to pick on. These kids were the ones with such full schedules that they had no idea how to "go play" without an organized activity. On this one particular, afternoon Noah and his buddy were wrapping up with a snack at the kitchen table. I was making dinner, and Noah curiously asked me what we were having, followed by his usual line of questions.

"How many bites do I have to take before I can have dessert?"

"At least ten. And that doesn't guarantee dessert."

"Then what's the point of eating it?"

"Because I want you to stay alive."

"What are we doing tonight?"

"After Gavin leaves, you have to take a shower because we are going to 5PM Mass."

(5PM Saturday mass was a huge score for me; I had all day to get the kids ready and Sunday to recoup.) The boys continued slurping their Capri-Suns and nibbling on Goldfish. His friend finally broke the silence with a surprising question.

"Do you go to church every week?" he asked Noah.

"Yeah, do you go to church?"

"No." He thought about his own response, then shot an annoyed look across the table.

"Why would you want to waste time on your weekend going to church?" he continued. I stood on the other side of the room, frozen at the cutting board, not knowing how my little scholar would answer this logical line of questioning, one even I was guilty of asking every once in a while as I rushed my family out the door.

"Because we love God," Noah informed him, as matter of factly as I'd ever heard. He didn't have to think about it or even question his motive. Just like that, my six-year-old had schooled his classmate *and* his mother, who at this point was wishing she were chopping onions to hide her overwhelming emotion over his declaration. What profound simplicity my son was speaking! His friend shrugged his shoulders, and the two of them continued on to new conversation. It is probably something he'll never remember, but it was one of my proudest mom moments, and it impacted my commitment to the Catholic church and my faith in an indispensable way. It assured me that they "got it" and that while I might be in the midst of a poor-me-losing-my-religion pout-fest, I was a good mom. I decided to knock off my bad attitude, forgive my spouse (again), and remember that it *is* worth it. Every time.

* * *

"Hello?" I answered, sneaking into the pantry one December afternoon. It was Tom calling from work.

"Hey, I have a Christmas Eve dilemma," he said, with a little spousal fear in his voice. I couldn't imagine a Christmas Eve "dilemma." We were elected to host the holiday for his brother and his family when we were dating, eliminating my favorite family tradition of having Christmas Eve dinner at my Grandma Foss's house. I'd spent over ten years making stuffed pasta shells and grimacing over their "we're running twenty minutes late" banter and my displeasure over rerouting baby schedules. I answered with a curious but unenthusiastic, "Huh?"

"The Lions are playing on Christmas Eve, so my brother is wondering if we can see them on a different day," he said, still on edge over breaking the news to me. I stood up from the wooden step stool and grinned. I could hardly contain my joy; this meant I was off the hook, and we could be with my family!

"Ugh," I retorted. *Not so fast, you don't want this to backfire.* "That's a bummer. I guess I could cancel our Christmas Day plans with my parents, but it'd sure be nice to do *something* on Christmas Eve."

"I know," he responded, relieved that I was not flipping out. "Can we see your family on Christmas Eve?" *Bingo.*

"Yeah, I'll call my mom. Tell your brother we are happy to have them Christmas Day," I consoled, while dancing around in my food-packed phone booth. I grabbed the jar of Nutella on my way out and called my mom. She was delighted when I told her we would be joining them at Grandma's for dessert, Bingo, and white elephant gifts. This would be the first—and maybe last—Christmas Eve with my side of the family, and the thought of sharing my childhood traditions with the kids warmed me to the core.

The eve came and went, and it was just as special as I'd hoped. Grandma was eighty-eight and still without her speech. She was thrilled to have us all together under her roof and was the perfect hostess. Her caretaker had helped her decorate the artificial tree, and everyone brought a dessert. Her condo was small; we were elbow to elbow but didn't care. In the good old days, we would have unwrapped real gifts that we'd then beg our parents to unbox and assemble while we ran around enjoying the freedom to eat junk and drink Squirt. It was always hot and sweaty, and we'd stay until after 11PM—late enough to fall asleep on our five-minute drive home yet early enough to leave cookies and milk by the wood stove for Santa. I had the best childhood. That night, I hugged my Grandma and told her I loved her. Then I thanked God for the Detroit Lions and their random home game.

Three weeks later, my Grandma passed away while tucking herself into bed. When my cousin called to break the news, I knew without a doubt that I'd experienced a Christmas miracle. I lost a part of myself that day and celebrated her life with the adoration that only a granddaughter could have. I knew I got the best of her from the day I was born: hugs, kisses, love, and life lessons that I'd cherish forever.

I spent two days with my family, mourning our loss and sharing the memory of Grandma and Grandpa Foss. I bravely stood in front of my peers at the funeral home and shared my favorite memory as a child. Every Christmas Eve, the Foss family would gather around the extended dining table (and card table for the kids) in their tiny dining room on Clarence Street. After the blessing, my grandpa would raise his glass and toast my grandma (who was at the opposite end, near the kitchen), and then say, "Beth, can you believe we started all this?" And she'd delicately take a sip of her white wine and smile, which filled my little heart with family love that I'll never forget.

Those days and weeks that followed stirred something inside me. It was like a slow growl from inside my soul that was begging to be fed. I spent a lot of time thinking about her life, who she was, and how she survived losses that made mine look like "a pimple on my ass," as Tom so crudely put it during our "Is this our reality, and what will we do next?" talks. She grew up during the depression and buried two brothers, her WWII war hero husband, her mother, and her best friend before she was thirty-five years old. She was a loving and loyal wife to my grandfather for fifty-three years and worked hard every day of her life. And she did it with a smile and class. It didn't matter that she lived in a small town or couldn't afford a luxury lifestyle; she was the perfect 1950s housewife and set an example that I only wish I could achieve. She loved her family unconditionally. She got through the worst of times ten times over, and I decided that I would do the same. I wasn't sure how to feed my hunger from within, so I channeled my Grandma's determination and loving heart to make the most of each day, believing that I'd be rescued in some way.

There were a few moments that took place that winter and spring that I didn't think much about at the time or the way they acted as precursors to events that would occur in the near future, but they're significant enough to share. After the funeral, I was rummaging through my grandma's kitchen with my Aunt Ginny in hopes of finding anything meaningful to take home. I snagged a couple of vintage 1950s serving bowls and her iron skillet. I use them both every day, which makes me smile. While chatting and reminiscing, I picked up a dated issue of *Better Homes & Gardens* and began thumbing through. I would devour *Redbook*, *Real Simple*, and *Parenting* on a regular basis, and over the years realized that, one, I knew this stuff inside and out, and two, I loved sharing my ideas.

"You know, I would love to contribute to a magazine one day. I eat, breathe, and sleep this stuff." I stated, as my aunt was organizing Grandma's 1970s ceramic brown coffee cups.

"That sounds like you. You'd be good at it," she replied, as she tossed a cracked one in the trash pile. And that was that. I don't know why this happened on this particular day, but it did.

The Michigan winter led to spring, which is really just more winter. My parents stayed in Florida until mid-March, and I usually ended up on the phone with my mom every afternoon during naptime. Nothing beats a mom talk. She's the only one patient enough to listen to (not to mention interested in) my rambling about my dreams. Tom is too, of course, but I have to consciously scale back my chatter or I lose him. This particular March afternoon, I was ranting over my discovery that I absolutely could not watch HGTV or any design show without feeling sick. I would turn on the kitchen TV or in my bedroom while folding laundry, and it was like watching the guy in high school who dumped you for a new girlfriend all day long. And I knew why: I loved these shows. These people were out there living my passion, and I couldn't have it. The problem wasn't that I disliked them; I loved them, and it was breaking my heart. I decided to indulge in stuff I couldn't do yet appreciated the artistic value. *Project Runway*, *What Not to Wear*, *American Pickers*...all painless entertainment. During this conversation with my mom, I casually said, "I've succumbed to the fact that I'll never be a designer in this lifetime (too much family responsibility), so I hope God has lots of mansions for me to work on when I get to Heaven." And again, that was that, and we moved on.

Around the same time, my dear cousin Jamie had written and published a Christian book about motherhood. It was called *Push*. Tom downloaded it to our Kindle, and I decided it appropriate to read while pushing the pedals on the exercise bike in my pre-Pinterest workout room. Jamie and her husband worked at my mom's church, had two little girls, and the absolute most balanced life I'd ever heard of. They had Fridays off and Grandma watched the kids all day so they could have a date day. They shared the exact same beliefs and she had an endless group of friends who supported their lifestyle, as well as only two kids; I know I just mentioned this, but to really bring it home, *two kids*. The book was supposed to inspire me to pursue my dreams as a woman. While she understood that motherhood is exhausting, it doesn't end our God-given destiny; you have to *push* through it. About two chapters in, I determined that she was disillusioned by a life on Mom Easy Street. *What qualifies her to tell me that she understood motherhood? I had two and a half times the number of kids she had. I should be schooling her. And date days? Really? She was not living reality, she was living luxury (not materialistically but emotionally).* It was the equivalent of reading about celebrity moms who attempt to relate to those of us on the front lines. I'd been in the trenches for at least four years without hope of climbing out.

By now, my pulse was racing, my chest tight, and I could hardly breathe. I was having a moment. A long moment. I put the Kindle down and tried pedaling through, but it was no use. Within seconds I'd put on the breaks and caved into a complete meltdown in front of my wall of mirror tiles flanked by my fashion collage. I cried. I sobbed. I looked at my pathetic self, slumped on a *very* stationary bike, my frizzy ponytail and red, wet face wondering why God was not rescuing me from all this work. I hated the frustration I felt toward Jamie and her book. She is the most faithful, kind-hearted woman I know, and I love her. She was the magazine contributor, the HGTV designer, the mom expert. She was also too close to home, and I wasn't sure how to handle my feelings. I wanted balance. I wanted to believe that I could *push* through this world of big responsibility. I understood that my experience was not the norm. I got it. I just didn't like it. I later vented to my mom during another naptime call and threw away my bitter cousin feelings, hoping she would continue to sing, dance, write, and love her life. Maybe her book would even inspire a mom or two. *But not me.*

Finally, it was the second week of May, an International Claudia Wednesday to be exact. We'd had our usual almost-an-hour chat while zipping through chores. It's funny, whenever we talk, we just go on autopilot and work. Our big talk of the day was the official end of the Hyundai dealership in Jackson, leaving Tom without a team to manage. The Kia dealership had been sold, and the new owner was renting the building. This left Tom and his brother office space to use, but the work ahead was basically dissolving what was left. There was casual talk with a few sources about purchasing new dealerships and even moving into other opportunities, but it was out of Tom's hands. He was just riding out the storm. Besides my parents, Todd and Claudia were the only ones who'd been through it all with us; they knew the details and never wavered in their support.

Once off the phone, I worked my way into my closet, which I'd painted Victoria's Secret pink (including the ceiling) when Tom was on a business trip as a revolt against Noreen. The ceiling was a few shades lighter, and the northern light that shined through the small horizontal window made the entire room glow. I had a full-length mirror on a stand in the back corner, my chocolate brown suede Coach bench running the length of the middle, and my coveted 1992 *Vogue* cover print, featuring Eva, Christy, and Cindy from the shoulders up, above. I'd had it framed in a solid wood, gold leafed, rippled frame that was four inches thick and cost me a day's worth of work in the design studio back in the day. I loved that picture. It made me feel like I was seventeen and invincible. I had a heap of my tired mom clothes on the bench and was hanging them once again on my black velvet hangers, mulling in deep thought about life. And then it happened.

It was the most powerful revelation I'd ever encountered. In one spiritual moment, or for those who need a different reference, an "Oprah Aha" moment, I was blinded from my mundane task. I had no doubt that it was God speaking to the depths of my being. He said (not audibly, but in a still, powerful, commanding voice that I'd never known), *"Show Them How You Do It."* And, in an instant, I saw my purpose, my life, everything I was, and everything I was meant to be in its entirety. I saw my childhood and my passion for design. All the little clues that I was meant to be a designer fit snuggly together like a puzzle. From the time I was three until I declared my major, it was all there. My devotion to excellence in college, my dream job, my marriage; I understood it all as if it were part of the perfect plan for my life. Add in my struggle to take care of my family while fighting the overwhelming need to be "me" again. It was all there.

All those hundreds of moments when strangers would ask me how I do it were meant for *this moment*. I saw my life as a beautiful tapestry, woven from three patterns, each representing a part of my life. Little girl. Designer. Wife and mom. For the first time, these three patterns wove themselves into one purpose. Only I could possibly care for my family in the unique way I had. I'd left design to be a mom. But in the end, Designer Hollie was the only one who could uniquely do everything I was doing. I'd been so blinded by the constant triaging of my own ER that I failed to see it for so many years. I was given this life and this story because I was being prepared to go into the world and share it! Everyone around me wanted to know, and the truth was, it was my inherent design skills that enabled me to be the mom I was and am! A childhood of clues, seven years in the field, and seven years as a mom had brought me to this moment in time. And here I was, alone, standing in my closet.

3AM Interior Design. A brand. A way out. The name came to me as I stood there, and I never looked back. Every moment of my complicated life fit together to create something beautiful and bigger than I ever imagined. I would fuse my design world with my mom world to create a brand that would change the way women think about their lives. It was interior design at its core: if you feel good in your environment, you'll naturally feel good about yourself. You'll be happier, healthier, and in the end, a better spouse, a better mom, and a better woman from the inside out. *My purpose was to inspire and transform lives just by being me!* I was instantly filled with so much excitement, energy, hope, and happiness that I felt as if my broken wings had been mended and I had taken flight, above all the problems, fears, and heaviness that hung in my heart, throughout my closet, and on the walls of my life.

Here I was, having moped around for a couple of years, struggling with feelings of oppression and laboring through a life I didn't understand. Nothing had gone my way. My family planning was on steroids, I was stuck in a house that was too big, I was physically working too hard to adhere to impossible standards, and I was bitter about getting the marriage agreement church shaft. What I overlooked were all the amazing things I had to be grateful for and how special I was in the eyes of God and my family! *Who else could have popped out two sets of twins plus one in four years? Who else could take care of all those babies, put meals on the table, keep the house together, and be a fun mom who found time to workout and leave the house with lipstick on? Who else could do it all on a dime? Without babysitters and nannies? Who else could pack up five kids every Wednesday and get to the zoo (besides Claudia, of course), and expedite a round trip against traffic to ensure a fast tour and have lunch before 11:30AM? Who else, when everyone in Bloomfield Hills was traveling to warm climates, would crank the heat up in one of the kid's rooms, fill the tub, play Beach Boys, and have a beach party complete with swimsuits, picnic lunches, and suntan lotion in the middle of February?*

I could go on and on with all the little ways I took crappy, hard circumstances and rose to the occasion to do what was best for my family. I never had a day where I just climbed into my bed in my pajamas and slept the day away in depression. I was on fire the whole time, and while life comes with challenges and disappointments, it can all be made beautiful for a greater cause if you follow your heart every day. And there, as I was still standing in my pink closet, having my holy moment, my supermodels looked back at me and I started laughing. Then crying. For the first time in almost seven years, I felt like *me*. I had been transformed. I was little Hollie Foss: Creative powerhouse. Artist. Designer. Cheerleader. Top graduate of my design class. Department store designer. Wife. Mom. *And it was glorious!*

CHAPTER 17

CURTAINS

"You have to take them all down!" my mother exclaimed with the kind of excitement I only heard after she sat through a good sermon. I was standing on the second step from the top of our twelve-foot ladder in the great room and had just handed her a three-inch mahogany drapery rod holding at least ten pounds of burgundy Schumacher fabric with the 1995 fruity border sewn along the inside, lengthwise.

"If I do, Tom will *kill* me!" I whined, envisioning his reaction to our two-story room minus Noreen's expensive draperies. I was in the midst of a pivotal marriage moment. It all started during naptime when we noticed the dust collecting on the fabric-covered rods. Seriously, who purchases wooden rods and then spends money to encase them in fabric? The drapery workrooms must have loved Noreen, her designer, and the hefty commission and simply let her have her way. Design disservice. So, I asked my mom if she was up to holding the ladder and the vacuum hose so I could suck some dust. Twenty minutes later, I'd conveniently discovered that the rods were not mounted to the brackets but instead just sitting up there! Of course, I had to just "see" what one of my windows looked like naked. It was the most beautiful nude window I'd ever laid my eyes upon. I didn't even have to get down for a ground-level view. She was perfect, measuring thirty-six inches wide and fifteen feet tall to the left of our fireplace. Her supermodel counterparts were begging to be stripped, and it was all I could do to contain my designer ecstasy. My mom could see it in my eyes, my delight in the elimination of any of the fabric that represented the chains of this house.

"He'll be mad, but he'll get over it. You *have* to take the rest down! Look at how happy you are! Besides, the ones on Noah's staircase are already in a heap in the garage." My mother was a bad influence. This was very out of character for her; she was a rule follower.

"Oh, easy for you! What if it were you and you had to deal with Dad?" I accused. "Would you do it?"

"I won't let you put them back up. You have to take them down." And that was it. Word from the mother. We worked our way around the room and took them all down. Even the heavy brass lion head tie-backs. Since I was terrified of what would happen when Tom got home, I folded them into Costco trash bags and stashed them in one of the basement storage rooms—the same one that hid all the rosettes, swags, chintz pillows, and other eyesores I'd snuck down since we'd moved in. When we were done, we beheld the room in its original architectural state. It was stunning! The double French doors on the west side opened to our bluestone patio; the mantel, millwork, and crown molding were finally center stage; and if you looked up and out the two story windows, you could see the tops of the one-hundred-plus-year-old pines, clouds, and jets streaming their way to Metro Airport.

I finally had a glimpse of this house as my home. I glanced into the kitchen and the hunter green faux finished wallpaper that surrounded my white cabinets, which were topped with the pear, apple, and grapevine border. I was just getting started. Stripping wallpaper, painting the dining room, formal living room, and removing those horrific funeral home draperies would be my next projects. I suddenly felt invincible. This was the new 3AM Hollie. My transformation had ripped me from my briar patch of endless mundane chores and given me newfound stamina to do it all. I backed off my cleaning standard and made room to take on projects that made me happy. I refused to let a laundry heap own me. I refused to allow the clutter and the toys to steal my time. I had a dream, a vision, and a business to get started, and it was taking root right here in my own home. I would eliminate things that weighed me down, and someone else's fabrics and wall coverings had been a source of contention since I'd walked through the house with our realtor.

As I soaked up my designer superpower strength, my mom had moved on to a cup of tea and playing make-believe with the kids. I remembered Tom, who I would have to explain all of this to. This was the first time I'd done something big without his approval. Our design relationship made my blood boil every time we had to make a décor decision. It would go something like this:

"This is the color I want to paint the dining room," I'd announce with authority, because I am the design professional. He'd glance at it immediately, thinking of every reason why it should be a shade or two lighter or darker, or a different color all together. He'd grab my paint deck and thumb through to select his choice. Fuming doesn't even begin to describe my mood in his designer moment.

"Why not *this* color?" he'd counter, completely clueless as to how insulted and unappreciated I was feeling. Clearly, this is not a conversation I enjoy having with my spouse. It is, actually, the only part of my marriage that is almost unbearable for me. How could I have married someone who would actually *debate* me on color choices? Could I keep my cool? Or find a warm way to psychoanalyze his need to control the one thing that identifies me as me? At this point in the conversation, I know how it will end. I'll yell at him, have a complete tantrum and tell him to forget the whole thing. I'll point out that I'd never argue or second-guess his automotive knowledge. My feelings would be hurt, and I'd spend the rest of the night feeling unappreciated.

I didn't want to face this argument over the draperies. He was not going to take it lightly. I silently prayed for the rest of the day until he got home from work (my mom had conveniently left after playtime). He came in through the garage door, through the mudroom, past the great room, and into the kitchen where he sat at the island amongst his mail, eating dinner. The kids had the TV on in the great room, and he looked into the space for over an hour without noticing the change. Ugh. How could something so meaningful to me, something that made me so happy, not even phase him? I think his obliviousness made me even angrier than if he'd walked in and flipped out over what was, in his mind, a $20,000 loss. My great room would officially be naked and afraid until the battle had been won.

I stood on the front lines for three full days, waiting for the attack. Nothing. The man came, went, sat, played, and had beer in that room without noticing. On the fourth day, in mid-August, we had a repairman at the house fixing the dryer. He was a heavy-set fellow in his mid-forties, friendly and exactly the kind of guy you'd expect to be working in your laundry room. Otto had no problem with him, which is always my indicator of a good repairman. He was crouched in the laundry room, and the kids and I were all in the kitchen. It was late morning, and Tom was heading toward the mud and laundry room to ask the repairman something. Then it happened. He caught a glimpse of the extra beams of sunlight shining through the windows and realized they'd been stripped of their wardrobe. He stopped mid-step and silently gasped while his cheeks flushed with anger. *Oh boy, here it comes.* I could feel my pulse quicken and little beads of sweat swelling at the top of my forehead.

"WHAT THE *HECK (but not heck)* HAPPENED IN HERE?!" My spouse, for the first (and last) time in the thirteen years I'd known him, said things I'd never heard him say. I knew he was going to be mad, but I had no idea he'd lose his mind over the ugly removal. I remained calm. I was embarrassed for our Maytag friend, but even more fearful of how I was going to win this war. Calm. Collected.

Wife. Equal partner. Mother of five. CEO of Homemaking. Interior Design Diva. Modern Day Rosie the Riveter. My armor was on, and I was ready to win. (In my mind, I'd already won.)

"I took them down because I was sick of looking at them," I righteously stated. He glared at me as if I'd killed his dog. My sister-in-law left the door open to the house when he was a teenager, and his dog ran out and got hit by a truck from the party store down the street. His dog died. I imagined this was the look he would have given the truck driver had he come face to face with him. I remembered my rights.

"How could you do something like this without even asking me? *How* dare *you!* How did you even do it without killing yourself?"

"My mom helped me three days ago," I countered. He was shocked. Three days ago. To think I could have done this years ago made me sick.

"I should have known! *You conspired against me!*" he steamed. And there it was. Right out in the open. This war was not about the draperies or the money I'd removed. What I'd taken away was his jurisdiction, and *that* was the issue at play. A steady stream of justified calm ran through me, and I knew that this was going to change my marriage for the better. I would stand strong and hold my ground. What followed was at least a thirty-minute battle of the facts, rights, and legalities of drapery aborting. Luckily, I had (of all things) a party to attend and had to leave him alone for the afternoon with the kids. When I drove away, I thought he'd never talk to me again. That's how betrayed he felt. I was allowed to make house decisions and should have been able to do so without begging for his approval. He should be honored to be married to a designer. It's not like I'd do something stupid. And I wasn't spending money; that was something I always cleared with him, even if it was just a couple hundred dollars.

In the end, the fight continued into the late hours of the night, all over whether or not I was in the right to do what I did without his input. I can happily report that it was the absolute best fight I'd ever had. If you can fight fairly and resolve problems, both parties win. We did not go to bed angry but instead with a new understanding of how I had the need to feel valued as a professional, and he needed to feel respected and not undermined by his co-conspiring mother-in-law. Besides, he was just trying to "express his paint color ideas" over the years and had no idea what I was always so upset about.

That night we established new house rules. Moving forward, I would continue with my proposed design projects, de-Noreening upon his approval (which he knew he had to grant unless I was being unreasonable), and I promised not to let my mother influence future decisions (she took one for Team Daughter on that one). Life at 34 Pine Gate Drive changed that day, and new boundaries had been set. It was good.

While all of this was happening, my mom and I made no correlation between the curtain corruption and some very real-life issues that had been taking a toll on our family. Papa had taken a serious turn for the worse and had been hospitalized, moved to a nursing home, and moved again to assisted living. He had terminal cancer that had moved to his brain, and the goal was to keep him comfortable for as long as we had him. Knowing that he would never return to his home was really hard.

Growing up, I could look out my bedroom window across the acre of grass in between our houses and see my grandma's bedroom window through the line of pine trees Papa had planted when we built our homes. I was four when I watched him bury the tiny saplings, and he told me that by the time I graduated from high school, they would be five times taller than I was. They'd grown so tall that they hovered above the roofline of our ranch-style homes, and their branches had grown into one another. My dad had to prune back a small area just to create a walkway through them.

It seemed like just yesterday that I could skip next door in the summer, climb the garage porch stairs, and announce my entrance as I took off my shoes in the small hall that led to their open plan kitchen, dining, and living room. My grandma was usually making dinner and Papa would have just gotten home from work and would be listening to WJR news radio. If it was a hot day, the draperies, hand sewn by my grandmother, would be drawn to keep the house cool and the heat seemed to amplify their natural house smell. Every house has a "smell." Grandma and Papa's emulated her amazing cooking, usually meat and potatoes, and the aroma of their heavy wood, old-world furniture. It's hard to really describe a house smell, but, like a fine wine, this one was priceless to me, and it held all of my childhood memories of my grandma, my Belgian roots, and my adulthood closeness to Papa within its walls.

When we moved him into assisted living, my parents asked if I could meet them at the house to decide what furniture to bring and what artwork/accessories we could use to make him feel at home. Their house was filled with oil on canvas paintings that my grandma had made. Still life, landscape, and everyone's favorite, an old man smoking his pipe in a rocking chair next to the hearth while his dog napped by his side. My grandma was so talented, and we appreciated her long after she was gone, as her artistic genes found their way through the generations. My cousins, most of us girls, all had some of her skills, from sewing to cooking, fine art, and of course fashion and interior design. Being in the house without Papa there was sad. And when this was over, it would be emptied, and the beautiful smell that took me back in time would be lost forever.

The door in the dining area led to a wooden deck that overlooked a large valley and beyond it, acres of wooded land. Cement block steps led down to what used to be a meticulously kept vegetable garden, grouping of apple trees, and my favorite, three large currant bushes. I could see my grandma bending at the waist working in the warm months, and days in my childhood sledding into that valley from my own backyard with my family and friends. Even before Natalie and Kate, we bundled up the Big Three and Papa met us outside for some laughs.

The dining room was separated by a half-wall to the living room, and I remembered all those Saturday nights watching *The Muppet Show* and sleeping in the blue room. I walked down the hall, smiling as I crunched on the clear plastic runner my grandma insisted laying on the carpet to keep it from wearing. My room was the first. I stood at the doorway taking in the memories. The crisp sheets. The tuck-ins. An oil painting of the European city street still hung above the bed. I glanced at the dresser and noticed two little canary yellow birds facing each other just as they had when I was four. I'd forgotten all about those birds until that moment. They were probably accessories she'd bought at Hudson's for the house on the lake, and in this moment, I knew I had to have them. It was like having a secret piece of my grandma and all those tuck-ins right at my fingertips through the eyes of those little birds. They came home with me that day and have sat on a shelf in my closet in front of my supermodels ever since.

Two weeks after we'd gotten Papa into his new apartment, his health took another turn for the worse. We lost him on a Tuesday morning. My mom and her three sisters were in the next room setting him up with hospice when he passed. It was peaceful. He'd been in a deep sleep for a couple of days, and Tom had gone with me to say goodbye to him over the weekend. He was the only grandparent I had a chance to be with at the time of his death. I was blessed to have been able to spend afternoons visiting him with the kids, having him for dinner, and saluting him with a fancy Belgian brew on many occasions. He was close to us all, and we'd seen him on multiple occasions over the weeks leading up to his passing. It meant so much to be able to tell him we loved him in the end.

Everyone called him Van, but his full birth name was Ides Adolph Baldes VanPachtenbeke, and he came from a family of fourteen. At the age of twenty-two, he immigrated to the United States to start his own American Dream with his nine-month pregnant bride. My uncle Ernie was born en route without proper medical attention and suffered oxygen loss to his brain, leaving him with severe brain damage, a tragedy they would not discover until he was a toddler. By then, Ernie had a baby sister (my mom) and later, three more. My grandma had four girls and one boy, just like I did. By the time Ernie was seven, she could no longer give him the care he needed at home, and he was placed in an institution in the late 1950s, a decision that grieved my grandparents every day.

My mom grew up going to 8AM Sunday Mass, followed by an hour and a half car ride to go visit her brother. The institution in which he lived was a miserable place. When I was born, I tagged along once every couple of months. In the mid-eighties, Ernie was moved to a group home, and that was a huge blessing for the quality of his life.

Papa was a hard-working electrician by trade. His integrity for getting any job done the right way was unbeatable, and he made a nice living to support his family as the foreman on many high-profile jobs in Detroit throughout his career. Hospitals, hotels, and the project of which we were most proud, the Detroit Institute of Arts. He was an adoring husband, loving and very "old school" father, and of course the best Papa to his grand and great grands. He was a high energy perfectionist with a "let's get it done today" attitude, one that many of us VanPachtenbeke's share, right down to my mother calling me the day of his passing to let me know that the viewing would be the very next day and the funeral the day after that. I remember hanging up the phone and finding it almost comical that the Dryer Funeral Home could pick him up at his facility, embalm him, and have him laid out in less time than it would take me to get my kids bathed and dressed in appropriate outfits with clean shoes for a day.

When Grandma Foss died in January, I left Tom home to watch the kids. Her service was held at the funeral home, and there was not an internment. My kids understood her passing, but didn't have the full experience, which was one I'd learned of at the young age of three when my baby brother died a week before his first birthday. I was never sheltered from death. It was part of life. Every funeral I'd ever attended took place at the Dryer Funeral Home. It was situated one

182 · HOLLIE GYARMATI

block west of Downtown Holly and owned by the Dryer family, of course. It'd been the same my entire life and was, in a very non-creepy way, "home" for me. I never felt out of place there. When I was three, I placed artwork in my brother's tiny white casket. He was followed by great grandparents, great aunts and uncles, the tragic deaths of family friends, a cousin, and now the last of my own grandparents. I was happy to have Tom and the kids there with me for the day, and curious as to how they would handle their first viewing.

Thankfully, grieving Papa was a beautiful experience for my family. My kids loved him and seeing him laid out was not scary. They fully understood that his soul was not there and that they were just looking at his "earthly body." At ages eight, eight, seven, four, and four, I thought they'd be afraid, non-social with the visitors, and bored of the Dryer Funeral Home within an hour. Instead, they were obsessed with using the kneeler in front of Papa's casket, so much so that at one point I caught them elbowing each other out of the way, and a vision of the casket spilling over flashed through my peripheral vision as I excused myself from a conversation. Yup, the Gyarmati kids made themselves right at home amongst the living and the dead. My mom's entire family spent the day there, and it was of course nice to see old friends whom I remembered from my childhood come to pay their respects.

My cousin, Jamie (the author) drove in with her brood from Denver, and I shared my workout meltdown story with her. I had no problem laying it all out there—my jealously, my depression, my hopeless situation as a slave to my house and family. And, in the midst of sharing this with her, I remembered that she wrote her book to inspire moms. I don't know if it was profitable or how many copies got into the hands of desperate women. But I, against my will, was one of them and maybe the one most impacted by her encouragement to pursue one's dreams even while a proud holder of the title "Mom." Just as I believe the Lions played that game for me, I believe that God inspired Jamie to write that book for me. I had nothing nice to say about that book, but my dear cousin contributed to the day I came out of my closet a new woman. Sharing that with her meant a lot to me, and she embraced me in a big sweet loving hug, just as she has her entire life.

Papa's funeral was a full Mass at St. Rita's, the small cobblestone chapel I'd spent my early years visiting when I'd stay overnight with my grandparents. I walked in with a full box of Kleenex in my Prada bag, which was, by this point, a glorified purse and only used it if we were out for the day, or in this case, needed to smuggle in large items like full boxes of tissue. My family took up an entire pew three rows back on the right side. When I was a kid, Grandma and Papa sat on the left. I'd only sat on the right for my grandmother's funeral, which was a giant blur. Today, while my tears continuously ran down my cheeks, I was proud for many reasons.

I was proud that I had been blessed with a wonderful relationship with Papa, and I had no regrets. I was proud that my children knew him and were sharing this important day with me. I was proud to be at St. Rita's, raising my kids Catholic because when everyone else was not exactly sure when to sit, stand, or kneel, my crew was. And not out of habit but because we understood the Mass, appreciated it, had a deep reverence for it. It was the first time I was proud to consider myself Catholic. Maybe it was all those years at St. Hugo's finally catching up to me, or the fact that I'd reached a point where I could sit through Mass without being exiled to the foyer with toddlers. Or, maybe my anti-Catholic upbringing was fading a little. The organist began to play Amazing Grace, a tearjerker at any service let alone a funeral, and I turned in my seat to glance up at the organist just as I had when I was four. And wouldn't you know, it was a volunteer from my own church up there in the balcony. What were the odds of that?

Following the Mass, we proceeded four blocks north to Lakeside Cemetery, where five generations of my dad's side rests, including my brother, my Grandma VanPachtenbeke, and now Papa by her side. The kids were perfect. They laughed, they cried, and Noah even cornered Father Dave to ask him his latest deep-thought questions about God, the Devil, and all his "what ifs." It was so nice to visit St. Rita's that we decided to make it a quarterly tradition and still drive out for Saturday 4PM Mass, Papa's favorite, followed by our favorite pizza at the Red Devil.

Losing my last two grandparents months apart marked the end of an era for my family. My parents were now the "old generation," and life suddenly felt short. Tom's career was still uncertain, and my drive to create a lifelong business with 3AM gave me a new reason to be hopeful that I had a bigger purpose than dishes and laundry. Yes, I know that raising five kids is a huge purpose and one I don't take lightly, but reflecting on the lives of my grandmas and seeing their personalities and talents in myself had ignited something. I was half Belgian and half All-American. I was, as in the closet moment, able to see myself with a different perspective, focusing on the big picture of who I was. And I decided to embrace it and live it for the rest of my life.

CHAPTER 18

SURPRISE MAKEOVER: SCHOOL & SPOUSE EDITION

It was a typical mid-February day in Michigan: overcast and cloudy with zero chance of sunshine. There were a few layers of old snow covering the ground, and the wind chill made even the dog want to stay indoors for the day. The big kids were in school—the twins in second grade and Isabelle in first. It was my favorite time of the day, naptime, and while my three-year-olds were snuggled in their bunk beds, I was sitting at the kitchen island working on a design project. Tom had been gone for a couple of hours. He'd gone to the office at the old dealership and apparently out to lunch with his brother, who'd been out of town for a few weeks. The months leading up to this day brought a plethora of uncertainties in terms of Tom's future role with his brother. In September, Tom had felt it necessary to ask for a few months' notice if their business relationship would be coming to an end. The response he received was, "Hang in there, we'll get something going." After months of lingering dealership discussions, it became clear that another dealership was not coming. Other conversations circled back to opening a pizza franchise, and we couldn't see supporting even *one* family on that. The strain of almost five years of dealer distress had taken its toll on both families. We suffered economic hardships in different ways, and open communication was at a standstill. The holidays came and went, and as of January 1, so did the paycheck. In fear that it was over (without clear warning, no less) we entered a Code Red on the career front. By mid-February, our savings were draining fast, Tom needed answers, and thankfully, he walked into the house on this particular afternoon with a very knowing—yet not surprised—look on his face.

"We need to talk. Come to the library," he said seriously, grabbing my hand as I stood up to give him a hug. I followed him through the foyer and into his office, sitting with my knees tucked into my chest in his brown leather, tufted-back armchair. He pulled the ottoman out a bit and sat on it, leaning in, his giant blue eyes focused on mine.

"It's over." I sensed some relief in his voice. "I met up with him for lunch, he told me he couldn't afford to pay me, and I asked if it was the end. He reluctantly confirmed with a very heavy dose of denial that it had to be. I confirmed that I would no longer be reporting to the office, handling bills, phone calls, or anything dealer-related, and he agreed. And that's it."

I kept my gaze directly on his, and I think we were remembering our "What if I had a normal job?" talk from our courtship. We didn't have to say it, but we were both relieved that it was over. It was really good in the heyday and very lucrative, but four years of a stagnant business was depressing. We could start fresh. Tom could do whatever he wanted, and anyone would be lucky to have him. That was the good news. The bad news was that we were officially unemployed, and we had a lot of bills and a lot of mouths to feed. I was already crunched with a budget and I knew how hard it was. Still, without a verbal reply, all in this brief moment, our eyes still locked, I felt giant tears welling up, and I started to cry. Not sob, just cry.

"I thought you would be happy that it was over," he asked, confused.

"I am; I'm just scared. What about health insurance? What about unemployment? Is that an option?"

"As of right now, he's agreed to keep us on his insurance, which is very generous. I don't think unemployment is an option since we've been out of business for so long. There's nothing official to make it worth pursuing. I think I'll be able to find something soon, anyway. I've already got a couple of ideas." That's all I needed. I knew I didn't need to have a meltdown over money. Money was *his* job. And out of my control. I was thankful that the small amount I was making with design work could contribute to groceries. Crap. I would have to let my cleaning girl go all together. The scrubbing of toilets and tubs was now part of the housework. *Blech.*

Announcing our unemployment was no surprise to our small group of friends and family. Of course, my parents, Tom's closest friend who lived in San Diego, and the Zarotney's were our biggest supporters and the only ones who knew that we'd already lost so much by this point. They gave us what would be unwavering support throughout our journey. Most reactions were, "Wow, sorry; I'm sure Tom will get a great job." It wasn't like we ran around telling everyone we knew, but it was also a reality we didn't hide. The hardest part was once again defending the fact that we lived in a beautiful house in the wealthiest city in the state. The assumption was that we were rich. I despised that. I felt the judgment from extended family. Most of my local friends got it; they could relate to an extent. The ones who *really* understood were the automotive acquaintances that Tom started contacting as he began his job search.

You'd think that Tom would have been a wreck, facing such an uphill battle at this point, but the reality was that he'd found his peace with God during all those weekday Masses, and thank goodness. The man I'd married had been refined by his faith and he had a calmness about this job loss that kept me from losing it. He'd started a men's group at church that would meet once a month at 7AM. This group of twenty or so men ages thirty to ninety gave him the emotional support he needed. Our priests were amazing, and considering the size of our church (3,000+), we had no reservations discussing our situation with a couple of them. Knowing that our family was in their prayers brought us a lot of comfort. We remembered Father Jim and his words to us on our wedding day: "It's you two against the world." And it was.

Within a couple of weeks, Tom had an interview lined up with a reliable entrepreneur who knew what standard of living we were used to, that we had a large family, and the details of Tom's background. The job was in automotive internet leads, and he was told that the average salary was six-figure plus; it sounded like the perfect rebound. I sent my husband out, giving him approval to buy a suit that made him feel like a million bucks. Even though we needed that money to pay the mortgage, I knew that he needed every bit of confidence possible, and if a Brooks Brothers suit would do it, I was in. Very unlike Frugal Hollie. I'll never forget the interview day. We were so relieved. So excited. We thought, "Wow, there *is* something better, and God is really taking care of us!" Just two weeks in, and we could possibly be getting back to good. It was a Tuesday morning at the end of the month, and I met up with Claudia and our preschoolers at the Henry Ford Museum. Warm weather was zoo day once a week; cold weather was the museum. I strolled through with Natalie and Kate thinking about Tom in his suit, shaking hands with his new boss, and envisioned returning to grocery shopping without tears.

When I got home that afternoon, I was greeted by a disappointed and confused spouse. He went through the entire morning, the multiple interviews, and the job offer. There was an offer! I was excited! Then he told me the starting salary. $40,000. It was a joke. It was sales, and he'd have to build his book of business. It was something he could have done when he was single with a hopeful outlook, but not with a family of seven.

That's how we ended up, later that night, sitting in the formal dining room on our silk Baker armchairs, painful reminders of what we now considered our past life, the good old days, and a bottle of Pinot Noir from my father-in-law's collection that had sat untouched in our basement for years. With our life spread before us, I took in the monstrosity of the house that had swallowed us up. I was sitting in what was once a $1,000 dining chair, the equivalent of six weeks of food for my family when new, but now worth only $100 at most. I was surrounded by luxury and felt nothing but poverty. It would have done us no good to sell our belongings; they were of little-to-no value after years of use. Even trying would take time that we didn't have.

My head was spinning before I'd even lifted my glass to my lips. I felt more than poor. I felt anger for the predicament we were in, and was overcome with fear, shame, and despair. Tom and I sat in silence for what seemed like an hour but was probably more like ten minutes before very rationally discussing our plan. We could pay for three months of the mortgage at most, and with the help of my design income and Tom's eBay sales, we could manage putting food on the table. Nothing more. No doctor's visits, prescriptions, life insurance, extracurricular family time, or gifts of any kind. And it wasn't guaranteed that we would even manage the bare bone essentials.

By the end of our meeting, Tom had shared his distaste for everything automotive and his desire to try something new. He'd always been intrigued by the medical industry and thought he'd have a shot at equipment sales. He lit up when talking about it, and with that he had my full support to pursue it. We had nothing to lose. Our hope was that he'd find a job within the next couple of months. The house would undoubtedly go on the market by May if he hadn't, and a fast sale would ensure us the last of our funds, which, because we'd put a substantial amount down, would be enough to live on until he got his foot in the door somewhere.

The idea of moving made my stomach hurt just at the thought of the massive quantity of overflowing basement storage and garage clutter that needed to be remedied. And I was no stranger to the stress of staging and house showings. But envisioning a regular house in a regular neighborhood excited me. I wanted less. We both did. It'd been over five years in the house of pain. We were methodical with it all and agreed that it had to be job, then house. It made no sense to put the house on the market not knowing where our employment would be based. It could be out of state for all we knew. We ended our executive meeting with a handshake and a hug under Noreen's $10,000 crystal chandelier and embraced our commitment that we would get through this together. We didn't really have a choice.

The very next morning, Tom started his reinvention in the library, and I continued to, as much as I hate the expression, "keep calm and carry on." Kids. House. Groceries. 3AM. Design was my outlet, and I embraced it more than ever. Nothing made me happier than to get the kids tucked in, set up my drawings in the dining room, pour a glass of Pinot Grigio, and listen to Louis Armstrong and Ella Fitzgerald—or anything from the 1940s for that matter. Tom would walk into the kitchen to refresh his drink and glance in at me in my glory through the butler's pantry before heading back to his work. He loved that I loved it, and I loved him for it. We were both pursuing dreams.

My 3AM dream was more alive than ever nine months after conception. I knew what I wanted to be, I had a short-term game plan, and like anything else in life, I plugged away at it every single day. The website was up and running. I had business cards that I'd carefully designed with Bodini font, the same as is used on the cover of *Vogue* magazine, white field, and one of my favorite color combos, poppy red and light teal. My official business name at this point was "3AM Interior Design *for moms*." Marketing myself as a hybrid-designer, I was ready to makeover every mom in Bloomfield Hills from her kitchen sink to getting her family out the door every morning. I was like a human version of *Real Simple* magazine, and I couldn't wait to share and answer the question everyone had been asking me for years: "How Do You Do It?"

I had successfully made over a couple of homes and consulted a nice handful of people on miscellaneous projects. In both cases, I solved their lifestyle needs and mom problems, and both women raved and even got teary over my understanding of what their needs were. I was a different designer. I was the educated, experienced, and much more talented version of my younger self, who spent the day making over my girlfriend's bedroom then standing back and asking, "How do you feel *now* in this space?" There was no doubt that I had a unique niche to fill in the design community; yet getting my message out there had thrown me for a loop. There wasn't anyone to compare myself to, and I was pioneering a new brand. Loving every minute of my client time and design work, I kept finding that women were afraid to be open about what they were frustrated with, or they thought of me as "Hollie, the one with five kids," only to discover that yes, I was, in fact, a real designer. So we focused on finding the right sofa or decorating, when what I *really* wanted to do was tell them to stop spending money on their over-scheduled kids, carve out thirty minutes to work out yet wear a real outfit to the grocery store, and buy the eight-way hand-tied English arm sofa from the design center because it *would* make her feel fabulous and it would last forever. No go.

It was much easier in the department store. I had the brand. I had the title. I could slip a business card into someone's hand that read, "Hollie Gyarmati, Senior Interior Designer." Easy. But those days were over, and I was going rogue. I needed to project who I was so people would appreciate and understand what I had to offer. I decided to start a 3AM Top Ten list that I would post on my website every month. Everything I was a pro at all wrapped into a theme that fit whatever month it was. It would be a great resource, and it was fun to compile my favorite fashion, beauty, design, and mom tips into one great article. I began in January, taking a couple of hours each month to sit and write. As it turned out, I was pretty good at it, and I loved writing.

I'd print copies for friends and family (who gave me rave reviews), and my mom immediately told me I reminded her of a modern-day Erma Bombeck. I was writing great material, posting it on my website, and had no idea how to get it out to the world. Back then, I was a virgin to all things tech and social media. Tom had to force me to get an iPhone when I started my business, and that was when I learned how to send my first text, take a digital photo, and send an email to multiple people at the same time. I'm not kidding when I say tech virgin! All those years the world was going digital, I was busy changing diapers—27,000 of them to be exact—and giving anyone besides my babies a second of my time was not on the list. So here I was, diaper-free, stroller-free, and the owner of 3AM Interior Design for Moms, writing my own Top Ten list for women around the globe.

While navigating my new destiny, I received a text from a mom at school that the PTO president was looking for an interior designer to help spruce up the teacher's lounge. I mulled over whether or not to contact her. If I got involved, it would be volunteer work, which I wasn't in a great position to give. If I didn't, I could miss an opportunity to leave my mark, spread some love, and possibly get some business. If I did, I'd have to work with the PTO president, Stacy Fox, who, for some reason, intimidated the crap out of me. I don't know why. I didn't even know her. But she held the title of Detroit's Best Chocolate Chip Cookie Maker, and when she was in the room, she was in control. Also, she was the president. I'd met the presidents of the automotive industry, both US and foreign, yet this little woman made me sweat more than a black-tie introduction. If I didn't take a chance, I would always regret skipping the opportunity to do something new, and so I decided to call her. Actually, I sent her an email—less scary.

She sent me a prompt response, and we met up within days in the lounge to scope out the project. Our schools are the best public schools in the state. The buildings are all meticulously maintained, and the classrooms are stacked with the most upgraded technology tax dollars can buy. The teacher's lounge, on the other hand, was the most depressing room in the building. I swung the heavy metal door into a narrow, eight-foot-long hallway that opened up to a tiny room for the more than thirty staff members to kick back in. It was about eighteen feet wide and twelve feet deep. There were two tall, narrow arched, brown brick, 1970s Spanish era, off-center windows. The cement block walls were dingy beige and covered with posters, bulletin boards, and some 1980s pastel watercolors in gold frames. A matching oversized sofa and loveseat were shoved into the left side of the room. They were boxy and broken in—like something you'd find in a fraternity house. You couldn't pay me to sit on them. In the middle of the room sat a laminated, maple-colored, bullet-shaped table with folding chairs around it, and the other side of the room held a kitchenette and a wall cluttered with carts holding a coffee pot, a crusty microwave, and cluttered paper and pantry goods covered in dust. By the looks of this sad scene, I don't think anyone had "lounged" there in years.

"I'm thinking we go to Bed Bath & Beyond, buy some slipcovers for these folding chairs, and get some accessories; what do you think?" the president asked with a "Let's get this thing done and crossed off the list" tone. I stood there envisioning what we could do to this room. It needed a complete overhaul and polyester slipcovers from BB&B were not in my vocabulary.

She stood there in her boho-chic long sweater and buckled boots. Her voice was ringing in my ears. It was sugary sweet like her cookies, which, by the way, *are* the best ever, and part of me wanted to go along with her little "spruce up" gig. I ran the options and then asked, "I have an idea but it's big. I need some time to put it together, but I'll do it for free and promise you'll love it. Give me a week." She shot me a smile and a dose of trust, and we set up our next appointment.

A few days later, I sat next to Stacy at the Township Library while our preschoolers got acquainted over coloring sheets one table over. I'd put together a complete design package, as I do for every client, because without it they can't visualize the final product. One look at my floor plan and glossy prints of the new furnishings had her wiggling in her chair. Her eyes lit up with excitement.

"I LOVE IT!" she exclaimed, and suddenly her presidential intimidation dissipated, and she became my new mini business partner. We snuck our plan to the principal, who gave us the thumbs up, and from there I plotted out final selections and started ordering. This was going to be a surprise makeover for the staff, so we decided that the smaller the design team, the easier it would be to keep it under wraps. Noah, Emma, and Isabelle thought I was working on someone's house. Emma even helped me select Michigan prints online without a clue. I partnered up with our local Sherwin Williams store, and they generously donated the paint and the service to give our room a complete overhaul. Tom was even a great sport about me taking on the project, as always. I was glowing yet penniless, and he loved me anyway.

While I was running my top-secret design project, Tom was spending his days locked in the library, methodically making calls and researching every viable career path that could land him a starting position in his new line of work. Thankfully, he had a personal list of approximately thirty doctors who were friends or long-time clients. Many were very helpful. He was already two phone interviews in with a company that specialized in dialysis and was interviewing about once every two weeks with local vendors. He'd purchased a fat orange hardcover book in which he plotted out his plan of action. He was online and on the phone all day, breaking only for lunch, dinner, and hugs from Natalie and Kate, who I am convinced kept his spirits high every day. Beyond his library lockdown, he was taking any consulting jobs that came his way and sneaking out for a couple hours in the evening to find things to sell on eBay. Cash flow was minimal. We were terrified, but the daily hope we held onto of getting a callback or the next interview kept us going.

By mid-May, our makeover weekend had arrived, and I had the entire installation planned down to the minute. I can proudly report that it went flawlessly. As soon as the teachers left on Friday after school, I had a crew moving every last dusty piece of furniture out and giving it a once-over cleaning. There were maybe eight of us in total; Tom came with the kids, and we made it a family weekend at the school. The painters started Friday night while we assembled Ikea furniture in the kindergarten wing and the cafeteria. Stacy had a friend in the printing business who helped us laminate an oversized mural of the Holland lighthouse on Lake Michigan, which would hang over a crisp white sofa, topped with a hand-made valence of roman shades, birch branches, and side panels, all white. It would completely transform the space to feel like a vacation spot, the perfect escape for a teacher on a gloomy winter day with a classroom full of loud, stir-crazy kids.

Sunday was final installation day, and I pulled in the big guns (my Dad, who can do anything) to come hang the draperies, wall shelves, and tweak whatever needed tweaking. The husbands worked hard, the moms did a lot of grunt work, and over the weekend I became friends with some very special people. It felt great to lead a team and see what started as a vision come to life over the course of just a couple of days. The final product was stunning, and we couldn't wait until Monday morning.

"Why is the lounge door locked?" an early arrival teacher asked her co-worker standing in the hallway.

"I don't know. Look at this sign they hung on the door. 'No teachers until 8:45AM'" she complained. "We won't have time to get our coffee before the buses get here." There were six of us huddled near the kitchenette, which was sporting a new grass green backsplash and a Keurig single cup coffee maker. The opposite wall (that used to be cluttered) showcased a white Ikea two-high cube unit on casters with storage bins, two brand new microwaves, floating-style shelves with baskets, and a row of sweet tin pots with grasses on top. We reused the maple bullet table but flipped it parallel with the sofa and added six white Ikea side chairs. I space planned so efficiently that we were able to squeeze a new four-seater rectangular table from Ikea against the wall on the kitchen side to serve as counter/prep space and seating. It was perfect. Over the nestled table hung the "old school" wall clock, and above, three vertical photos on canvas of close-up Michigan fall, winter, and spring foliage, representing the seasons of the school year and balancing out the beautiful mural on the opposite wall.

There was quickly a lot of chatter outside the heavy blue steel door, which had been painted bright red to match the lighthouse from the inside for a pop of color against our white getaway. Stacy gave me a wink, and we decided it was time for the big reveal. It was better than Christmas morning with the kids. Christmas morning surprises are heartwarming and filled with love, and this was *better!* I knew that this makeover was going to bring some joy to every single one of these hardworking teachers at some point over the years. Whether it was having a nice table to dine at, relaxing with a cup of coffee on the sofa, or even taking a moment alone to regroup in the midst of a bad day, that room would be a safe-haven from that point on.

Stacy snuck over to the door and peeked her head out. The hallway buzz had created a mini crowd by this point, and when she opened the door all the way, Susan Payne, the school librarian of thirty years, headed the line. Her reaction was jaw-dropping priceless; thank goodness my friend Jaclyn captured the moment because it was featured on page two of our county newspaper the next day. As the teachers poured in with excitement, I overflowed with the kind of happiness that only comes when you give from the heart. Many were so happy that they teared up. It reminded me that if what I did as a designer could result in tears of joy, I would keep designing.

In the end, we left our school in a better state, and had pulled off a newsworthy surprise that became one of my favorite portfolio pieces. Did I have school parents lined up for design work? Nope. I think a couple of small projects came through as a result, but it was not a moneymaker for 3AM. It was okay. I knew it was something worth investing my time in, and even though we worked through the whole thing while Tom was wishing he'd had a job, not one person involved ever knew that we were in the midst of a crisis. Design jobs always had a way of landing in my lap when I really needed the money, and we believed that Tom was just weeks away from his new career. We decided to trust the life design process.

CHAPTER 19

ESTATE SALE

"Mom, I have good news: we're finally putting the house on the market," I announced over the phone. It was late June, and we'd just gotten off a call with our realtor, who said she could get us listed within a couple of days. It was a Friday morning, and with our listing came a to-do list about two pages long to get the house "show ready."

"Thank God!" she exclaimed, understanding how anxious I was to see an end to my big house problems.

"Here's the deal: we have some major purging to do, and the front door needs to get stained. There are a lot of jobs to get done, and we have the weekend to do it. Can you and Dad help us?"

"Of course! When would you like us there?" she asked, ready to start taking orders from yours truly.

"We're starting now, so whenever you can be here. We're grateful for your help," I responded, scanning my legal pad and envisioning an executive buyer walking through my house within the next week, loving it, and throwing out an offer that was within range so we could take a breather. Our realtor, who we also used for our previous home sale and had known for years, gave us every indication that it was a seller's market. She wanted to list our "estate" right back at its original value, its new-build price from 2000. We trusted her input and research and went with it. She felt it would be a quick sell, and with the profit she was dreaming about, we could buy an average-sized two-story colonial outright and call it a day.

The six weeks leading up to our real-estate call were excruciatingly humbling for Tom. My husband has been an overachiever his entire life, and his makeover wasn't going as planned. He'd been through a full round of interviews with his number-one-choice medical company, which took three months, only to hear back in a voicemail that they'd decided to "hire from within." This phrase was one that he'd read in multiple emails from HR departments, and to hear it after months of what he felt were successful interviews made us want to vomit. If it was obvious that he was not the right guy for the job, we wanted to know with real feedback, not lies and "fluff." The man was putting everything he had out there, and all he wanted was honesty. He received anything *but* from those in the medical field. He met with various industry owners for coffee, and they all threw out a gratuitous, "Oh, yeah, I'm looking to expand into this area. When I do, I'll give you a call."

All these phone calls, email exchanges, and meetings were recorded in his orange Career 2.0 notebook, and after five solid months of rat-race work, we sat together in the library and took it in over a glass of wine. (It's a good thing Tom's Dad left us a wine collection to last a lifetime; we never imagined how much we'd need it.) Tom opened his makeover book. It was like a giant book of heartbreak and failure. We looked over his starting list of contacts. It seemed so easy in the beginning. As we flipped through the pages, we saw the dead ends, the scratches through names, the friends who didn't call back, the lives that were all running their own race while here we were, paralyzed without direction in terms of how we would take care of our family of seven. That night, we decided to burn that book, start over, focus on the house sale, and get back to automotive.

A few months earlier, Tom had the privilege of meeting up with a couple of very influential men whom he admired. They were kind enough to have a cup of coffee with him and share their life lessons.

One was a former Detroit Lions football coach turned successful businessman, the other a former Chrysler VP who'd known Tom and his family since the mid-eighties. Both men, well into their later years, told Tom to "stick with what you know." Which is everything automotive. They shared their own stories of failures and rebounds. They inspired him when he was at rock bottom not to give up. While they provided no job leads, these men gave my husband the determination to once again *be* a car guy and pursue a rewarding career.

Within days, our library transformed from medical sales to corporate automotive control center. A new book was opened, new names were written in the first few pages, and Tom was back on the phone making every connection he could with anyone pumping a pulse in the Motor City. Previously naïve to the power of social media, he joined LinkedIn and was immediately connecting with people he hadn't heard from in twenty years, discovering the benefits of having a stellar reputation as a former dealer. Most of us are happy to get a couple of endorsements or a great review when needed. Within just a few weeks of joining this new digital resource, Tom had personal recommendations from at least three top automotive executives and a full graph of endorsements from his 500+ LinkedIn connections. I was happy to see him making progress, and we both felt like we had this unemployment thing under control.

On the design front, in the midst of the summer of dead-end interviews and the decision to sell the house, I had jobs landing in my lap left and right, both commercial and residential. With Tom home to keep kids alive (my only standard for working outside the home), I could take on these wonderful projects, and with my income and Tom's internet sales, we miraculously squeaked by every month. The workload I was managing was not humanly possible. Somehow, I mustered the supernatural ability, for which I take *zero* personal credit, it was ALL GOD, to feed my family three real meals a day, provide those meals on a ridiculously low budget, take care of the kids (who were all under the age of nine), clean my 7,500 square foot house, maintain the exterior to the best of my ability, *and* be an interior designer, who, when stepping out for an appointment, looked like she had her game on and never once indicated that she feared she may be living out of a cardboard box within the next few months if one of two mountains didn't move out of the way.

Looking back, the joke was again on me. A year earlier I had a vision of branding who I was and inspiring women around the world, with the singular financial hope to supplement our income enough in the beginning to pay for my housekeeper. Here I was, just months later, cleaning twice as hard, being the designer, wearing all the mom hats—and even some of the dad hats—that had cluttered up my closet in the first place! Deep inside, I held tight to my dream, but the reality of what I needed to do to get my family through each day forced me to put it on hold. My life at home, with Tom in it full-time, was more work than it had been when he was out. His physical presence didn't change my routine (maybe my sanity at times) but him being there yet incapable of providing equal partner help made it difficult. My number one job during this time was allowing him to spend every minute finding work. This meant that I had to pick up the slack. I didn't ask for his help with the kids, in the kitchen, or even to run an errand. If I could do it, I did, and I tried my best to be his lifeline with encouragement and support every day. I was Tom's biggest cheerleader. If he was frustrated, I could whip out a list of all the reasons he was the most brilliant man on the planet, why I loved him, and why anyone would be nuts not to hire him. And I meant every word of it. It was during these times that I would walk by my kitchen island of mail clutter or stub my toe on the shoes he'd left in the middle of the doorway and realize that life was too short to focus on the little things that used to get my blood boiling.

More wedding day "us against the world" moments would echo in my soul as I rushed through my tasks. "Remember darling," Tom's frail Biggy told me with a serious smile and her little hand gripping mine before I walked down the aisle, "It's all about the love. Love, love, love. Just love each other and that's all you need." Wise words from a ninety-year-old who lived through both World Wars, the Hungarian Civil War, and survived three husbands plus her only daughter (Tom's mother). When she shared this life secret with me, I was standing in my Ralph Lauren wedding gown and had my suitcase packed for a honeymoon in Paris. I didn't give much thought to what she was telling me. Of course it was about love. I was IN LOVE with the man waiting at the altar. It would be a decade before I truly understood what she was telling me. Giving yourself entirely to your spouse means that you have to love them unconditionally through it all. I was guilty guilty guilty of putting conditions on my love over the years. I'd let all the little things get to me and sometimes had complete meltdowns over stupid things. My life lesson during this hard summer of unemployment was that I needed to love more. The more I loved, the more hope I had that something would give, and maybe we wouldn't have to live in a box.

Back to getting the house on the market. My parents saved the day by taking on big tasks like refinishing the front door, wiping down window screens, organizing the garage, and handling spring-cleaning tasks like washing walls and baseboards. Even the kids were excited about selling. Our expectation was to get it on the market, have a couple of showings, and be out before the beginning of the school year. I'd been through the house showing routine just six years earlier. The only difference this go 'round was that our lives depended on a sale, I had double the house to clean and stage (and I am serious about staging), and there was the small addition of two extra kids and a dog to evacuate along with the original three. No biggie.

The day of our first house showing had me on my hands and knees, not just scrubbing dog slobber off the patch of wood floor the sun was beaming across but in deep prayer that I would not have to again go through the work I'd endured over that last twenty-four hours. That was our advance notice request: no phone calls with a "We'd like to show the house in an hour" message. It was twenty-four hours' notice or nothing. And within those twenty-four hours, my family learned what "house showing ready" meant. I had a to-do list scribbled within one minute of my realtor call with names attached to each task. My kids knew how to clean windows, hide toys, fluff pillows, dust the spindles on our four staircases, and stage our seven bathrooms with my signature hotel folded toilet paper. Tom was allowed to work in the library until the last hour, when he'd jump into last-minute vacuum mode. He could clean an entire floor with our Dyson in less than twenty minutes. The biggest challenges, besides all the cumbersome prep work, were leaving the kitchen spotless and getting everyone out for a couple of hours—including the dog—and finding something to do. The first time it was McDonald's for dinner. We hoped it would be our last.

So there we were, packed in the minivan, hot and grimy after cleaning all day, wishing we were at a pool instead of an air conditioned vehicle we could not afford, smelling Otto's dog stress farts. That's right, our poor Springer got so worked up during the evacuation that his digestive tract went nuts once he was crammed in the car with us. Unemployment was taking a toll on the dog too. I looked at Tom as he was driving residential side streets looking for houses in our budget and noticed that he'd gotten really grey in the past year. Then I looked at Otto and noticed his ears were showing early signs of aging as well. The phone rang. It was Shilpa. The showing went well. It was a professional athlete. Young, single guy. Qualified buyer, but the house wasn't what he was looking for. I cringed at the thought of keeping my house clean for more showings. It was going to be a long summer.

Within four weeks, our realtor realized she'd overpriced the house, and we reminded her without sounding too desperate that we needed a sale. By this point, we were into August and had missed the prime season to sell. School was on the horizon, along with my usual school prep work. Historically, August was not my favorite time of the year. I had supplies and clothes to purchase, and the lesser income made that very challenging. That year, I scrounged up anything on the list that I had around the house, purchased the bare minimum for the kids, and was deeply embarrassed that I wasn't giving my two third graders and second grader my full attention so that they'd feel ready for school. My kids were amazing. They didn't complain, and humbly made do with what they had.

The showings came about once a week. Reluctantly, we went along with an Open House, which had us once again roaming Bloomfield Hills for a couple of hours on a Sunday afternoon, discussing Tom's latest business leads and the possibility that we'd hired the wrong realtor while the kids shared iPads on yet another hot day in the car. For all the naysayers when it comes to allowing kids to use mobile devices, I am the spokesperson for the other team. Without Apple products, we couldn't have survived keeping preschoolers and school-aged kids occupied for an hour here and an hour there while being absent parents, fighting for the right to provide a home and income for our family. By the time we arrived back at the house, which had been "open" for three hours to anyone out for a Sunday drive, nosey neighbors, and possibly the prospect of a real buyer, we'd decided to terminate our contract with Shilpa. We loved her as a friend but wanted a heavy hitter. We needed to bring in the big guns, the multi-million-dollar agents who had the money to market our home and get the job done. We walked in through the garage door as one family was roaming the second floor. We sent the kids to the basement to play, and Shilpa was excited to share that a nice couple came through who wanted to come back the next day with their entire family.

Just then, the doorbell rang. I wished my house were closed, but we agreed that if they were coming, we were showing, even if it felt weird. It was a good thing that I'd taken all signs of Noreen out of the main floor, painted the kitchen a beautiful French chardonnay, my formal living room citron yellow, and the formal dining room a fleshy neutral. All draperies had been removed, and my main floor was as up to date as it was going to get with a few gallons of paint. As the new family roamed the house, not minding my kids running through the lower level, the doorbell rang again. This time, it was my neighbor, Rasha, who'd moved into the previous Kmart CEO's home at the end of my street a year before. I met her briefly outside; she had a son who was Noah's and Emma's age and three older children. She very politely reintroduced herself and asked if she could take a look for her nephew who was moving from California.

I decided to give her an official tour, and by the end we were sharing the woes of caring for our gigantic homes, the difficulty of taking care of our large families, and even laughing over our husbands and their unrealistic expectations of what it's like to be a homemaker. This woman, who was Syrian and a devout Muslim, was the last person I would have expected to have a bonding moment with upon our first acquaintance. She then changed her tone and shared with me the news and tragic loss of their immediate family members in Syria and her commitment to helping the refugees, her own sister being one of them. It was a sobering reminder that while our problems were serious, there were people going through harder times who lived in an even bigger mansion, just two doors down. I told her I'd be praying for the safety of her family in the Middle East. She teared up and embraced me in a hug. It was a powerful moment for me. Once again, Biggy's little frail voice from Heaven whispering, "It's all about the love, darling." And here we were, a Muslim and a Christian, holding on to each other because of the love. I called her "friend" from that day on. When we "closed" the house that day, we broke the news to Shilpa that we wanted to end our contract with her.

Back to the drawing board once again. Tom and I were exhausted on all levels. We knew who we wanted to hire to sell our house. Her name was Cindy Kahn, and she was a top producing Sotheby's Realtor whom we'd met a few months earlier when we brought the family through one of her houses on the market. She was probably in her late fifties, highly professional, dressed to the nines and used to upper class clientele. If our assumption that she was Jewish was correct, we felt very strongly that she'd have the understanding, integrity, and work ethic we needed to get results. Tom and I liked her the moment she greeted us, and within a day of contacting her she was sitting with us at the kitchen table with a realistic marketing plan to move our house. We were open with her about our situation, our need to sell ASAP, and our frustration over missing out on the summer market. I had a bit of a meltdown (a few teary-eyed moments), but by this point I was so exhausted by keeping up appearances on the outside that the walls of my home provided a safe haven in which a tear could roll whenever it needed to. My mom-in-distress call didn't scare her away, and we could feel that she was the right choice. It was business, but there was a mutual respect. Within ten days, our house would be professionally photographed and back on the market, ready to sell.

The first official Wednesday working with Cindy, we were scheduled for a realtor's Open House in the late morning. By then, I'd been through about twenty house showings and could do it blindfolded. I hated every minute of it, and if you've never had to take your home, make it look like no one lives there (at least not a family of seven and a dog with muddy feet), leave for an hour, and return only to get everything back in place to continue on with the day, consider yourself blessed. It is truly grueling, and doing it after breakfast is even harder. It doesn't matter how "picked up" or clean the rest of the house is, the kitchen needs full attention, and all the beds have to be made for a showing—a full hour's worth of work right there. Any way I sliced it, prepping for people stressed me out.

Cindy and her fellow Sotheby's co-workers would arrive between 11AM and noon, which gave me a full two hours to finish the house. I had the basement done, the beds were made, and the upstairs bathrooms were wiped down. My last push of time was desperately needed on the main floor. Besides the kitchen, I had stacks of kid crap and Tom clutter piled in the hall outside the formal bathroom that needed "filing," and the laundry and mud rooms were a mess. They looked like I'd just shuffled a family out the door (because I had). I was picking up in there when I heard my phone vibrating on the kitchen island. I ignored it for at least ten minutes because I was in a groove. When I got to it, there was a text from Tom, who was at a job seminar on the other side of town. It was a screenshot of a text from Cindy that said, "We're on our way; will be there just before 10." I looked at the kitchen wall clock, my go-to in every "down to the minute" situation, and it read 9:45. It's a good thing I'd given up breakfast years prior, or I would have hurled right then and there.

I never—not even in my craziest, most harried mom moments—felt the pressure to pull off the impossible like I did in that moment. I had five minutes to do something, I wasn't even sure what, but I had to MOVE! I stayed in the kitchen, got everything into the sink, stashed the toaster and usual everyday counter stuff in their usual spots, then ran a towel as fast as possible over the black and green marble island. I then ran to the stacks of clutter and threw them into a laundry basket that ended up parked on the laundry counter. I had just enough time to stage the great room and ended my two hours with a two-minute drill and an armload of miscellaneous items that I piled into the washing machine—on top of a clean, wet load of whites. When I say "items," I mean things like dirty socks, Barbies, remote controls, Tom's fall coat that'd been left on the island barstool, and other items that should have been put away. But in this moment, they were topping my clean clothes. As I turned around to sprint up the back staircase, across the upstairs, and into my closet to grab my jewelry, I noticed that there were muddy dog prints all over the white tile floor. My mudroom was actually muddy. These realtors would have to accept that this was a working house, not a show house. I could hear the cars pulling up the driveway.

I opened my front door with beads of sweat on my forehead. My new realtor, my multi-million-dollar Sotheby's star, didn't know whether to laugh or cry at what stood in front of her. I was wearing a baseball hat, diamond earrings, my pajama top, cut off jean shorts, and flip flops. My diamond engagement ring glistened in the morning sun, a 1980s Rolex (which was Tom's mother's; I didn't have time to lock it up) wrapped my left wrist, and I was holding a dog leash and collar in my right hand. There were at least ten realtors just steps behind her, and I heard more cars pulling in, doors opening, and idle chatter between well-dressed Bloomfield Hills professionals ready to appraise my home. She gave me a quick smirk, and I motioned for her to call me as soon as she was done.

I ran back through the foyer, past the formal powder room, onto the hardwood floor, down the hall, and through the mudroom, grabbing Otto on the way out. Pulling down my baseball hat, I drove past the line of black, white, and silver luxury cars in my circle. Once onto Woodward Avenue, I didn't know what to do or where to go. I was a hot mess and couldn't be seen in public looking the way I did. I hadn't even brushed my teeth! I drove two streets north to my friend Heather's house, where I sat in her kitchen with a bottle of water and bawled my eyes out. Heather Fairbanks was a newer friend, and the mother of Noah's best little buddy, Walker. Walker had become my "sixth sense" over the last year. It was easier to have him in my house as I discovered his presence eliminated girl screams, which, in my opinion, is priceless. I blubbered through the whole morning saga as I worked through a box of Kleenex in between sips. Heather was the perfect friend to comfort me through my crisis. Always sweet, sincere, and full of empathy, she agreed that what I had on my plate was more than anyone should have to handle, and as I'd heard many times over, she "didn't know how I did it." At this point, I didn't know how I could possibly do it for much longer.

210 · HOLLIE GYARMATI

CHAPTER 20

ASHES, ASHES, WE ALL FALL DOWN

I'd become a Twitter girl over the previous few months. I liked that it was short and sweet, and many of my contacts were national. Most were strangers. I wasn't after mass following, but just kept a steady little pace to feel like I was in the game. I wasn't, however, a fan of Facebook. I was connected to more local people, and my "friends" all seemed to be leading normal, happy lives, constantly posting photos of outings and little quotes about love and life. I didn't have a huge network there, but felt it was a good idea for business, so I made an effort to make posts related to being a mom or things that I hoped would bring a smile to someone having a bad day.

One particular day, I decided to share the secret that I was horrible at ironing button-down shirts. I'd usually grab a few "likes" and move on, feeling like I was part of the Facebook world and had a pulse. The reply I received from someone who was very much—as in the very most—removed from the personal loss we were struggling with, went something like this: "Be grateful because it means your husband has a job and he needs that white shirt you are trying to iron." In that minute, I became a ghost on Facebook. I didn't take it personally, but if there were a way to scream a reply back, it would have said, "MY HUSBAND HAS BEEN OUT OF WORK FOR TEN MONTHS, WE

HAVE FIVE KIDS, WE MAY LOSE OUR HOUSE, WE DON'T KNOW WHERE OUR NEXT MORTGAGE PAYMENT IS GOING TO COME FROM, AND THE WHITE SHIRT I SUCK AT IRONING IS MINE!" I reserved my self-control and put my laptop to sleep.

This closing of the laptop was the last straw of my attempt to hold on to being "normal" in my non-normal life. The reality was that we were at the end of our rope, and something had to give. Tom and I faced every day with the same attitude of thankfulness for our family, our health, and the roof over our head. We trusted that God had a plan for us. We both knew that we had a special purpose in life, and living in poverty was not it. We worked together to get through one day at a time, and in a weird way, while romantic date nights or stress-free quality time hadn't been in our deck for a long time, we grew closer. We'd become dependent on each other to get through the days like a retired couple in their eighties. We were emotionally fragile and appreciated our companionship with new perspective. I counted on him to make my coffee in the morning, and he knew that every day around 12PM I'd stick my head in his office to ask for his lunch order. If I needed tech support, he'd drop his job search to help me, and if he needed to make an important call, I'd get Natalie, Kate, and Otto out of the house to ensure complete silence, so that whoever was on the receiving end wouldn't know that he was working from home. When the kids got home from school, he'd help me keep them in line, and at the end of the day when we'd all cram onto the sectional in the lower level to watch an episode of *Gilligan's Island* or *Green Acres*, we'd push kids out of the way to sit next to each other and hold hands. At this point, we were all the other had. The testament of our wedding vows was undeniably real; it was "us against the world."

On the job front, Tom had reached a point of complete humility. Not that he wasn't humble from Day One, but now he was talking to every human who would give him the time of day. His automotive list had been scratched through one name after the next, and at best, his "interviews" were actually morning Starbucks meet-ups with anyone in the industry who was willing to meet him and get his name out there. They were people he'd connected with on LinkedIn or executives he was referred to by personal friends. I'd never seen him work so hard, and all for nothing. No paycheck. No Career 2.0 as planned. At this point, he'd placed over 1,000 applications online only to get lost in cyberspace. It seemed like everything required an engineering degree. We knew there had to be *someone* out there who could use his unique set of business skills. But how would we find them? With all this exhaustion, we started living by a quote Claudia had hanging next to their mudroom door: "Do Your Best, Let God Do The Rest." Who can argue that point? If you are doing everything you can possibly do here on earth, the rest is out of your hands. And, if you are a believer in God, you must believe that He is bigger than our puny little brains and can guide us through our toughest times. We had no idea what *He* was doing, but we continued to keep the faith.

I'd mentioned to someone close to my family that Tom really needed work, any kind of management work. The company they worked for owned multiple fast food chains and was expanding like crazy. Tom reached out to their source, and they set up an interview. Once again, we prayed, he put on the suit, and he met up with their manager. The interview was held at one of the new restaurants, which was still under construction. He said he looked like the executive who should have been conducting the interview. To his embarrassment and theirs, he discovered that he was interviewing to be a manager at the actual *fast food restaurant*. That was his lowest of lows. It was humiliating for us both. We couldn't believe that our "source" didn't take our urgency seriously enough to sort through their chain of command to see if they had openings that fit his qualifications. It was just another reminder that everyone was busy with their own lives, and someone like Tom, who was considered the top of the food chain in our circle, was disregarded as someone in need.

All this Debbie Downer dud employment had me racking my brain to move 3AM into a more profitable position. While I understood "interior design for moms," my clients did not. Actually, the "moms" were not even my clients. I was landing small commercial jobs and working on some high-profile local residences, all miraculous considering my lack of marketing or cash flow into the business. So I dropped the "moms" and ordered new business cards that made my Hudson's cards look like Vista prints. My new cards featured a beautiful photo that encompassed all things "me," (I shot it myself, and it took over twenty hours since I know *nothing* about photography!) They were printed on thick cardstock and were Euro-sized (like a pillow). I'd morphed into 3AM Interior Design, LLC and pushed forward as my personal best.

I applied my "best business practices" to my school mom etiquette and all things social. I could walk into the school office with a smile or chat with other moms in the parking lot like everything was normal. Noah and Emma were now in third grade, and I'd put them in the same class to take some stress off communicating with multiple teachers. Also, I felt like they needed each other. The kids were, at this point, feeling the stress. No matter how hard you try to get through the day (as though meticulously calculating grocery lists or calling the gas company to ask for a hardship break on your bill were normal parent tasks), you are in full understanding of the situation. But when you're a kid, you just know that your family is different. and your parents are under pressure and say no to just about everything. You adapt and try to fit in even when you don't. You stop asking to go to the birthday parties or after school activities. You learn to be silent when your friends are discussing their country club pool parties, Taylor Swift concerts, and shopping with their moms. You understand that you're probably a great athlete but won't get the chance to show off your skills until your parents can afford to pay for sports. My kids never once complained about not having money to do what everyone else was doing. They went to school and religious education (which the church allowed us to attend free of charge that year) and spent the rest of their time surviving house showings.

I hated living in our big house in the Hills. I hated that my kids were surrounded by such a high standard of normal that even "normal" made middle class kids feel poor. There were days when I wished we lived in a trailer park because it would reflect what our income could truly afford that year. At that point, we were at such high risk of losing our home that our only consolation was that my parents were comforting us by saying, "If the worst happens, you will not live on the street, you can live with us." *Really?* How was it possible that less than seven years prior, *I was the giver*; the one hosting the cocktail parties, the bridal showers, family dinners, donating time and money to the starving kids in Africa and the poor in our community, and here I was, almost one of them? I was haunted by the comment I'd made in the car in the parking lot of Whole Foods when Noah and Emma were babies. The time I confided in my mom our financial security, my gratefulness for having money to shop where I wanted, and the chilling fact that if Tom lost his job, he could pay our mortgage by flipping burgers. What a sick twist of fate that only seven years later, he was offered a job at a fast food restaurant. It made me sick. It made me angry. If it all had happened to us without kids, I could have handled that. But waking up every morning and looking into the eyes of my beautiful children without a bit of security to offer them except the knowing that we would last at least another week with food and a bed was terrifying.

The only thing I had to offer my babies besides my love was my faith. We learned during this period, this gloomy Michigan fall, that when you have nothing, you have to have hope and faith, or inside you will die. Our devotion was more prevalent then than ever. Mass was the one hour of solitude and comfort we had every week. We would sit, stand, kneel, and pray, hand in hand, the seven of us—Tom at one end and I at the other—and we knew that God would empower us to get through this storm. It was "us against the world," and "all about the love," and it didn't matter *what* church I was sitting in, God was going to reach me, love me, and give me what I needed to survive right where I was. All the pressure I'd put on myself, my marriage, my life to live up to an impossible faith standard was just wasted time and effort. Most important was the man flanking my five and the fact that we had each other for the rest of our lives here on earth.

God was leading me, guiding me, and comforting me through every moment of every day during this time. You know when you hear about people who are blind or deaf having supernatural ability with their other senses? That's the only way to describe what it was like in this darkness. The blind are guided through touch, something most of us take for granted. I was guided every day by God's supernatural power to make little things happen that made my life easier. I was in tune with things that I used to appreciate, but not need: a sunny day, a powerful storm, a friend who called to see how I was doing, or a front row parking spot.

The clearance rack at the grocery store became my little secret miracle every week. It didn't matter what was on my list, I'd find it on the stainless steel clearance rack hidden in the back of the store next to the bottle returns. Funny that an area most people wouldn't even bother with was the one spot I got excited about every week. I'd come home from the grocery store with a trunk full of groceries that would have cost me $300-$400 back in the day of Whole Foods, and now I was feeding my family for our budgeted $200.

I was walking a faith walk that freaked me out and thrilled me at the same time. I was learning that I couldn't out-give God. I was going out on a limb with things that seemed absurd to the average person in our society. One day, I marched into our bank with a 3AM check for almost $5,000. I promptly took ten percent of it and gave it to the church. I handed the rest to Tom to make our mortgage payment. And I secretly prayed that this whole ten percent thing wouldn't come back to bite me in the butt; it could have fed my family for a month. I was finding happiness in helping anyone around me in need. I'd hold the door open for a mom with a stroller or rush to the aid of a frazzled woman who'd dropped her purse in the parking lot. I had nothing, and I had nothing to lose. And giving humanity everything I had was the only thing that made me happy. So that's what I did.

One Saturday morning in November, I was scrounging up Noah's gear for his flag football game. The weather that day was bitter cold, and he needed layers to stay warm. Flag football was the one thing we decided not to eliminate. It was $150 for the season, Noah desperately needed an outlet for all of his boy energy, and it got our entire family out for the afternoon. The girls loved running around the high-school track and playing on the bleachers, and it was good for Tom and me to be together in public. You could look at the $150 as a seven-for-the-price-of-one event. As I shuffled through Noah's closet drawers, I realized that I didn't have an under layer for his legs to keep him warm. I'd gotten him by the year before by sneaking a pair of Emma's fleece leggings under his sweatpants, but today I had nothing. And I knew I couldn't afford even a $20 pair if I ran out to find him something. I stood in his closet and prayed for a solution. Then I remembered my friend Patti dropping off a couple of large garbage bags in July filled with winter gear that her son had outgrown. They were sitting in one of our storage rooms in the basement.

I ran down the two flights on the back staircase, still in deep prayer that there might be something in those bags. They were right where I'd left them on an old area rug in the kid's craft area. I ripped open the thick Hefty plastic in a panic. And then I started to feel my face flush as my tear ducts, active on a daily basis, began to flow. There, at the very top of the first bag, was a set of boys Hot Chilly's, top and bottom, size eight. An exact fit for Noah. And as I dumped out the entire contents, I discovered four sets of pink North Face fleece under layers for the girls.

Patricia McCalmont and her sister had become my guardian angels in the kids apparel and shoe departments during those last couple of years. The sisters had only three children between the two of them, but thankfully they were bulk shoppers, and when the sales were on, they bought doubles, even triples, of everything in every size. They had no idea that their savvy shopping sprees were going to clothe my five needy kids with like-new outfits and even, get this, *matching* ones for Natalie and Kate, on many occasions!

I met Patti during the first semester of kindergarten during afternoon drop off when she offered me a box of diapers she'd found buried in a closet. I was never one to turn down anything for the kids, and from that day, Patti and I were friends. A couple of times a year she'd surprise me with her bags of overflow from closet cleaning, thinking we were just happy take it off her hands, but the reality was that she was saving us hundreds of dollars we didn't have, and she would never understand how much she blessed our family during that time. She had a forever friend in me.

I'd never known a Patti growing up, but I think that if your name is Patricia, Patty, Patsy, or any female form of the name Patrick, which means "noble," you were meant to be an angel to me while I was walking through the fire. I had one clothing my kids, one who'd given us an open invite to swim at her pool, which saved us during the hottest, most humid Michigan heat (and gave us a safe haven during house showings), and another who had just moved to the Hills and was good for a nice dose of "easy" friendship when I needed low key. My three P's proved their nobility during some of my most challenging days, days when I was holding it all together on the outside yet feeling like I'd fallen into the deepest of holes from which I'd never climb out on the inside, and they probably had no idea how indebted I was to them for just being my friend.

It was November, almost the end of the fall season. For most, it was a time to begin preparing for the holidays, decorating, shopping, and spending time with family and friends. December 1 would be the one-year mark of the last real paycheck Tom had received, and we had no idea how we would get through December. At this point, being in the company of anyone besides my parents was so painful it was nearly impossible. There is no common ground when your entire existence revolves around trying to stay alive. We were overly tired of playing the game. Tired of running in circles. Tired of falling, over and over. But the game was all we had, and the only thing we knew. We would keep playing until we could no longer fall without getting back up.

CHAPTER 21

MIRACLE ON PINE GATE

It was cold and blustery as I got out of my minivan in the Target parking lot. My mom got out of the passenger seat, and we pulled up our collars as we swiftly walked toward the store, our eyes focused on the frosty ground. We were embarking on our annual Christmas shopping trip, the one that used to involve a leisurely day strolling through luxurious Somerset Mall and having lunch at Nordstrom. Today, the bulls-eye was on Target, my old employer from the design studio/Marshall Field's days, and it made my stomach churn just watching the crowd of happy shoppers coming and going from the store.

I missed my corporate paychecks. My 3AM paychecks were getting us by, but design work lightens up quite a bit in November and December as the average family turns their focus to celebrations, parties, gifts, and glitter. I was particularly bummed because I'd been taken by an old client, someone I'd trusted when I'd worked at the store who'd hired me to rework some drawings for a couple of jobs. He was a contractor, a puny little man both in stature and character. He'd call me, fast-talking big business and wanting me to turn over drawings for him overnight. He knew our predicament and that I was probably the only designer out there that would do it. The first job was successful, and the client ended up hiring me for commercial and residential work; it was a great fit. The second, in which the client and I had no relationship, never progressed further than drawings before they walked away from the deal. And the contractor decided, amidst our long-standing relationship, invoices, emails, and phone calls, that he would ignore my small bill of just over $500. These things happen, and I let it go, however that money was going to provide Christmas for my family.

When I shared this information with my mom, she called me back the same day and told me that my dad, my real Santa, wanted to give us that money to have for the kids. I graciously accepted and debated whether or not to tell Tom. I felt horrible enough not having money for the kids, and I know he must have felt worse. I could only equate it to having a baby with a miserable runny nose and sore throat and knowing that there is nothing you can do except wait it out, that you'd take the pain for them if you could. That's the worst feeling as a mom. So I decided not to tell.

We actually had good news on the job front. Over the course of the previous couple of months, Tom had connected with a charismatic entrepreneur in downtown Detroit who owned a digital marketing company. Much of his business was focused on the Big Three. He invited Tom into his office in November, they hit it off, and he expressed his intrigue with Tom's resume and experience as a dealer. He told Tom that he could be his "secret weapon" with tier two sales, and Tom agreed. Tom lit up about the idea of digital marketing. It was new, it was "sexy," as they put it, and it was here to stay. Twenty-seven years as a dealer made him the perfect fit for such a position, and he was hooked at the thought of it. Within a month, he became a digital expert. He dove in with everything he had, and within a few weeks, had met with the owner's wife and business partner to discuss a future with their firm. She loved Tom, and after a two-hour lunch meeting, she expressed her need for his expertise, offered him a job, and they shook hands on it.

We were, of course, delighted! He'd finally found his fit, his foot-in-the-door to the Career 2.0 that we'd been praying for. But, alas, there was a catch. The kind businessman was leaving the country for three weeks over the holiday and would be in contact with Tom upon his return to move forward with the plan. This left us with uncertainty that felt like rocks in our stomachs. We were in yet another round of our game where you can't tell the outside world what's in your hand. We had to play it cool and wait. It would feel like an eternity, and we decided to cling to the hope that it was a real deal. That was the only hope we had as our beloved Christmas came to pass.

As I pushed my giant red shopping cart through the busy aisles of what used to feel like a budget store, my Christmas spirit had checked out. It was like when we lost my Grandma VanPachtenbeke on December 5 during my senior year of high-school. We made it through Christmas, but it was a blur. We were grieving a huge loss during a time of happiness in the world around us. We tried. We went through the motions, gave the gifts, had the dinners and the desserts, but I remember looking back in the family photo albums of that year, and you could see the hurt in our eyes. That's how I felt as my mom and I muddled through my list of wishes I couldn't afford.

We were standing in front of the candy. I was calculating the cheapest way to fill five stockings and realized I couldn't do it with ten dollars. My Santa money had gone toward a gift from the Saint and one from Mom and Dad. It broke down to a hundred a kid, which, divided by two, is a $50 gift from each. The stockings had to come out of my grocery budget, and I didn't know how to do it. I could feel my breath increasing in speed and couldn't bear the thought of asking my mom to buy it for me. Suddenly, my phone started vibrating in my handbag. I fumbled for it and held it out to view the screen. Ugh. It was the school.

"Hi, Mrs. Gyarmati?" I recognized the twenty-something voice. It was Miss Harris, our third-grade teacher.

"Yes?" I replied, dreading what she had to tell me in the middle of the school day.

"Noah and Emma both have a horrible cough, and I'm worried about them; is there any way you can pick them up? I really think they need to see a doctor." My heart sank. I can't remember what I told her, but it wasn't the truth. I couldn't tell her that we'd run out of health insurance a month ago and had no coverage. I couldn't tell her that I was drugging them up on cough suppressant at night so they would sleep and praying that they wouldn't get a fever or need a prescription for a cough that sounded like they'd been smoking cigarettes for twenty years. I think I asked her to keep them for the rest of the day and promised I'd take care of them when they got home. Whatever I told her, she was very kind and forgiving, and what she thought about me in that moment paled in comparison to what I thought about myself.

As I tucked my phone away, I felt my fingers trembling, and I looked up at my mom who was waiting to hear what bomb had been dropped onto my perpetual battlefield. I could feel shoppers all around me, all in the safety of their financial homeland, at least to the outside world. Most were probably running up credit card debt, but their cheerful smiles concealed any struggles they may have had. Whatever they were, they were not shaking the ground, they were walking like mine were in that candy aisle. I could hardly get the words out without breaking into full sobs of a mother in distress as I filled her in. The happy shoppers were now trying to politely push their red carts around me during my quake. My mom guided us out to the main aisle and over to a tiny two-seater table at the Starbucks by the store's entrance. I sat. I cried. I let it out with as much composure as possible as my mom grabbed us drinks. I knew my eyes would be puffy for a day and my nose raw, and I wasn't sure how I was going to go home to Tom, tell him that my annual shopping trip was unproductive, and dump the load that we needed to get health insurance set up through the new Obamacare program.

As my mom sat across from me, she encouraged me, as she always does, that we had to keep our faith and that we would not fall. That something really wonderful was on the horizon. That we were strong and would get through it. I slowly caught my breath and my calm. My life was the epitome of a really sad country song: My man ain't got a job. The feds are going to take our house cause we ain't got no money to pay the bills. We got five babies and can't take care of them no more. Two was sick, and we ain't got insurance to take them to the doctor… Maybe I had a future writing sad songs. We sat in silence for at least a half hour. It felt good to just be with my mom. I could just "be." And she grieved with me as we sipped our coffee. She understood everything.

When I returned home, Tom and I sat together in the library, as we had for many spousal meetings in times of sorrow, and once again tried to make it work. I spilled the Santa news and confessed that my dad had given me money for the kids. He took it with stride; as much as I know it pained him, he had no choice. He was making healthcare progress, and our family doctor would see us without insurance in good will. I'd stopped thinking about the debt we were drowning in long ago; owing money to our doctors was just another battle wound. We'd been losing on life for a full year, but hope remained for the dream job that he'd been promised.

I'd come up with an idea to make Christmas better for the kids by refurbishing an old air hockey table that had been left behind by Dave and Noreen (I guess they weren't so bad after all). It was sitting in the basement covered with junk since we'd moved in; the kids had no idea it existed. I had a hunch that Tom and my Dad could get it started, I could clean it up, and we could move it to the play area in the lower level before they woke up on Christmas morning. They would love it! Tom was in. So we kept moving through December with at least two house showings a week and our "It's a Wonderful Life" mantra, refusing to give up.

The following week, I received an email from the school sharing the sad news of a family in need. One of the parents was undergoing chemotherapy, and they had three children. I didn't know them, but I followed the link to find myself signing up to deliver them a meal within a few days. I made a nice pan of mostaccioli, bought a Caesar salad kit, and made a pan of brownies. They needed this, and while I needed it too (yes, there were kitchen moments when I had a bad attitude, the "poor me" thing working against me), I couldn't imagine how scary it must be for them, especially this time of year. I made my delivery; it was a quick exchange, and they accepted the box with a smile and that was it. I didn't introduce myself; I just told them that I was a school mom.

The following morning, Tom and I were in the kitchen refilling our coffee mugs while Natalie and Kate colored in their Barbie coloring books. Their four-year-old fingers were still sweet and chubby and we'd watch them like prized possessions, amused by every interaction of their "twinhood." As we smirked at each other while pouring our cream, we noticed a bright red cardinal eating out of the green bird feeder hanging from the Japanese maple outside the kitchen window.

"Girls! Look! There's a cardinal on the birdfeeder!" Tom announced with excitement.

They ditched their crayons and ran over to us as we lifted them to view the red beauty. It was bitter cold and still gloomy outside. No snow. The trees had lost their leaves, and the evergreens that lined our backyard had become diseased. Even they were feeling the economic crunch as they held onto the brown branches that covered their lower half.

"See Daddy," Kate stated in her high octave little voice. "God is making sure the birds have food now that it's too cold to eat the worms." I nearly lost it. It was a precious moment and we both agreed that we needed to keep buying the birdseed to fill the feeder. From that day on, waiting for a little sparrow or two to show up to nibble became our daily bread, a reminder to believe that we would be provided for every day. Nothing more. Nothing less. During Mass that weekend, Tom and I exchanged a knowing smirk after a homily when we learned that the cardinal represents the ultimate promise that our faith will carry us through life. If these had been richer times, we may have thought nothing of this comparison, but during poorer times, it gave us continued hope. Our family clung to it without discussion; we knew it in our hearts. Natalie and Kate would always end our bedtime prayers thanking God for "feeding the baa'ds in the baa'd feeda," and every once in a while, we'd gather around the kitchen sink to watch a beautiful cardinal gracing our patio.

December had always been a month filled with so much social activity and preparations for Christmas that Tom and I would look at each other around the nineteenth or twentieth and say, "Wow, we can't believe it's almost Christmas! There's so much to do and never enough time!" and move into high speed finishing up our shopping, baking, and last-minute decking out before our celebration. This year, a week before Christmas Day, our giant house was not boasting a year of prosperity but one of sorrow and loss. Our tree, always real, came from the grocery store because we couldn't afford an up-north spruce from the nice family from Manistee that set up on the lot in front of Costco. I didn't hang the garland, or bake the cookies, or wrap gifts for anyone. Tom and I were thankful for our Secret Santa gifts stashed in the basement, and the kids had been rescued from our tired hearts by Noah's best friend and his family who, during the last couple of months, and especially the last few days, became our personal team of elves.

The Fairbanks family decided to bless us with the twelve days of Christmas. Every night after dinner, the doorbell would ring, we'd hear a car rolling down the driveway, and the kids would race to the front door to find a package left on the step with a poem and a small gift for each kid. We never let on that we'd figured out the secret, and they deny it to this day. The thoughtful gesture to take the time and money to buy gifts forced us to keep our heads up. At this point,

Noah, Emma, Isabelle, Natalie, and Kate didn't really care so much about being like everyone else. They'd accepted our hardship. They didn't gripe about not having a normal holiday season. They knew we were tired. What they needed was love, and that's exactly what they got. And with the Fairbanks, it didn't stop there.

Remember the mostaccioli dinner I'd delivered to the family in need? Remember my struggle with it? My grocery bill fears rising to the surface and my gripe of wanting a break in the "feeding the family department?" Well, one of those twelve days, Heather—on a separate trip to our house—delivered about three days' worth of dinner to us. Ham, macaroni and cheese, and boxes of cereal that had been on sale at Costco. I could hear my mom's famous saying, "You can't out-give God." She was right. My one delivery came back to me, and much more. I profusely thanked her, and she insisted it was "nothing" and left me with a hug and an appreciation for her kindness.

It was Monday, December 23, and I was cleaning up the kitchen after breakfast. My phone buzzed, and I noticed a text from the pastor's wife. She had been a design client I'd helped a few months earlier with a renovation at her church as well as her home. She was the sweetest little lady I'd ever met, and to be in a room with her made you feel radiant love even in the gloomiest of days. Her text read: "I have something for you; can you please come to my house today to pick it up?" I had no idea what it was, but Tom was in the library as usual and didn't mind watching the kids so I could make the twenty-minute drive. I replied with "yes" and was on my way later that morning.

She lived two towns north, and I trekked my way on the back roads to her northern Oakland county subdivision. When I pulled up to her house, there were multiple cars in the driveway, so I parked in the street. She lived in a nice two-story beige brick home that was built in the late 90s. I hurried to the front door, which was decorated in greens and adorned with beautiful planters on each side. I rang the bell. I could hear that there were conversations, music, and preparations taking place in the kitchen, which was situated on the other side of the home behind the garage. I saw a woman through the frosted glass window making her way to the door. She cracked it open with a smile. She was medium in build with long dark hair pulled into a ponytail. Probably about my age. I think she was a relative of the Syrian pastor's wife visiting from out of town. Just a guess. They had a huge family.

"Hi, my name is Hollie; I'm here—" and before I could finish my sentence, she handed me a small but heavy gift bag and wished me a Merry Christmas. I thanked her with a smile, wondering what in this little bag could be worth the drive as I walked back to my minivan. Once I was out of the subdivision and at a red light, I reached into the bag and felt around. There was some candy inside, a card, and many tiny envelopes. I slid one out from the handles that were tied together with curling ribbon. It was gift-card sized. The light turned green, and I set it in my cup holder until my next stop. I opened it to find a Walmart gift card for $25. Walmart. I wouldn't have stepped foot into a Walmart five or six years prior. But it had become part of my scavenger shopping, as it sat next to Meijer, the most affordable grocery store I'd found to supplement my Costco trips. I put the card back into the bag and read the tag attached to the handles. It read: "Unemployed mom with five children." I knew immediately what this was, and my daily choke-up began.

I arrived home during lunch; Tom had gotten quite good at rationing out yogurt, goldfish, and apple slices. It made me nuts that he would dig out the push-down apple slicer, which never cut straight through the core and was a pain in the butt to clean, but I'd learned to pick my battles. He'd even figured out that you give the kids half glasses of milk, and if they want more, there's always a refill option. He'd had come a long way over the years. When I walked in, everyone was excited to see me and wanted to know what the pastor's wife had given me. My eyes were telling, already red from my drive home, and I pulled Tom into the library to tell him what she'd done and open the rest of the gift.

I sat him in his executive chair and handed him the bag. He wasn't impressed. I'm sure he assumed it was a candy assortment with a card. I debriefed him before he opened it.

"The pastor's wife included us in their Christmas outreach. You know how our church has the giving tree that I used to participate in? When I'd grab the paper ornament with a description of a community gift and I'd shop, wrap, and deliver the gifts back to the tree?" (I always grabbed the nursing home request and would put together ten gift bags filled with a variety of things like socks, playing cards, large print word search pads, lip balm, and hand lotion. I so missed the days of being the giver). "Well, this is *us*. We were part of their tree as a family in need. Nobody knows us. Whatever is in this bag is from complete strangers, all who wanted to make our Christmas special." He raised his eyebrows, and I knew he was feeling the same humbling embarrassment of our Bob Cratchit reality.

"You open it," he said, as he passed the bag back into my possession. I took it and sat on the carpet in front of the desk. He sat back and watched as I pulled out a gift card: $50 to Meijer. Then the next: $20 to Walmart. Then eight to ten more. Some were generic Visa cards. Others were for Target and Kroger. With each card, as I read it aloud, I'd look up at my husband, who, for the first time since we'd lost his dad, had tears welling up in his eyes. When I'd finished exposing each card, I opened the large one attached. It wished our family a Merry Christmas, and there were dozens of signatures from members of the non-denominational Christian church where the pastor's wife led this wonderful outreach. I stood up with the handful of cards and walked over to Tom. We knew this money meant putting food on the table for a couple of weeks at our house; there had to be at least $400 of value there. But more than the monetary value, the gratitude for feeling the love from complete strangers was what blew us away. Money makes everything easier, but we needed the love just as much.

"You know this is a miracle, right?" I said. Tom was the guy who'd silently roll his eyes when I'd come home from my grocery missions and share all my little "Hollie miracles." He never acknowledged, up until this day, that miracles come in all sizes. We were in the midst of our own Christmas miracle. And I say "in the midst of" because it didn't end there. About an hour later, the mail truck was making its drop at the mailbox. Tom booted up and walked down on our ice-encrusted driveway to retrieve the usual bills, bills, and more bills. No mail was good mail at our house. When he stood at the kitchen island, sorting the pile, he called me over.

"Look at this. Someone put this in our mailbox. And they spelled our name wrong." People always spell our name wrong. I grabbed the card from him. It was a gift card from Target without an envelope, just the attached "To and From" backing it was glued to. It said, "To the Gyarmaty's from Santa's Elves." I flipped it over to see the $100 value printed on the back. "Who is it from?" he questioned in disbelief.

"I have NO idea!" I answered. I didn't recognize the writing. It looked like teenage girl writing, pretty and puffy. It didn't match any of my Patti, Patsy, or Patricia personalities, and I didn't know many people who understood our destitute state. He gave me a look. The one where he thought I was holding back information. "Honestly, I really don't know!" I retorted. "It's part of our miracle!" I announced. And then it hit me. The unpaid design bill from the slime-ball contractor! This gift card combined with the others had to be close to $500!

"Tom! I need you to give me an exact total of these gift cards. Don't ask why. I'll meet you in the library in two minutes." He took the Target card and headed back to the library, this time playing some Christmas music through iTunes, which made me happy. I scurried to my traveling 3AM file boxes that were currently stashed in the butler's pantry. I dug out the unpaid invoice. The total was $550 even. Unpaid. Scum of the earth. I would forgive him. But he still deserved my Scrooge label because he *knew* my family. We *were* the Cratchits at that point. I marched my invoice to the executive chair. Tom was just finishing totaling up the gift cards.

"$550.00," he announced, sounding like he'd just been given a trip to Paris, which, back in the day, was a regular occurrence. I stood in front of him with an "I told you so" smile and handed him my invoice. He looked at the total that was circled in my irritated fine point Sharpie with an "unpaid" note next to it. He looked up at me in disbelief. Or maybe it was belief, but he was shocked nonetheless.

"I TOLD you this was a Christmas miracle! How can you explain us receiving gifts from two different sources on the same day that total the EXACT amount I missed out on from my client?"

"You win," he said with a smirk. "It's a miracle."

Christmas 2013 turned out to be the most special, love-filled Christmas I'd ever experienced. It was quiet (by celebratory means, not actual noise). My parents came over on Christmas Eve and brought *Despicable Me 2* and Minion T-Shirts for the kids to layer over their ratty mish-mashed pajamas. We had popcorn, candy, and Cokes while giggling our way through the movie. My mom brought a bag of leftover gifts from her church outreach for the kids, which was fun for the little ones to have a little more to open. We left milk and cookies out for Santa next to our wimpy tree, and Grandpa and Grandma stayed overnight.

On Christmas morning, the kids were delighted with their scaled-back gifts and were led downstairs by a string of notes that revealed the air hockey table wrapped with paper and a giant bow. They loved it! Air hockey tournaments lasted all morning before our annual trek to Christmas Day Mass, the most beautiful Mass of the year. That day, we decided not to worry about the maybe job, the debt, the non-house sale, the medical bills... we remembered the famous words from Kris

Kringle in 1947: "Faith is believing when common sense tells you not to... Oh, Christmas isn't just a day, it's a frame of mind."

CHAPTER 22

DON'T CALL ME DICK

As it turned out, Christmas really *was* just a day. It was the last I'd see my parents until spring (due to their annual migration to Florida), and unlike most years, I cried for days because I was afraid and wanted my mom. I'd become childlike in this way. I had Tom every day, but I couldn't vent to him; I had to be *his* cheerleader. So I'd vent to my mom, and she would be *my* cheerleader.

They left us with the comfort of knowing that if we lost the house, we could live in theirs; my dad would probably be happy to continue traveling the country until we vacated. This idea, while a relief to know we wouldn't be gathered around a trashcan fire in a back alley in downtown Pontiac, scared us astronomically. We brought in the new year with a crapped-out hot water tank and another mini miracle of a reimbursement check from one of the utility companies for the exact amount we needed to replace it.

In an effort to continue his eternal optimism, Tom decided to take on the task of recruiting a prominent Catholic speaker named Matthew Kelly to come to our church in August. Tom had seen him a couple of times at men's conferences with Todd, and was so inspired by his enthusiasm about faith, family, and the need for the church to make some changes, that he went out on a limb to see if he'd consider a conference in Bloomfield Hills. My husband used his executive persuasion and demure people skills to secure a date with just a couple of phone calls. This was fabulous news for our pastor, who'd casually mentioned he'd love to host such an event. It was also fabulous news for Tom's men's group, and fabulous news for Tom. He now had what would be a part-time job until August as event planner at our church. This was the *last* thing he needed to be doing, donating his time to something when he didn't even have time to be a husband or a dad due to his eighteen-hour-a-day job search. I gave him my full blessing like a good wife would do. End of story.

After the first week of January, we started to get squirmy that Tom hadn't heard a peep from his future employer, who by now would have been back in town preparing for the largest social event of the year, the North American Auto Show. Another sit down in the library left us with the decision that an email to the gent would be best. Within a day, Tom received a reply that went something like this:

Tom,

The year is off to a bad start as we've lost some contracts that we'd planned on renewing. Unfortunately, I will not be able to bring you on, but as you know, God has a plan.

Blessings,

The Kind Business Man Who Flaked on the Job Offer

This was, as you can imagine, a *huge* blow. We thought December was rock bottom, but it suddenly appeared that January would be worse. Once again, we grieved our horrible loss. Our circumstances had to change immediately. We needed to sell the house. We needed a bailout. And we ended up getting one. A family, whose name I will not reveal, came along right about this time and laid it all out there for Tom. They said they'd wished they had known our circumstances all along and insisted on helping us so we wouldn't lose the house. They told us that it was nothing; it didn't make a dent in their bank account, and they knew that we'd do the same for their family if they were in the same situation. Tom promised we'd pay them upon our house sale, yet the bailer refused to discuss terms until we were situated. And that was that. We survived another round of staying in the fight, but we felt like bottom feeders and hated what we were amounting to. We had no choice. Without the sale we'd lose the rest of our savings, and that would be it. We would be homeless and unemployed. We had to try.

The house showings continued to take us away from life about one day a week. There were a lot of second and third-timers, and the intense preparations had left me with back pain, cracked cuticles, aching varicose veins (thank you second twin pregnancy), and a lot of frustration. I'd been running in this circle for seven months, and each time I gave it my all. I'd be a little grumpy after I'd get the "house showing tomorrow" call but took a lot of pride in my home and left it staged perfectly every time. It seemed there'd always be a last minute "surprise" as the vacating time came to pass. We'd always leave through the garage, usually just as Cindy or the buyers would be pulling in. One freezing morning, we got all buckled in the minivan as the Lexus and the Range Rover were parking in the front circle, only to discover that the battery was dead. It was like a Chinese Fire Drill combined with the sneakiness of the Von Trapp Family eluding the Nazis. We had to silently, with the dog and the garage door closed, squeeze out of the van and into Tom's car, which was totally unsafe, and sneak away. How embarrassing would it have been to tell the buyers, "We're sorry, but we have no money and our battery is dead, so we'll sit in the cold garage praying that you'll buy our house." Keeping up the constant public lie was killing us!

Topping our list of chaotic showings was one in early February. It was a Thursday morning, and I will *never* forget it. I was mad at Tom for lingering in the library too long while I martyred my morning to hard labor. We had a good system, but because I was me, I did more work; it just had to be that way. So this particular morning, I decided to storm through the house during the last hour to make my anger known. In the last twenty minutes, Tom had started up the Dyson, and I'd begun putting finishing touches on the bedrooms and bathrooms upstairs. Did I mention we had *seven* bathrooms? I was wiping out the undermount sinks in our master; mine first, then Tom's. I was giving his an extra clean scrub, or maybe I was taking my anger out on the cleaning rag, but as I was wiping it out, I heard an odd, soft, cracking sound and there, just ten minutes until show time, the sink fell two inches into the cabinet, caught only by the plumbing underneath. I am not a woman of profanity unless I stub my toe or have a true "OH SH*T!" moment, and this was one of them!

"TOM!" I screamed. "WE HAVE A 911 IN OUR BATHROOM!" Assuming that he'd missed a spot with the vacuum and feeling guilty about his lack of morning responsibility, he ever so politely ran to my aid. I was terrified of what his reaction would be, but to my amazement, he was very chill, and together we created a faux construction zone. He ran down to his eBay stash and grabbed large bubble wrap. We covered his entire side of the sink and taped a sign to it that said "In Repair," which looked way better than, "Oh, and this is the master bathroom, covered in 1995 green marble from floor to ceiling, a beautiful seamless glass shower for two, luxury tub, and oops! The "his" sink has fallen through the cabinet. This mansion is falling apart. Make them an offer, any offer, and they'll take it." We drove away that day with our precious Natalie and Kate in the backseat (and, of course Otto, with his butt gland stress) and tooled the back roads on the dreary, snowy, Michigan day, wondering when it would end.

While the house showing saga continued, we did get a break financially; it dawned on me that I could sign the kids up for free lunch at school. While I filled out the online forms, I realized that we were about as poor as poor gets. I resolved to having *no shame* in applying for this luxury, and when I announced to Noah, Emma, and Isabelle that they could have hot lunch every day at school, you'd think I'd given them a lifetime supply of Halloween candy. It made me sad. They jumped up and down with excitement and discussed how they would finally get to use their school ID to get lunch like the other kids. They only bought lunch once a month, if that. And since Tom's job loss a year earlier, they hadn't bought at all. The only comfort I had was knowing that it was private, and the other kids wouldn't know mine were the poor kids. Also, I didn't have to pack lunches. I was humbled once again. I wasn't sure how much more humbling I needed, but this was a level I never thought I'd reach.

Later that month, exactly one year to the week that Tom had dissolved the partnership with his brother, he found himself accepting a job at a new dealership as the finance manager. He was not happy about any of it, however the owner was a reputable business and family man who, knowing that Tom had to support seven, hyped up the opportunity to grow with his business. Tom had actually gone to meet with the dealer to discuss his career goals and maybe get an "in" with someone in his circle, but the owner had no interest in Tom's goals, only to fill the one position necessary to hang an Open sign on the front door.

There wasn't *one* thing about this position—with the exception that it was a job—that was beneficial to my husband. Finance manager was a title Tom had held when he was in his twenties; he knew the role it inside and out, had hired many of them over the years, and knew that, if sales were outstanding, the commissions could possibly pay our mortgage. In the days of the dealership, Tom disclosed that their finance managers made a really good living. But it was all relevant to the overall numbers. And the numbers generated by a small, new dealership in a down economy would not cut it. All the morning cups of Joe he'd had meeting with executives who'd been coaching him over the last six months to "not take just any job" and to "hold out for one that you know you're worth," all the hype, the LinkedIn connections, the consulting gigs, the promises of "I'll talk to so and so," and the insincere job offers had come to this: Finance Manager. We felt hopeless.

This new job was about an hour's drive from home. Tom would be working dealer hours: Monday-Saturday, 9AM to close. There were late nights. And, unlike the good ol' busy days at the Dodge dealership, this dealer kept the doors open until the last customer left, even if it was 1AM. This inevitably made *every* night a late night. Tom would be gone eighty hours a week, working a desk job that he despised, making money that would *not* pay the bills, all with the hope that it would either A) bring in extra money through his savvy sales techniques, or B) use it as a stepping stone to get a better job. It broke my heart to think about him taking this job. Tom acted like he had one foot in the grave. I thought about how all that money we were saving on school lunches would now be spent on gas and carry-out lunches for my hard-working spouse. On his first day of work, the owner, whose name was Richard, handed Tom a set of keys to the building. In this moment, Tom's other foot stepped into the grave; he knew it would be the end of his sanity. Any other guy, excited at this wonderful opportunity, would have thought it a compliment to be entrusted with a set of keys. Tom knew it meant that he would be responsible for locking up the building, in other words, the *last one to leave.* It was a death sentence for my once Vice President husband.

On the home front, it meant that I was about to go from retired life (at home with your spouse 24/7) to single-mom life. I would now be responsible for the kids full-time. From the moment they woke up until tuck-ins at night. Their dad would get home in time to kiss them on their foreheads as they slept. I would be flying solo on all house showings, doctor's appointments, and errands. I would have to figure out how to squeeze design clients into Sunday afternoon appointments or hire a sitter for Natalie and Kate until my parents came back from Florida in April. I would also have to figure out how to wash and press Tom's new casual work pants. There are many things I can do well; laundry to my husband's standard is not one of them. I looked at the bright side: this job would just be temporary, and once the house sold, we'd have money to make decisions again.

Within the first two weeks, Tom was already plotting his next move to get out of the dealership. It was just as he expected. I shouldn't say that—it was *worse* than he expected. Traffic was a bear. He was spending three hours in the car six days a week. The building was an existing older dealership, just under new ownership, and it was small. There were only three salesmen on the team, as well as the owner's manager, who he'd be reporting to. Neither had proven dealer experience, but they were happy to boast of nice salaries. Tom's office was across from the conference room, and just feet from the sales floor. It was maybe nine feet by nine feet, could hold a U-shaped workstation, and had no windows. There was a camera in the upper corner that he was instructed to turn on to record every transaction he made with customers. He may have walked in wearing his shirt and tie, but the reality was that he was wearing a full black and white jumpsuit, accessorized with a ball and chain.

The computer system was about fifteen years out of date, which, as an Apple junkie, made Tom nuts. He spent hours troubleshooting ridiculous problems he had no control over and helping his "managers" manage basic dealer skills. Richard was in his late sixties, maybe early seventies, slim and fit. He had white hair and a white flashy smile to match. He traveled a lot, but when he'd make an appearance, he made sure to bop his head into Tom's office to cheer him on. The dealership environment was frustrating, with sales goals that were too high and would never be met in the blue-collar demographic of the city where it was located. Tom quickly realized that he would never make the extra commissions. So, he simply made the best of the situation every day. The hour-plus drive there and back gave him ample time to either dwell on his career purgatory or press on to 2.0. We both knew that this was not going to work and did not want to accept this as part of the plan.

There were so many ridiculous expectations put on him that we didn't know whether we should laugh or cry about it in the few waking hours he was home. Not only was he the finance guy, he was also the "manager" whenever the buddies were out of office. They wanted him to do his job, be the manager and even greet customers in the service department at 7AM with a smile as though he were a Walmart greeter. His smile wasn't nearly as flashy as Richard's, but he respectfully did his best day-in and day-out, and I have never been prouder of him. It was harder than not having a job. I know he earned more money selling on eBay and freelance consulting than working at this dealership. One day, Richard walked into his office with a pair of scissors and requested that he take the time each week to trim the fraying edges of the old tattered carpet in his doorway to keep the place in tip-top shape.

Tom made two friends at his new job: Peggy, the office manager, who had worked for the man for over two decades, and Scoots McGregor, the old cat who lived in the service department. My husband was a sucker for nice older women who appreciated his kindness and would repay him with pretzels and stray cats. He'd send the kids video clips of the mangy kitty perched on the roof of a customer's warm car in the back. There'd be paw prints winding across the hood, and if you asked him what he was doing up there, he'd lift his orange furry head and belt out a loud *meow*. These little videos helped him cope with the misery of his days there.

One night, after a very long day, one where he waited past 11PM to lock up due to a late-night browser with awful credit, he came home in an especially foul mood. Frustrated with the continual late nights without good compensation, overtime, or even a thank you, Tom was venting over his day while enjoying a Bud Light in the kitchen. He proceeded to tell me about the comedic relief he enjoyed over Richard's hallway introductions to all the buyers. His family owned multiple dealerships. His father went by "Dick," so, naturally, people off the street concluded that Richard, Jr. would also accept this nickname; it was, after all, printed on signs all over the city.

"So," Tom told me after he took a sip of his beer (I was standing in my usual spot in front of the kitchen sink, leaning over the island intently, listening to his story) "Richard has supernatural hearing. He can be anywhere in the building, and if he smells the blood of a possible buyer, he's right there in the hall outside my office door greeting his prey like a shark with a firm handshake and a flashy smile." I was thoroughly enjoying this story, because Tom, for the first time in weeks, was sporting a smile on his face—one I hadn't seen in months. I leaned in closer to hear the punch line. "'Hello, Dick, it's nice to meet you,' they said as they shook his hand. And you know what he says EVERY time?"

"What?" I giggled, envisioning Tom working like Bob Cratchit at his desk trying to keep a straight face.

"He says, very firmly, *'My name is Richard. Don't call me Dick.'*" Tom burst into childlike laughter and I joined him. All the annoyance of this workplace, this horrible twenty-year setback position, one that was paying him less than a fifth of what he used to make when we met more than ten years earlier, was somehow manageable if we could have a good laugh over it. This comic relief would refresh his soul so he could continue his search for the "meant-to-be" career into the wee hours of the morning. And, when it was just the two of us, when the exhaustion of long commutes and loud kids and empty bank accounts had us spent, we referred to his employer as "Don't Call Me Dick." It guaranteed a smile every time.

CHAPTER 23

CLEAN HOUSE

"Good afternoon, ma'am," a nice young gentleman greeted as I pulled my minivan up to the drop-off doors. I'd become a Monday afternoon regular. And Tuesday. And Wednesday. They all knew my black Honda and nice mom smile, and they were happy to help me unload my trunk and whatever I'd wedged into the back seats. I spent as much time making drops to the Salvation Army as most moms did waiting in the pick-up line at school, which I'd sworn off after one try when the twins were in kindergarten. It was the end of March. The only nice thing about March in Michigan is that we are one month closer to May, which is when we get our green back and hopefully some warmth as well.

"Hi there, how are you today?" I asked as I jumped out of the driver's seat. It was cold and damp and the back of the building was lined with piles of dumpsters, folding tables, and old chairs that needed a match. Once in a while, I'd spot a vintage piece that grabbed my attention such as a 1960s wooden arm chairs with teal tweed upholstery. I have to admit, I thought about adopting these heirlooms once in a while because I loved mid-century modern and they reminded me of Grandma Foss and her house on Clarence.

Unloading my minivan one day at a time made me feel like Andy Defray digging his way out of Shawshank Prison with a spoon. One of my favorite movies, I never imagined relating to *Shawshank Redemption* before then. Our house wasn't selling. Tom was making the mortgage payments with the help of our bailout guardian angel, but we both knew that it couldn't go on forever. We dropped the price of the house every month, hoping we'd hit the sweet spot Cindy told us about—the one where our house would be the right buy for a multitude of buyers, where we'd have to let go of some of our investment, but one that would make enough sense to just "let it go." Coming up on a year on the market, I'd gotten an inner motivation to start emptying the basement, the closets, the storage areas, and the shelves crammed with almost ten years' worth of baby and kid crap along with Tom's life-long collection of mish-mashed memories.

I'd become extremely savvy over my years with this "more is more" guy. Falling in love with the "less is more" girl had saved his life in many ways over the years, and he hadn't a clue that she was single handedly eliminating over a quarter of the estate, load by load, week by week, month by month. I'd take days to clean, organize, and very strategically eliminate anything I knew he hadn't touched or had an emotional connection to by stashing it in bags, out of sight, then dropping it to the Salvation Army if it wasn't missed after six months. If he was out of town on business during one of my "makeovers," I would expect him to come home and be so overwhelmed with its splendor that he'd whisk me off my feet like he had on our wedding day. Instead, he'd get home, throw his bags on the floor of his side of the closet, oblivious to my clean house, then crab about not being able to find the jeans he wore three weeks earlier with the Ralph Lauren belt on them, at which point I'd resolve to never organize his "areas" again (which include the kitchen island, the laundry room, his library, and the corner in the foyer).

It took me *years* and a lot of pouting to realize that you can de-clutter your man, organize a space, and scrub the floors, but if it didn't bother him before, he wouldn't appreciate it once it was complete and would probably even complain about his piles being placed into complete logical categories like a store. I learned the hard way with this one and knew that there were a few things that would save me from living with "more is more" grief. One: if you stop cleaning his crap and just make your side beautiful, he'll eventually follow suit, at least to a tolerable extent. Two: if you must clean a pile, accept that you are doing it for yourself, not for him or his acknowledgement or gratitude. Three: when you are experiencing the "worse" half of your marriage vows, eliminating pile irritation will make you love him more. Four: remember, "It's all about the love."

All this said, the junk that had accumulated in our gargantuan estate was *not* downsizing with us, and it was up to me to do something about it. I knew what he'd miss and what was junk. I'd put in my time and had no fear over donating half the everyday drinking glasses from the old house, the coffee pot from the bar, bags of clothes that had been stashed in the garage, or anything offspring related. I knew my limits. Anything pre-Hollie or from his dad's house was untouchable. While my husband was trekking to his miserable job every week, I was silently scratching, chiseling, and scooping away our clutter, one pocketful (or trunkful) at a time. And it made me smirk, just like Andy.

It was around this time that my new friend and colleague, Matt Pfeiffer, the owner of a luxury flooring showroom about twenty minutes north of Bloomfield Hills invited me to a special event that he was hosting. Emmy Award Winning celebrity designer Mark Brunetz from The Style Network's *Clean House* was making an appearance to pitch his book *Take the U out of Clutter* and share with designers an opportunity to enter a contest to win a makeover for the charity of their choice. It was on a Thursday evening in April, and I was lucky that my mom would be home from Florida so I could attend. Matt was pushing me hard to enter this contest because, as he put it, I was a "firecracker." I'd met him in the fall and fell in love with his business logic, sharing his passion for putting people first. However, the idea of entering a charity design contest gave me a headache; I couldn't imagine squeezing in the time for more pro bono work, but an opportunity to listen to a celeb designer had me intrigued, so I busted out my fancy handbag and threw on my skinny jeans, a drapey white T-shirt, and my cheetah print open-toed heels that had seen me through seven years of fashion and never let me down. They were like my lucky socks.

The event was nice; it was open to the public, and it was followed by a private presentation for the design community. I grabbed a seat in the second row and got acquainted with the professionals around me. They were friendly; it was a diverse crowd. I think there were college students behind me; the designers were mostly women and mostly older than I. It was the first event I'd attended with professionals in years, and it made me miss my department store once again. Mark was finalizing his setup, and I removed my focus from the past and settled in to learn something from exactly the TV design type I'd sworn off years earlier.

I sized him up. He was about six feet tall and fit, with chiseled features. His eyes were hazel, maybe more bluish green, and he had a tall forehead (like me) with his brown short hair combed straight back. He had broad shoulders and was wearing a mid-season sport coat layered over a casual mini-plaid button-down with a pair of dark blue rinsed jeans and what I assumed were Italian brown leather dress shoes. The wardrobe was pressed and perfect, not stuffy or star-like, but well-thought out for the crowd of Michigan designers, moms, and grandmas excited to hear his secrets to ridding their lives of clutter. I was impressed.

By way of introduction, he stood in front of me and smiled while giving a little bit of background on his award-winning show, *Clean House*, and how working with hundreds of families inspired him to write his book. At this point, while I was hanging on to every word, waiting to learn something, I instead found myself embracing his story and passion for changing lives. His eyes lit up every time he went from the Before photo to the After. He was a dynamic speaker, handsome, and the old ladies were gushing over him. I was secretly gushing over him, too, but not because I wanted to take him home, clean out a closet, and serve him a pot roast. It was the design gene. You are born with it. This man was born with it. Unlike me with my early childhood design declaration, he drove his career to LA after college in the early 90s, and it took him ten years in the business to pursue interior design. Hmmmm. He was as old as the supermodels hanging in my closet, which proved to be my most admired age bracket.

I liked him. Though he wouldn't teach me how to get rid of clutter. "Less is more" girl is a pro at piles. "Should I keep this or get rid of it? Maybe I'll use it one day," my husband had been asking for years. "Throw it out. Or donate it. Or eBay it. Just get rid of it. And the rest of everything else you're going to ask me about," I'd retort, annoyed that I was stuck being the pile therapist. Mark Brunetz had seen his share of piles over the years, much worse than mine, but I'd been *living* with mine, which, by the grace of God, ambitious eBay sales and my rendezvous trips to the Salvation Army, had dwindled to a respectable size over the last year.

There was a short break. I grabbed a glass of white, said hi to some old friends and carpet reps that I hadn't seen in a decade, and stood in Matt's showroom amongst the carpet samples while nibbling on red grapes and chocolate. Mark was surrounded by old ladies like a missionary who could wash away decades of design dust. I watched his interaction with each of them as they professed their love, confessed their emotional connections to their trinkets, or blamed their husbands, parents, or the mailman for their unkept home. He was kind, smart, and knew exactly how to steer the conversation in the right direction of "answer-hug-move-on." As I stood there sipping my wine, I decided that I was 100% right in my judgment of all the network design stars. I was in love with them all because I was one of them. Not that I belonged in front of a camera, I don't think my shiny skin would last ten seconds without powder, but I wanted to share my design skills in order to change lives. It had always been about the transformation, big or small. That was where I found my joy. Mark was the real deal. I settled back into my front row choir seat so my preacher man could move me to enter his contest.

To the designers only, he introduced the pro-bono work he'd done a couple of years prior in South Africa. A friend had invited him to head up a charity makeover, and the transformation was life changing. He shared his feelings on giving back to our communities and his idea to bring charities to the forefront focus of designers. I thought about my time making over the teachers' lounge. I remember the feeling I had when they walked in that Monday morning. It was a design high that transcended just another beautiful space. It was spiritual. As I listened intently to Mark motivate us to enter Design for a Difference, I was thinking about getting that design high one more time. I knew I would submit an entry or two, but I was charity-less. This would require some strategic planning, and in that particular moment, I was thinking about driving twenty minutes in the dark (horrible night vision), relieving my mom, tucking my crew in, and making Tom dinner.

Once he was finished, I made my beeline to buy his book, get an autograph and photo op, and then make *myself* back over to *mom*. I was one of the last in line, but I didn't mind waiting. When I got to the front, I introduced myself and thanked him for a wonderful evening.

"My name is Hollie, with an ie," I added as he Sharpied the inside cover of my newly purchased book. He smiled. Suddenly, my chest tightened, and my head felt woozy. And it wasn't the wine. I was actually nervous! I was feeling it more than my Donnie Wahlberg moment! *How could this be?* It just snuck up on me out of nowhere. *I didn't want to BE Donnie. But I wanted to BE design Mark.* I was enamored with him. Great, I'll be sweaty in my photo. I coaxed my business card out of my clutch and handed it to him. I could tell he was impressed. My business cards *were* awesome.

"3AM. Why 3AM?" he asked, purely amused.

"I had two sets of twins and one in-between in less than four years, so I've accepted sleep deprivation as part of life. It's a way to relate to moms," I blurted out. *I sounded like an idiot.* There was so much to my world that couldn't be condensed into a sentence that fully explained why my business was called 3AM Interior Design. But what he *did* get was the simple "Live Who You Are" that was printed over my vignette photo. He understood that I was one of them—his kind. I could just feel it. His assistant kindly took my iPhone and a photo of us together, which turned out horrible under the fluorescent lights casting shadows over our faces. I blubbered a "thank you" to him once again, and as I turned, I thought about how I wanted to see him again.

"I'll see you on the other side," he pointed with a smirk, and I shot him a wink and a very sincere and uncalculated smile as I waved goodbye. As I walked out of Matt's showroom, I wondered how in the world I would find the time to enter a charity into this international contest. Crap.

Weeks passed, and I was spinning on the carousal of working hard on what seemed to be hardly working. Kids, design jobs, calculated grocery trips, cleaning, house showings, all while watching the deadline to enter Design for a Difference as a blur on the calendar every time I zoomed by. Nothing was getting easier. To say I was exhaustion would be an understatement. Natalie and Kate were so neglected as at-home preschoolers that I was starting to feel resentful toward our situation. It wasn't fair. I should be spending my days enjoying motherhood, not parking my kids in one room then the next, begging them to play Barbies for just a few minutes (at least twenty) or color just one more picture or play their iPad just long enough for mom to make dinner. I was a crappy mom. But you know what? Those two were happy together and never complained. They never threw tantrums or had expectations of parental entertainment. And, when their daddy got home, he'd play with them enough to make up for my workaholic habits. I wasn't a crappy mom. I had happy kids and reminded myself that I, with my super childhood memory, didn't remember *any* day-to-day moments. Just the important stuff. My kids would be alright.

Tom, on the other hand, was not. I'd get through each day, exhausted by the time I'd finished cleaning the kitchen after dinner when my phone would start buzzing. I could see "Tom" on the caller ID, and my heart would sink because I didn't know if I could muster up the strength—as I did every night during his drive home—to stay positive and listen to him vent about his miserable job. I would lock myself in the pantry, sit on the heavy maple stepladder my dad had made a few years earlier, and listen. The story was the same. Every night. Six nights a week. I would remain silent and calm through the call as he'd discuss the frustration of finding time to continue his job search under the radar when he was putting in so many hours. It seemed hopeless. Once tapping the red "end call" icon on my phone, I would stay seated in there, as I had so many times in the past, and silently cry for my spouse. Was it possible that this was *worse* than having no job at all? He never knew how many tears I shed over his labor, but he understood that I cared most about his happiness, and finding a fulfilling career was again head-to-head with our effort to sell the house.

While Tom focused 500% of his efforts on the career move, I realized by mid-May that the contest deadline was at the end of the month and I still needed a charity to embrace, visit, and write a short essay about, summing up their worthiness and my vision for a makeover. There were a gazillion charities out there, but I was set on finding the right fit or I wouldn't enter. I had to believe in them and their cause. I had to see their conditions and feel like their space needed a makeover more than any other charity in the country. Those were my conditions for spending even an hour of time on this. All or nothing. I gave regularly to a homeless shelter, but they had an army of followers and support in the Detroit area. We supported everything Catholic through church, which, while always close to my heart, wasn't right either. Like all good things in life, my answer came in the most unexpected way and in the eleventh hour. My mom had a lightbulb moment, called me up, and told me that my Uncle Ernie's daycare program was a non-profit, allowing it to qualify for the contest. I had no idea they were a non-profit organization, but what I did know was that the facility was old and stinky, and I loved my uncle, so my design game was on.

The following week I drove out to Ernie's adult daycare, which was about twenty minutes north of my house on Dixie Highway, a four-to-six lane, forty-five mile an hour road that runs from downtown Pontiac all the way to the Flint area, north of my hometown. Pontiac and Flint were major mid-century players in the automotive industry, but today are void of production and have become cities filled with vacant buildings and poverty. The drive covers four townships and is slow moving due to the busy intersections of local drivers out running errands or nine-to-fivers using Dixie as a shortcut to avoid the interstate. It's not a pretty drive; everything is concrete—mostly shopping centers, fast food chains, and in some areas, leveled properties with new construction erupting. My destination was the old courthouse built in the 1960s. It was brown brick with skinny vertical windows lining the front, barely enough light to see whatever dust particles might be floating in the air of the dingy offices upon entry.

I parked along the south side of the building and entered through the heavy steel door which had an automatic lock for the safety of the clients. To my right was a small room cluttered with old furniture, a table and chairs, a coat rack, and some metal bookcases that looked like they might fall apart if you only nudged them. This was the room I knew. It had two of the narrow windows along that south wall that were frosted with bumpy glass. It reminded me of an old bowling alley. I'd met my mom here with the kids on numerous occasions to visit Ernie, and this was the room we would use. They'd escort him in, now well into his 60s, and sit him in his heavy wooden rocker that Papa had bought him years earlier. Ernie had the busy gene. Just like my mom and her sisters. And myself. My Belgian roots kept me moving, which served me well as a busy mom, but for an old man with the mentality of a toddler, they called for a rocker, the perfect way for him to expend his energy.

There was a deep metal shelving unit along the same wall as the visitors' room, filled with lunch boxes, bags, and personal belongings. Ten steps inside opened into the large thirty-by-forty-foot community room. There were no windows there. The floor was covered in old dingy vinyl floor tiles, many of them broken and stained. The walls were beige painted cinderblock with old torn posters taped in areas, more rickety bookcases, a large TV, and entrances to the women's and men's restrooms that I would later determine were in worse condition than most prison facilities. There were a few old vinyl sofas lining the walls and some folding tables with mismatched chairs in the middle of the room. An overall glance at the ceiling uncovered years of water damage as well as a few brighter tiles that had been patched in for a quick fix. The stench of urine, adult diapers, and canned vegetables filled the air as I stood in the middle of this community space, viewing it for the first time through the eyes of a designer. It needed a gut job.

Bill was sitting crossed legged on one of the sofas, I'd known him for over twenty-five years. He lived in Ernie's group home. He was unresponsive and would sit this way during his waking hours with his eyes rolled back and his head swinging back and forth. He'd been a prisoner in his own body his entire life. I never got close to him because I knew he was a biter. From the back room, I could hear more clients making themselves known with sounds like screaming, groans, and other loud noises that sounded more like those from a barnyard than an adult daycare. Most people would be afraid, but I'd been exposed to these unfortunate souls my entire life. As a child, this existence brought me fear. As an adult, it brought me compassion. And now, as a mother, it brought me pain. I couldn't imagine what my grandmother endured every day of her life knowing that her baby was institutionalized. It broke my heart.

"Hello, you must be Hollie," a heavy-set woman greeted as she walked out of the back room.

"Yes! It's nice to meet you. Sharon?" I questioned extending my right hand.

"That's right. You are Peggy's daughter? I love your mother; she's always such a joy to have visit our clients."

"Yes. Did you know my papa too?"

"Oh goodness, Van? He was a celebrity around here! What a gentleman! He was always in such a good mood every time he came with your mom or her sisters, and funny! We have so many pictures of him hanging in our back office. He was a very special man."

"Thank you, he was the best and was always fond of your staff," I offered. In his later years, Papa would see Ernie about once a month. I loved seeing Ernie's face light up like a child when his papa walked in. And Sharon seemed very sweet. She was gentle. I could tell she was busy, and I decided to get down to business. I explained Design for a Difference and that only five designers would be selected to receive funds for their makeovers. I also told her that I believed I had a chance of helping them. I wanted to tell her that I would be the national winner and would have $25,000 to better their space, but I had no idea how many designers I'd be up against. One thing was certain, however: this building was a dive, and the deserving category had my full attention.

"Do you have a few minutes to give me a quick tour?" I asked, beginning to walk toward the back noisy room.

"Of course, Ernie is back here," she smiled as I followed her to a double room about the same size as the community area. I was greeted by Ernie himself, sitting at a table playing with some old wooden children's blocks. There was a pile on the table, and he'd pick each one up, inspect it, and place it gently in the old cardboard canister as he rocked back and forth. This was his favorite way to pass time. "Ernie! Look who's here to see you!"

"Hi, Ernie!" I smiled and bent down to embrace him with a hug. I know he knows that I am a familiar face, but his response does not contain the same joy of seeing his mama or papa, or the comedic response that often came with seeing his sister—he's either excited to see them or sometimes grumpy; he'd been dealing with them his entire life. With me, he let out a sigh of contentment, which meant he was copacetic with the situation, and it was all good. "Can I give him a chocolate?" I asked, as Sharon stood back enjoying our little reunion. She nodded. Ernie loved chocolate. He was Belgian after all, so it ran in his blood. I reached into my bag for a Hershey bar and handed it to him. Watching him eat candy was our favorite thing to do. He was so meticulous and careful as he'd open the end of the wrapper, and his first bite was pure ecstasy. He'd close his eyes and smile with another sigh of happiness. Chocolate makes everything better.

I had to keep moving. Ernie was one of the easier clients at Lahser. He had full mobility and could understand basic instructions. The "noise" that filled the expansive room beyond my uncle made my heart ache. There were at least eighteen adults, most in wheelchairs parked either at folding tables or in the middle of the room, being cared for by a couple of employees. Their mental capacity was pre-school at best, and they'd sit and play with toys. However, many had severe brain damage and were trapped within their bodies without the ability to see, hear, talk, or otherwise communicate. The staff was small, and they tried their best to keep everyone happy.

This room, like the community room, had no windows. It was in the same condition as the first, and the air quality made me want to vomit. The furniture was in worse shape than what I'd seen along the dumpsters at the Salvation Army. I paced around the room, keeping an arm's distance from all clients as I didn't know their personalities or strength. It wouldn't be unusual for a man to reach out and grab your arm or try to hug you. Having my physical guard up didn't prohibit my social mood, however, and I smiled and said hi to everyone as I made my way through. This was so much worse than I thought. The building hadn't been maintained and was in its original state, soiled on every surface. No matter how hard the staff cleaned, the stains would not go away nor would the air smell fresh.

There were at least thirty-five adults in this facility who lived in group homes and spent their equivalent of a forty-hour work week in this dump. There was no sunlight. There was no art. The furniture needed to be thrown to the curb. I didn't think I would see worse. She finished off by unlocking the door to the staff kitchen, which did me in. Another room without light, maybe 10 x 10 with freestanding appliances that were about forty years old and a freestanding metal table against one wall to provide a bit of counter space. Every corner was covered in grime. The ceiling tiles were stained, and the walls, once a light yellow, were muddied up with grease and age. As I wrapped up my meeting with Sharon, I promised her that I would provide the best entry possible, and if a win was not in our future, I told her that I had some ideas to ask for some donations from the community. They were located in a very giving area yet had no social presence. They were operating on minimal funds as it was, and it was obvious that there wasn't anyone rallying or fundraising for further support. She teared up at this suggestion and embraced me in a hug, saying they were honored even to be considered for such a nomination.

The drive home was one I will always remember. I was thankful for all the wonderful things I had in life: my healthy kids; my clean house; real food; my ability to walk, talk, see, and hear all the beauty of the world around me. The reality for these adults with severe disabilities was an existence of imprisonment, yet they were among the most innocent souls on earth, without a malicious thought or action, all dependent on care from another human in order to stay alive. Pain was probably part of everyday life and feeling the love from a caretaker (if they were lucky) was the closest they would have to complete happiness. I envisioned them in Heaven one day, free of their bodies and free to be who they were created to be. I thought about my Uncle Ernie reuniting with Grandma and Papa as a healthy man. Believing in Heaven is the greatest way to take your focus off the hardships we face during our short life here on earth; it puts everything into perspective, usually making the daily obstacles look small. Especially today, my personal hardship felt embarrassing compared to the standard of life my own uncle lived. I drove through downtown Pontiac, past the vacant lots and dilapidated houses. Even in full bloom, this city was gloomy and depressed. But was it worse than the conditions I'd just left?

It took me a week of deep thought to collect my feelings, sit down, and write up my contest entry. Words alone had to set me apart from what I assumed would be hundreds of designers. Who would I be up against? What started out as design competitiveness had turned into a desperate need to really make a difference for these people. The panel of judges would only know that I was a designer; they would not know my age or see my photo, experience, or portfolio. I had to design this project with words.

THE MOTHER OF ALL MAKEOVERS · 259

CHAPTER 24

REDEMPTION

"Our Father, Who Art in Heaven, Hallowed Be Thy Name…" We prayed every night before tuck-ins. From the moment we became parents, family prayer before bed was a must, and we always gathered on the floor. I think that tradition started because Noah and Emma were in their cribs, leaving Tom and I sprawled out in-between them in exhaustion. Nine years later, we were still on the floor and still exhausted. But now there were seven of us all sitting every which way in Natalie's and Kate's room with Otto by our side. We would passionately pray the Our Father, then ask for blessings upon those we loved, and finish with open prayer for special things. This open prayer time could go either way. When they were really little, and hadn't a care in the world, it would get silly. When she was under three, Isabelle once thanked God for Bud Light. Not my proudest mom moment, but it did bring out a giggle. Every night since June 1 finished with "Please let Mom win her contest." This was added to the usual "Please help Dad find a job that he loves and help us sell our house." In short, it had become contest, job, house. In that order.

The prayer varied depending on who was the speaker. When it was Emma, it was much more detailed, like, "Please let the judges love Mom's contest entry so we can win a makeover for Uncle Ernie, and help Dad find a job he loves that is not so far from home and he can be with us on Saturdays and make enough money so we can do fun things like go to Cedar Point and take vacations and swim in the summer. And please make someone buy our house so we can move into a better house that's not too big and not too small, but just right. With real neighbors and a place for us to ride our bikes." By this point, Isabelle and Natalie would be fighting over who was kicking whom, and Noah would be playing with the dog, but we never cut little Emma off. Something had happened that summer, and we decided that worrying about the horrible "what ifs" was going to kill us, so we gave it all to God. It is *so* much easier said than done, but we did it.

Tom and I still had more responsibility than time allowed. Everything remained the same. It was the second summer being a slave to the house and real estate showings. On the Fourth of July, we had the entire entourage of out-of-staters, the new Lion's football coach, and a buyer (with a relator other than Cindy; she never would've let it fly) who actually brought their little rat dog in my house and left tiny footprints all over my freshly vacuumed cream carpet in the formal living and dining rooms. Cindy was in the process of switching real-estate companies, so we unanimously agreed to take a break for a month and let it rest. This was the best thing we could have done. It felt like vacation having four whole weeks to live without having to "unlive" our space every few days. We mulled over listing it ourselves but knew the property value was too high to take on such a responsibility. We would loyally stick with Cindy, and when she was set up, we would relist it and press forward with an aggressive price drop. It was like the back half of the Titanic bobbing in the ice cold Atlantic before plunging to its resting place on the bottom of the ocean floor. This was it.

This break also allowed us to focus on other things. I had the August meltdown fast approaching (the usual school prep), over six more weeks home with all the kids, creatively keeping them occupied and happy while managing the house *and* design appointments. My parents were lifesavers during this time, as they would take them by twos and threes on camping trips. Ages five, eight, and nine were awesome. Kids that age think you are the best. They can do pretty much anything the adults do, and my mom and dad loved being able to ride bikes and take them kayaking and swimming. My kids were happy. Tom was finally connecting with some digital automotive execs and sneaking out to the car lot with Scoots McGregor to take interviews by phone. He was also busy with the late-August Matthew Kelly event at church, which was sneaking up. They had to sell over 1,000 tickets for a semi-full house, and that added another challenge to his plate.

August 1: Contest Winner Announcement. I pretended like it was just a normal day, but the anticipation of receiving some kind of notice by email or phone was killing me. At the end of June, I'd received an email informing me that my entry had been selected to move to the final round of judging. Huge deal. If I didn't make it past that, I was happy knowing that someone out there appreciated what I was about and planned to get something going for Lahser regardless. We were playing outside all day. I knew that if I was inside, I'd be grabbing my phone and overthinking how sad I would be if not selected. We were on the driveway. All the bikes were out, the gator, the sporting equipment, and the sidewalk chalk. The girls had the vintage Barbie GMC camper in the yard. Our play-structure and swing set had gotten crushed by a tree during one of the severe storms that month and was off limits. I thought it was sign from above that the end was near.

I ran into the kitchen to refill my water and did exactly what I planned *not* to do. I glanced at my phone sitting on the edge of the kitchen desk. One missed call. I unlocked it and checked the caller ID. It was from New Hampshire. New Hampshire! The IDG corporate headquarters were located in Manchester! I gulped some water as I carefully tapped my voicemail. There was a message, and my heart started to thump. I couldn't remember the last time I was so excited.

The pounding of my organs had been panic-driven for so many years I wasn't even sure how to handle something good happening in my life. I mean, really amazingly good. Better than free food and front row parking spots good. Was this it? I ever so gently tapped Play and pressed the phone to my ear.

"Hello Hollie, this is Krista Eliason, President of International Design Guild. Could you please contact me at (613)-555-1212 regarding your Design for a Difference Entry? I look forward to talking to you soon," she concluded, and that was it. This was fantastic news! They wouldn't have called to tell me I wasn't a winner! Alone in the kitchen, doors and windows closed, central air on, and the kids' voices from outside permeating the brick walls, I bravely made the callback while I had the chance. I had to calm down. The basement was the only safe place to talk without interruption.

With my phone in my sweaty palm, I skipped down the stairs and locked myself in the workout room, now void of my magazine wallpaper. It would take them at least ten minutes to find me down there. I listened to Krista's message again. And again. One more time. Then I tapped the callback icon. Ringing. Ringing. Ringing… Voicemail. Ugh.

Within thirty seconds, I was sitting on a cooler in the garage, laptop open, Googling the IDG website. And there it was. The official announcement of the 2014 Design for a Difference Contest Winners. It was the one-page contest promo featuring a cute little boy rolling bright blue paint across a gray concrete wall as the header. Today, instead of the contest rules and regulations, it was topped with the National Winner: Stephanie Stroud from Kansas City. Below were four regional winners. I quickly scanned to find my name next to the South-Central Region. I was representing thirteen States-worth of entries. THEY PICKED ME! LAHSER! PRAYERS ANSWERED!

As the kids zipped around me on tricycles, I quickly closed my laptop, ran back into the house, grabbed my phone, then jumped into the middle of my circus and yelled, "KIDS! I won, I won, I won!"

Winning anything in a house with five kids grabs attention. It didn't matter if I'd won free French fries at McDonald's or a trip to Hawaii. A win, whatever the level, would stop all activity and create an instant crowd of gawkers. It was as much media attention as I would get, so I played it up.

"You won your design contest?!" Emma screamed.

"YES!" I screamed back with a smile as I jumped up and down with them.

"Hooray for Mom!" Natalie and Kate screamed and started chanting. Chanting is the gold standard of celebration at our house. Isabelle stood there with a smile but very little emotion. She does this when she approves of me or a purchase so much that she is actually jealous. Or when my hair looks good or I score a great pair of pumps. I take her silence as a compliment and dream of her being my right-hand business partner one day. Noah was sharing in our excitement, but already plotting to score something for himself. Little entrepreneur.

"Can we go out for ice cream tonight?" he asked with an angelic smirk as he batted his thick lashes. He was waiting for my usual "We'll see…" reply.

"YES!" I yelled, still hopping around in the middle of the driveway. "Let's have ice cream for DINNER!" This, of course, set the tone for my children that it *was* a reason to celebrate, and they would be my biggest fans throughout my Design for a Difference Experience. I called Tom right away, who gave me huge kudos from his desk under the fluorescent lights, and my mom of course was thrilled. Sharon at Lahser couldn't believe I really won, and even admitted out loud that she thought she'd never see me again.

I felt like the old me for the first time in years. Design Hollie with one of the top three portfolios in the state. I'd dug my way out of the never-ending workload of mom, had claimed my identity as a designer, and was free to be the new 3AM me! It was my 3AM Redemption! Once the excitement settled, I began to focus on my task at hand, and how amazing it would be to have the resources to really transform this charity that had stolen my heart just a couple of months earlier. It was truly a gift to have this opportunity, and deep down, I was dedicating whatever was to come to Grandma and Papa. I knew that they were proud of me from Heaven.

Within a couple of weeks, I had a conference call headed up by Mark, Krista, some IDG team members, and the other three regional winners. The goal was to have our makeover completed by the end of October. As a winner, I'd receive $2,000 to put toward goods and services, flooring donated by Shaw carpet, and be flown to Kansas City with the other designers to install the national makeover. There was no hand-holding here. If it was going to work, I had to grab this project and manage it the 3AM way—like a mom with her game on. This was the beauty of my life. I was in total harmony with who I was and what my capabilities were to get through every day. It usually started with prayer, was filled with surprises and impossible tasks, and in the end, I got it done. My design skills saved me through the crazy baby years, and now the mom skills I'd acquired were about to navigate me through uncharted territory of crowdfunding, soliciting goods and services, and installing a complete project within a fast-tracked timeline.

Matt Pfeiffer, my IDG showroom partner, was the absolute best fit for this mentorship. He was connected to a gazillion wonderful people who would step up to provide paint, custom cabinetry (built to my specifications), lighting, and of course, the beautiful vinyl, wide-planked faux wood floor. I cranked out a complete design package, created a full marketing plan for our Crowd Rise that included a photo shoot with our mini design team (Matt and myself), Sharon, another staff member, my uncle, and two other women who attended Lahser. Chelsea, my new favorite at IDG, was darling and patiently guided me through using Crowd Rise. Our goal was to raise $15,000 to pay for the makeover, which would leave the Lahser building with a beautiful room (the "visitors" room with the only two windows) and a little slush fund for continued repairs.

My local art gallery was kind enough to donate the artwork, which would be oversized color prints of various landmarks from San Francisco to a quiet village in Austria to the rolling hills of Kentucky. It would be a room filled with beauty and peace; I couldn't wait to see it all come together. Here I was, in the midst of what I expected to be a melt-down month prepping for school on a tight budget, and somehow, I was able to do all the back-to-school *and* find time in the evenings to work on the makeover. The house being off the market added hours of time to my week, and everything fell into place.

During all of this excitement, there were other things falling into place as well. Tom was getting job interviews from automotive digital companies that seemed to have the exact kind of work he needed to move forward, or shall I say, to be rescued from the dealer life. He wanted corporate America. There were two contenders, both of which he would have been happy to work for. The salary would be just enough to squeak by, and both jobs involved calling on dealers, servicing their digital marketing plans. One was local; one was out-of-state travel Monday through Friday. We were thrilled to be actually getting somewhere in this year-and-a-half job search, and the local company sent Tom an email extending an official offer. Tom, while very capable of making financial decisions on his own, still ran everything by me.

"Should I respond right away or wait a day? If I respond, do you think it means I'm accepting the offer?" he probed from his executive chair. Hating to see him jump into anything, and feeling a little coy, I gave him my opinion.

"You need to jump on this offer, albeit lower in salary than you'd like, but I would let them sweat it for at least a day."

"Okay, I'll respond tomorrow," he conceded.

The next morning, he received an email from the company notifying him that the position he'd interviewed for had been filled. I felt horrible; he was miffed. He'd gotten along really well with the gentleman that interviewed him, and while he didn't blame my wifely advice, he did wonder if they'd been expecting an immediate response. He followed up with a call and found out that they hired someone with less experience because they knew that Tom was over-qualified and looking for more meaningful work. If they only knew. Another blow. He focused on the other opportunity, for which he had an interview scheduled a few weeks out.

Riding right alongside my makeover, job interviews, and school prep was the Matthew Kelly event at church. Ticket sales were in the multiple hundreds, and Tom needed to sell 1,000 to honor his commitment. Going about it from a business perspective, he lined up some volunteers and decided to speak at every Mass for a couple of weeks before alongside an employee of Mr. Kelly's non-profit, Dynamic Catholic, and make tickets available in the foyer. Frazzled about the lack of excitement from our parish, he had a heart-to-heart with Father Eric, who, in so many words, told him not to worry about it, that "God would work it out."

After an exhausting eighty-hour, six-day work week, Tom drove straight to 5PM Mass on Saturday evening, then attended the four services on Sunday. Noah tagged along because he was intrigued by the sale of *anything*, and the hand-held credit card machine became his favorite device. By 6PM on Sunday evening, Tom, Noah, and an exhausted twenty-something Jessica from Dynamic Catholic, who drove up from Ohio, were having BBQ on the patio while counting ticket sales. Great success! They sold over 500 tickets in two days and only needed to sell 200 more within the next two weeks for a full house. Father Eric was right.

The following week, on a hot August morning, Tom called me on his way to work.

"I just had the weirdest experience," he said. I didn't like him having weird experiences while driving; they were usually the bad kind of weird. One time he witnessed a horrible accident and looked in his rearview mirror to see a woman get thrown from her vehicle and land in the middle of the expressway, right in the path of a semi-truck. The fatality made the ten o'clock news. He'd just recently gotten stuck in the west side of downtown Detroit on an empty tank of gas while the city was flooding. It took him over two hours to get home. I couldn't imagine what he had for me this morning.

"What," I answered, taking a sip of my coffee while cleaning the kitchen.

"I was driving on Telegraph (which is a four lane, forty-five mph highway), and just out of nowhere, a white dove appeared next to my driver's window! It flew with me for over a mile then swooped up into the sky and disappeared!" he exclaimed. I knew his blue eyes were twinkling.

"That is crazy! Where would a white dove come from? I've never heard of such a thing!"

"I know! It was like a sign from Heaven reminding me to keep pushing through this miserable job, that something better is coming." Birds seemed to be our messengers that year, and I decided to let the peace be with me. And also with Tom.

Appropriately enough, the Matthew Kelly event came and went and was a huge success. Ticket sales soared during the final two weeks, and our church was at maximum capacity with over 2,000 in attendance. It was a beautiful event, and I was really proud of Tom for all the behind-the-scenes work he did in the midst of our private crisis.

On Friday, September 19, the house was back on the market, and we had a house showing at 4:30, right around the time the bus was to arrive. Unlike most laboring days of house prep, I was basking in the glory of Career 2.0! The last string of interviews had developed into a real job offer, and Tom had put in his two weeks' notice that morning. It was a day of celebration, just like August 1, except this answered prayer came with a parental promise to our five that "When Daddy gets the job that he loves, we will go to Cedar Point the next day." I had the day to prep the house for a showing and was waiting at the bottom of the driveway for the bus, with Otto in the front seat and the windows rolled down to control dog stress odors and allow me to enjoy the summer air.

Within minutes, I heard the bus's diesel engine as it turned off of Woodward Avenue and onto Pine Gate Drive. As it rounded the corner and screeched to a halt, I wondered what the kids' reactions would be when I told them the good news. My trunk was open as well as one sliding door (I *love* the minivan's automatic everything), and the kids knew the drill: put backpacks in the trunk, load from the side, and promptly buckle, allowing me to shift into drive. Natalie and Kate, now in full-day kindergarten, followed the routine like little pros. I drove around the corner, then pulled off to the side of the street and put the van in park. I rolled up the windows for privacy.

"Kids! I have NEWS to tell you!" I teased, waiting for them to silence their chatter.

"What!" they screamed. When I say "screamed," I mean REALLY LOUD, but for normal people it would be ear piercing, so the word "screamed" is appropriate. It was Friday. Pizza/movie night tradition. Since we were kicked out of the house, they probably expected me to be surprising them with a dining out pizza experience. They were not prepared to hear what I cheered next.

"DAD GOT A JOB THAT HE WILL LOVE AND TODAY HE QUIT HIS JOB AND TOMORROW WE ARE GOING TO CEDAR POINT!" What proceeded to happen in my minivan was joyous. The kids were, at first, in shock. They didn't know how to handle this amazing news. My design contest win didn't affect them; their prayers were simply for the sake of Mom's happiness. But a "job that Daddy will love" meant that life was about to change. Their dad would not be miserable, and that was worthy of screaming as loud as they could. So they screamed. Then they cheered. And after that, they cried tears of joy. My little troopers, my prayer warriors, were witnessing another miracle and life lesson in perseverance. The car was rancid from Otto's stench, so I rolled down all the windows and opened the sun roof. That Friday, while most were focused on the weekend and getting out of traffic, we happily merged onto Woodward Avenue like we were on streets of gold in another realm. We were untouchable, blessed, and rejoicing in the freedom of real employment.

The next morning, as we drove to Cedar Point, I sat in the passenger seat of my black Honda, Tom at the wheel, the kids belted in behind, and Otto sleeping on the floor at their feet. Coincidentally, it was our wedding anniversary, and as I watched the Ohio farmland stream by, I realized that I couldn't remember the last time I enjoyed the view. Old white, gable-roofed two stories with red barns and giant silos. Acres of green corn rows, tall and sun-kissed by the Saturday morning rays. Dirt roads separating one farm from the next. A peppy song by Train was playing on the radio, and I put my bare toes up on the dashboard and sipped my coffee in pure contentment.

We say that we are strong and fearless through the storms, and maybe we are. We hold on, we don't give up, we make it through. But when the storm finally passes and the waters are calm (in our case, it had been almost seven years since we'd had calm), the contentment is euphoric. It felt foreign, and the only way to describe it would be the feeling you have when you're sitting in the back of the car as a kid without a care in the world except how long it will be until you get where you're going and how great a Coke will taste once you get there. When I was little, that drive was across the country pulling the pop-up camper to the next state park. As an adult, pre-kids, it was sitting in the window seat next to Tom on a Boeing 757 en route to Whistler to stay in our ski-in ski-out condo. As a mom, I'd never before experienced this euphoric travel state of mind. With babies, toddlers, and preschoolers, drives were usually anything but peaceful. But the drive to America's Roller Coast was two hours of Heaven I will never forget.

What I didn't plan was a day of bizarre gifts from strangers as if the angels sent a message down to everyone at Cedar Point and the surrounding area to take special care of the Gyarmati family. We stopped at the Dairy Queen right outside the park for an early lunch and to start our day of spoiling the kids. There was a new lady working the front who messed up our entire order. Completely relaxed about the whole thing, we ate whatever they gave us, with our focus on getting into the park. Taken with our little pack of five, the manager came out with extra food and announced that she was refunding half our bill. Just because.

Tom and I grew up going to Cedar Point. I went annually, he more often. It's truly the biggest amusement park in America, situated on a peninsula on Lake Erie in Sandusky, Ohio. It's not Disney World. It's not glamorous. But it's clean and ever-changing with the removal of small, older rides that are replaced with the most thrilling roller coasters ever engineered. When you go to Disney World, you feel the magic. Every detail is considered and every employee trained to make that happen. At Cedar Point, the international ride operators wear the same red and blue overall shorts, and you are lucky if you get one that gives the "Welcome back riders... Please wait to unbuckle your seatbelt until the ride has come to a complete stop, exit to your left and enjoy your day at America's RRROOOLLLLLER Coast!"

On this day, you'd think Walt Disney himself was operating each ride. Everyone was happy, which in turn made the hot sweaty riders waiting in long lines happy. Our family was happy whether we were riding the Gemini or the Scrambler. Or sitting in the back of a Tin-Lizzy while Noah and Emma drove us in circles on the one-lane wooded track. The only disappointment was that Noah, now tall enough to ride the real coasters for the first time, didn't have time to wait the hour and a half for the Millennium Force, the tallest, fastest coaster in the park. We moseyed into the Cedar Point museum to take a break and get into the air conditioning. As we sat on rows of wooden benches enjoying a historical movie about the park, this kind man (whose name was Ken, and would become our regular museum go-to), walked over for no apparent reason and handed us seven passes to ride anything in the park by entering through the exit lane. The EXIT lane!

This was like VIP backstage passes at your favorite concert! At least, for Noah it was. And my son promptly ran with his dad to the giant ride and rode it not once but three times to get it out of his system.

The day was beautiful, and when the sun had set a storm rolled in, catching us by surprise. Luckily, we were able to take shelter under some giant 1970s umbrella-style canopies near a food station. I sat with the girls as rain poured around us, splashing our feet and legs. It was late, past 9PM for sure, and I pondered how we would get out of the park without getting drenched.

"Mommy, I'm HUNGRY," little worn-out Kate announced in her squeaky voice. She wasn't really starving. Ready for a snack, yes, but it hadn't been hours since she'd had a meal. I looked down at her and smiled with my arms around her to block the rain. All of the sudden, I heard a voice and a gentle tap on my shoulder.

"Excuse me," said a sweet woman from behind me. I immediately feared that I was about to experience another public scolding as I had during the date night concert. I smiled as I turned, hoping I wasn't in her seat or that my kids were too loud for her amusement. It was a mom, a younger mom who didn't mind the extra thirty pounds of baby weight because she loved her babies more than she loved her body.

"I heard your daughter say she was hungry, and I can't imagine having four little girls; we just have two. Anyway, we have a meal plan with free food that we will not be using, will you allow me to use it for chicken fingers and fries for your entire family?" Amazed by the generosity of this stranger, and shameful of my initial judgment, I knew that our gifts today were not just coincidence. Things like this don't just happen.

"Are you sure?"

"It would be my pleasure," she smiled, and we exchanged an unspoken mom-style look of endearment. Then, off she went into the rain to gather food for my little birds. By the time Tom and Noah found us, they were starving, and Tom profusely thanked the family for their generosity. As soon as, and I mean the very minute, we finished our nibbles, the rain stopped as though the water had simply been turned off. It was the perfect conclusion to our first day as a free-from-grip-of-the-dismal-dealer family. Life was going to be better.

CHAPTER 25

DESIGN FOR A DIFFERENCE

When you pop out five kids in less than four years, lose everything from your retirement and financial security to your once-healthy body and mind, and are *still* able start your day with your dreams intact (even when they have been hijacked by important responsibilities like feeding those people, scrubbing floors for house showings, and trying your best to rally a community that hardly recognizes you as a designer to donate funds to a charity they've never heard of) you think a lot about life. You appreciate more than you did before it all started. You manage your time as if it is precious gold. You don't feel bad about opting out of school events, parties, or giving opportunities that come your way. You understand your purpose and grow into a more focused human being. You know that the dream will happen in due time, and you are patient to wait. Topping all of these little lessons is the one that expectations will set you up for failure. Very difficult for the Type-A personality, however the most valuable schooling I'd gotten over the years.

When you set expectations for people, they will let you down, and it's not their fault. It's yours. When you set expectations for the perfectly planned day, it usually gets derailed, so you have to be willing to adapt perfect to make it practical. Whether your expectation is on humanity or circumstance, the only thing you can do is be the kindest version of yourself, take the knotted chain, untangle it, and remember that it's all about the love. Sometimes, if you keep your attitude in check, you even realize that when people let you down, it's okay. People you never *dreamed* of helping you may help you untangle the chain, and when it's all said and done, your knot may end up being part of the most beautiful chain you've ever seen.

At the beginning of September, when I started emailing our digital flier to my family, friends, and clients, I understood that some would give, and others would not. I was okay with that. My dream was that this group of people would take the time to actually read what I was trying to accomplish and share it with their friends and family so that our makeover would be funded by many small donations, leaving the givers with a sense of satisfaction that they contributed to a worthy cause without breaking the bank. That was my plan, the plan I worked every night when the kids were tucked in. I was receiving donations and promptly thanking everyone with a personal email while continuing to concoct new ways to continue distributing my email flier without annoying anyone. We didn't have time for fancy fundraising, so online donations would have to do.

A few family members donated. A few friends. Teachers. Clients. Some were extremely generous, and it blew me away. My college roommate, who lives across the globe and hasn't talked to me in years, donated $300. The same amount came from a school parent. The funds were growing, and Matt had contractors lined up to donate their time, which was worth hundreds of dollars in and of itself. I had recruited my parents to be on call to help with the install—my private DFAD design team—and I prayed that my crowd would rise just enough to purchase the office furniture from Staples, a glider rocker, and two adult-sized bean bags. Mark Brunetz and the team at the International Design Guild had no idea that I was a one-man show, a mom of five in the midst of some pretty challenging times. They didn't need to know. I wanted more than anything to transform the space at Lahser, but I was feeling the crunch of my single act. Things like Design for a Difference need a community of people with the same mindset to make them happen. Here in Detroit, I was determined to make it happen with my mini team, who was as committed to the project as I was.

The hardest part for me was that I was a mystery designer. My talents had been archived with the Dayton Hudson Marshall Field's Corporation or were mere consultations or half-jobs not worthy of photography. I hated that. The people in Bloomfield Hills knew me as "Hollie with five kids," but hadn't a clue that I'd been drawing floor plans since I was ten. While the fear of funding failure crept up daily, I'd say a prayer and count on more miracles. By this point, I figured that God would be bored if I didn't ask for miracles every day, so I had nothing to lose.

My mom called me up one afternoon in response to my daily miracle request. "The most amazing thing happened today!" she exclaimed. I was so tired I honestly had no idea what to expect.

"What," I responded, once again standing at the kitchen sink.

"I just got a letter in the mail from my friend who your father and I walk with, and this couple, who doesn't even know you, wrote you a check for $500 toward the makeover!" I took a break and sat down for this; I was in shock. "She wrote the most inspiring little note in a card; I want to read it to you." I was listening, and felt my heart overflowing with gratitude...

Dear Peggy,

John went to the bank a few days ago and felt the need to get a purchase order for $500. He knew in his heart that he wanted to give it to someone in need but had no idea who it would be. He came home and shared this with me, and I thought he was a little nuts. Only two days later, you forwarded Hollie's charity makeover to us, and we both knew that the money was for your daughter and your brother's daycare facility. Please forward this to her! We wish her the best of luck.

God Bless,
Diane

I was blown away. By what happened afterward as well. Not only was I praying for enough support to pull off my beautiful space but I also wanted good photos to share. I remembered the previous fall how much I enjoyed the photographer Cindy sent to the house to do the photo shoot. She was awesome, a true artist who photographs multi-million-dollar estates. We had a lovely time together; I assisted her in staging every room, which was extremely atypical for a million-dollar-plus homeowner, and it took the entire day. We bonded over design, art, architecture, and people. Her name was Anna. She was in her mid-fifties, I'd say, with salt and pepper hair and a very sweet demeanor. An email followed, and within a day she gave me a call and told me that she wanted to photograph the makeover—and would do it for free! Thank You was not enough. I had nothing to offer this woman, and she not only remembered me, she told me she wasn't surprised that I'd won such a competition. She said it all felt right. So Anna, the renowned photographer of the rich and famous, was coming to our dilapidated building to work her magic. I was thrilled.

By the end of October, it was install week, and Design for a Difference excitement was hanging heavy over the kitchen sink (where one can clearly find me and my deep thoughts throughout the day). Tom and the kids were looking forward to my "design" making the "difference" in their world because they would have their wife and mom back. Looking back, I still cannot believe I made it through those six weeks. House showings, getting kids into the school routine, religious ed on Monday nights (and this year, I'd volunteered to teach a sixth-grade class), and the makeover. Plus all the usual mom stuff I used to whine about like dishes, laundry, grocery lists, shopping... Thank God Tom was engrossed in his new job and beginning to bring in real income because I had to take a break from clients in order to get the makeover finished in time.

Monday, October 27

Day One. The room had been emptied and floors prepped. Matt and his installer met me there around 9AM, and the three of us got to work. I unboxed the planks and made sure the pattern stayed random. I love watching people come to Lahser who haven't before been around adults with disabilities. Just walking in the building is a shocker, but once you're there for a while and get used to the stale air and sad space, you become immune to it and begin to enjoy the beautiful people being cared for in the facility. Ernie was happy to see me and had gotten used to my frequent visits. He sat in the community room just outside our makeover space so he could watch and play with his blocks. Most of the clients were in the back rooms, but there were a few independents that became favorites as the week went on. Topping my list was Joe, who was a client with Down Syndrome. He was in his late forties, used a walker, and spent every afternoon shuffling from the shelving unit outside our makeover entrance to the back room. He'd stop to show me his dance moves while ripping open his button-down to reveal his coveted Superman T-shirt, one he insisted on wearing daily. It reminded me that feeling great was often found in the simple pleasures in life, and if a superhero T-shirt was it, who can argue with that? Sharon and the staff were in high spirits, and once the floor started going in, they began to see my vision of the vacation space they were about to receive. I loved every minute of it!

Besides assisting Matt with the planks, I took note of the ceiling tiles, which were in poor condition. "Are we going to leave the ceiling?" Matt asked. I knew what he was thinking, and I was on the same page. It was grimy and would ruin our fresh look.

"I don't think we have enough money to replace the tiles. How much do you think we'd need?" I asked as we began counting the stained 2 x 4s hanging in the old grid.

"Probably about $300."

"We won't have enough; I need cash to finish accessories."

"I think we need to do something," he said, grabbing the ladder and poking a corner up. About forty years of dust came flying out and we both started coughing. I was in deep thought. It was like coming up with enough winter gear for the kids when we were unemployed. I had to be frugal and smart and find a way to make something out of nothing. I had a 3AM solution.

"Let's count how many bad tiles we have; I have an idea." He tallied the grime, I did the non-grime, and we compared. Just as I thought—about half the tiles needed to be replaced. "This can work, but it will be just that: work. Are you in?"

"You're the boss lady. What do you want to do?"

"We need to pop all of these out, get rid of the bad, wipe down the salvageable, and buy new ones to match. I know the color will be slightly off, but we'll reinstall them in a checkerboard pattern and it will all look new!"

"Genius!" he complimented. Not genius. Just a design-mom solution. Right on cue, a young twenty-something well over six feet tall kid from Matt's business group popped in to help. He was exactly what we needed and my new best friend. Between the two of them, they handed me the old tiles and I walked them out, making my two piles. This afterthought was going to add hours of work to the week, but it had to get done. Just as we'd calculated, my two piles were just about the same size; the stained ones went to the dumpster and I went to the local lumberyard with an existing sample to match up. As with any other 3AM task, what should have been easy snowballed into a nail-biting time crunch because the closest matching tile was out of stock—but "should" arrive from the store two hours north tomorrow afternoon. We didn't have time to try a big box store.

I went with my gut, made the nice bearded guy helping me wish he hadn't asked to assist my lumber needs as I had him quadruple check and call everyone involved in ceiling tile shipment right down to the truck dispatcher in Saginaw. Satisfied with my confirmation, I placed

THE MOTHER OF ALL MAKEOVERS · 279

our order and paid the frugal $60 for the tiles, then snuck through downtown Pontiac to get home in time to meet the bus.

Tuesday, October 28

Day Two: Paint Day. Getting this job done without the help of generous contractors would have been impossible. Matt's friend, Greg, met my mom and I on-site to get the dirty walls coated with a cool off-white. Paint is like the mascara of a project, instant gratification. It was looking fabulous and the fumes of the latex eliminated the stale air. My mom and I spent the morning washing the ceiling tiles in the "keep" pile and coating the ceiling grid with our neutral. Joe continued his afternoon routine of the back and forth, which I found out involved transporting the forty-plus lunch bags from the back room to the shelves, one by one. My mom and I also made a run to Target and Homegoods to shop for accessories. I was exhausted by the time I got home. I fed the kids PB&J with smoothies and *Uh-huh*-ed my way through our evening routine. I was online making one last attempt at finding bright green Sunbrella pillows for the built-in benches flanking my custom wall unit. I'd grabbed some cute accent pillows at Target that afternoon and realized that I'd need oversized lime green to pull off my look. Not going to happen. I decided to reach out to a friend who owned a drapery workroom in Oklahoma. She was happy to oblige my rush order and promised to have two thirty-inch lime green Sunbrella pillows with a knife edge on their way the next day.

Wednesday, October 29

Day Three: Installation Day. Another round of applause to Matt's friend and colleague, Mike, who whipped up my back wall of custom cabinets exactly the way I'd drawn them. Excitement levels were running high as our room was carved into shape. My dad's brother (an electrician) graciously stopped in to hang the new white ceiling fan. I supervised and ran to the lumberyard to pick-up the ceiling tiles. My kids were happy to accept pizza and Sprite for dinner and cheered at the thought of an entire week of super-fast kid food in their bellies.

Thursday, October 30

Day Four: Furniture and Artwork. We had a lot of furniture to put together, and my parents took on that job while Matt and I took a stab at installing the ceiling tile in a checkerboard pattern, one old and one new, which when it was finished (not without the help of my dad on a few difficult fits) looked exceptional. Our goal was to take the eye away from the dingy ceiling, but what we ended up with was a beautiful focal point that enhanced our completed design! We were all pleasantly surprised! The old tiles, since they'd been wiped down, didn't miss a beat sitting next to the new bright whites, and actually looked a tad like our wall color. The slight tone-on-tone pattern brought a fun element to the space, and it looked like it'd been part of the plan all along.

Scott from the art gallery arrived in the late morning to hang the artwork. I'd known him for years, and once he got the pieces into the room, I gave him a quick tour of the facility to gear him up for his role. He, along with anyone else getting the tour, was saddened by the reality of life at Lahser. It's hard to take it all in when you see so many people in need in at once. My little walkthroughs were like the pep rally before the big game. Newbies to this world embraced the need for our makeover, and their excitement to take part in transforming our one room was as thrilling for me as the actual work being done.

I tossed Scott a DFAD T-shirt, which he wore almost as proudly as Joe did his Superman T-shirt. (By Thursday, Joe was still dancing in the spotlight with his walker and had professed his undying love to my mom multiple times). Watching Scott install our giant foam-backed poster prints of my selected Technicolor landscapes was different than any other job I'd worked on with him. The DFAD magic had gotten him, and there was a little sparkle of pride in his eye as he carefully mounted the art to the cement block wall. He understood the importance of art, but turning this room into a beautiful space for the trapped souls he'd just met brought a new meaning to the concept of *living* with art. This art would be the only traveling that these residents would do outside the walls of their group homes, vans, and the gloomy walls of this building. It was beautiful.

Our last wall install before my dad was to begin to install furniture was the special order bright blue wall pads along the west wall of the room. A half-round activity table from Staples was popped in front of the cabinetry to create an executive-office-meets-kitchen-island look. It was multi-tasking perfection. An employee could sit in their swivel chair, working with up to four clients at a time on fine-motor skills, reading, listening to music, or even feeding them lunch. Standing in the doorway, Sharon was grinning from ear to ear as she envisioned how this would help them day-to-day. We created a seating area in front of the activity table that sported a comfy cream-colored gliding rocker, the perfect antidote for someone having a bad day as well as two adult-sized bright green glittery bean bags for the clients who have a hard time sitting in chairs and need the versatility of a soft landing.

It was late afternoon, and I had to get home for the kids, but before we split, we took a couple of group shots of our small design team. The makeover was almost complete, and to my team, it looked finished. But it was missing the accessories, the jewelry. I planned to bring them early Monday morning before the reveal party. I thanked everyone for their time, and we broke for the weekend. The next day was Halloween and that required full-time mom detail for costumes, the school parade and parties, and our traditional Grandpa and Grandma evening of trick-or-treating in downtown Birmingham. When I drove up the driveway that afternoon, I was greeted with a giant UPS box containing my bright green pillows. I unwrapped and was admiring them before I even took my coat off or unloaded my van. They were perfect! I heard the bus rounding the corner and realized how exhausted I was. Four solid days of leaving the home front meant a busy weekend catching up on laundry, cleaning, and groceries. Exhaustion was part of my everyday life, but this day's felt like I'd just wrapped up a week's worth of house showings or general life with five under four.

As I stood on the porch guarding my new pillows from grubby hands entering the house, I thought about how blessed I was to have had the week run so smoothly, for all the help we had, and for the excitement brewing inside Lahser. The employees acted like it was Christmas over the course of the installation, and I couldn't wait to see the reaction of the clients and their families, who were all going to attend our luncheon on Monday. I was grateful for the lack of real-estate interest in the house that week. A house showing would have done me in. All the worries of selling the house had faded with the excitement of the makeover and Tom's new job. His employment gave us a little more time to wait for an offer, and we hoped it would come before Christmas. Everything was falling into place exactly as Emma had prayed it would. Contest. Job. House.

Four days later, I was sliding baskets under the benches and placing my pillows in the corners. I added some greens to the top of the cabinets and a wooden bowl filled with fresh apples to the countertop. My mom and I had selected some board books and brightly colored toys to use in the room that matched the beautiful colors in the artwork: Golden Gate Red and Kentucky Rolling Hill Green. I finished just in time for Anna to sneak in to take her After shots. Even she was blown away by our end result. It was far from a $10-million estate, but a reminder for us all that design makes a difference in the humblest of forms.

During her visit, we let a few Lahser clients experience their new space. My Uncle Ernie was the guest of honor, sporting a suit and boutonniere. He was adorable. Sharon brought in Suzy, who was in a wheelchair, as well as a few others. Joe of course got his Superman groove on. Matt had snuck in, and we stood back to enjoy the reactions of Ernie and his friends. It was awesome. We were teary-eyed and amazed at their instant mood change as they entered the space. Those who could verbalize their joy said things like, "This is pretty," or "Horses!" as they viewed the artwork. They touched everything, including the freshly painted walls and cabinets, taking in the "newness" of it all. Ernie stopped in front of the photo of the Switzerland countryside and let out one of his sighs of contentment. Anna zoomed in on that moment as well as a few of Sharon interacting with Suzy before she left. She promised to have the photos edited and sent to me by Friday, the first day I'd spend in Kansas City for the national makeover.

I leaned against the doorway admiring our work. "Thank You, Mark Brunetz and the International Design Guild, for this wonderful gift," I thought to myself. This was going to impact some very deserving individuals for years to come. Even though they would never be able to talk about it, these blind, deaf, mute, and severely mentally disabled sons and daughters would experience life a little better through this room. I pictured Grandma and Papa and how happy they'd be to know that we were taking care of Ernie. Overwhelmed with gratitude, I heard five familiar voices running into the main gathering room as if they owned the place.

"WHOOOAAAA!" Emma exclaimed as she rounded the corner. "THIS IS AWESOME!"

"Thanks, Emsie," I replied, as her twin and his sisters roamed around testing everything out. Before I knew it, my made-over room was filled with Gyarmati kids occupying the bean bags, gliding in the rocker, and opening the small refrigerator built in to the new wall of cabinets. They probably said everything the Lahser clients were thinking, and it gave me reassurance that we created a dream room for the young at heart.

That Monday was one of the most gratifying days of my design career. It was nestled right up there with my teachers' lounge reveal. It was gratifying, not because I had created and installed a beautiful space, but because I was allowed the freedom to be who I was created to be without abandon. I think we are all happiest when we feel free to be who we are at our core. For me, it is not just as the wife of Tom and the mom of Noah, Emma, Isabelle, Natalie, and Kate but also as Interior Designer. As someone who cares about impacting lives. As someone who will design until she dies. And as someone who will follow her dreams, even when they are being held hostage by the most difficult circumstances.

CHAPTER 26

OPERATION BREAKTHROUGH

"Too straight," I thought, as I glanced into the large oval mirror over the bathroom sink. I grabbed my flat iron and strategically ran it through pieces around my face to create a slight wave. I stepped back again. Much better. It was a perfect blow-out, which I hadn't taken the time to do in months, and it was imperative that it was just so. It was Friday, November 7. I'd finally made it to Kansas City, and I was relishing the extended alone time I'd had for the afternoon at the historical Raphael Hotel in the heartland of America. Having arrived early in the afternoon, I spent the day enjoying the luxurious amenities of the renaissance, revival-style architecture and luxurious room overlooking the riverfront running through the exclusive Country Club Plaza. I had no idea that Kansas City was so enchanting and stylish! And I had no idea that I would feel a little lonely after a long day of traveling solo. It had been hours since I'd talked to anyone, and almost an entire day since I'd worn my mom hat. I had ten minutes to get dressed before dinner and was looking forward to meeting my new friends.

I did a quick run through of the other designers as I slipped into my new black wool and leather sleeveless sheath dress with an exposed hardware zipper running up the back. Dani Pollidor: bright blonde, glasses, bright lip color. Rochester, New York. Realtor and accomplished designer. Okay, I was guilty of a little Google investigation in the days leading up to my travel. Lucy Penfield: Minneapolis. Dishwater blonde. Fabulous wrap dress and coveted fun-yet-professional-sitting-in-a-stylish-chair designer photo. Nicole Zeigler: Salt Lake City. ASID president. More blonde. More fabulousness. Stephanie Stroud: National Winner. Kansas City. *Zero* Google information or social media presence. She was a mystery. I knew she would be amazing and wondered if she'd be blonde. I reached my right hand behind my neck and finished pulling up my zipper. Dani, Lucy, Nicole, and Stephanie. And, of course, Mark. And Krista Eliason, president of the International Design Guild. I'd heard Krista's voice during our conference calls, and she seemed very nice. She left me my congratulatory voicemail in August, and I couldn't wait to meet her.

Smoothing another layer of lotion over my knees, I glanced at the digital clock radio. 6:55PM. Dinner in five minutes downstairs. My stomach tightened a bit. I slipped into my patent leather Cole Haan pumps, slid on a few gold bangles, and grabbed my black evening clutch. *I can't believe I'm here.* I turned at a forty-five-degree angle to the full-length mirror in the small hall by the bathroom and struck a red-carpet pose. *Narcissist or nerd.* Whichever I was, I ignored my insecurities, focused on my overwhelming excitement, and strutted out of my room, making sure my key was snug in the side pocket of my bag.

"How are you this evening?" a dark-haired young man greeted with a sincere smile.

"Well, thank you. I'm here for the International Design Guild dinner," I smiled back, trying to not look as fidgety as I felt. He escorted me through the dimly lit bar area and down a couple of carpeted steps before I could take a much-needed yoga breath. Our party was set up in the back of the lower-level restaurant. There was one long banquet table separated from the rest of the formal dining area by a half-wall, making it hard to get a look at those in the back.

Mark was standing front and center and knew me by name as soon as I joined the group.

"Hollie, it's so good to see you," he said as we met with a light hug. Stylish as expected, he was wearing a dark button-down, dark jeans, and brown shiny loafers. Polished like a model in a Ralph Lauren ad, approachable like an old college friend.

"Thank you for having me, this is a beautiful hotel," my jitters immediately settled. I quickly forgot about what I looked like or whether my hair was too straight and immersed myself in the honor of being selected to take part in Design for a Difference.

"You look amazing," he complimented, and like the old ladies during his presentation, I was at his design disposal.

"Thank you," I blushed.

"Can I bring you a cocktail?" a nice waitress asked after making her way over with her tray. Mark was holding a lowball glass as he continued to greet his guests. I decided to stick with my usual.

"A tall Captain Morgan and Diet Coke with a lime, please." This had been my drink of choice since college. I enjoyed a glass of red or white on a date night, an ice-cold beer from the cooler if I was seated around a campfire, and my rum and diet when I needed reliability. In that moment, I needed reliability, no matter how sorority sister the situation looked. The waitress smiled and walked away, and I was greeted by a small handful of people either seated or arriving to the table, all very nice, most of them from the Guild. I situated myself to the right of Mark as I chatted with Frank Chiara, a digital marketing expert for the parent company. Frank was Italian, from Boston, in his early forties, and lit up the room when he smiled. We talked about everything from my makeover to his love of classic cars, newlywed life, and the dynamic of his Italian family. Before I knew it, Mark was standing with a glass in hand, making a toast and beginning introductions around the table.

Krista was seated at the far end of the table and exuded ear-to-ear pride and gratitude as she thanked everyone for traveling to Kansas

City. There was a group from Madden-McFarland Interiors (Matt's equivalent) surrounding Krista. They all greeted us with friendly waves. Lucy and Dani were at that end, their faces matching my Google research, and Nicole was to the right of Frank. Stephanie was seated diagonally across the table to my right, and wouldn't you know, she was blonder than us all! She was tall and slender and had a very sweet demeanor. Her straight golden hair fell below her shoulders, and her posture would make any nagging mother or chiropractor proud. My online probing had served its purpose, giving me a quick glance into who was who, but that was it. First impressions were made, all wonderful, as we enjoyed a nice evening of small talk, great food, and delectable dessert.

The evening flew by, and before we knew it, Mark was giving us our morning instructions and introducing us to the camera crew who was seated in the overflow area near the bar. Brett, Howard, and Joe from California. They looked really nice. Everyone was just *incredibly* nice. Had I been removed from society for so long that I found it surprising to be in a large group of people who all gave good warm and fuzzy vibes? As I stood up from my chair, I determined that I was truly surrounded by thirty-plus people who were golden from the inside out. I could feel it. As our party broke and we all parted ways, I walked with the other designers through the hotel lobby, continuing our dinner talk. They towered over me, Dani at supermodel height and the other three not far behind. I chuckled inside as I realized that I'd been around little people for so long that I forgot I was short. It had never bothered me, nor did it that night. I was happy to be away from my tall role on Pine Gate Drive, finished with my own makeover, and excited to be of service to Stephanie at Operation Breakthrough.

The next morning, we reconvened in our bright blue DFAD T-shirts and work clothes promptly at 8AM. We were all in jeans with the exception of Lucy, who casually sported relaxed khakis. She was probably in her late forties, the eldest of us designers, and the owner of Lucy Interior Design. She had four designers in her group, and her portfolio had a national presence from the twin cities to Phoenix to the Florida Keys. Her work had been featured in numerous publications and made my heart skip a beat it was so beautiful. She was an artist of our trade, one to be admired and praised, and I could tell that Nicole, Dani, and Stephanie felt the same. Much had been established during our short time together. Everyone knew that I had my own "twin city" at home and was a pro multi-tasking mom who spent her earlier years in the field. Stephanie was a mom of three, in her forties, and had taken up design ten years earlier. Nicole was our "mom-to-be," and we adopted her five-month bump into our team. She was from Michigan, a Michigan State grad, and also had a partner in her firm. Dani was a design powerhouse and filled with joy. If I didn't feel like a shrimp just standing next to her, I certainly did as she shared her recent success stories and big business plans for future projects. She was a mom of two and a pioneer in our industry. I appreciated them all and was happy to add my unique view to the that of the group.

While we chatted in the lobby, the IDG team members and camera crew packed up their gear and went over some last-minute details with Mark.

"Ok, designers," he greeted, as we huddled in for instruction. Just as quickly as I'd gotten past my initial Mark Brunetz celebrity jitters, I switched to business mode. Mark had my undivided attention.

"Good morning! Direct your attention to what you look like *right now*. You need to look EXACTLY like this tomorrow morning. If your hair is curly now, wear it curly tomorrow. Wear the same pants, same shoes. We forgot this detail in Spokane last year and had to get creative with our footage." Crap. All the straightening fuss for dinner last night had to be recreated for tomorrow. I'd have to get up extra early. "We are going to hop in our van, drive to Operation Breakthrough for a quick tour of the building, and then a full work day. That's it. I'll give you more instructions as needed throughout the day."

I loved it. He was smart. Information was on point and delivered on a need-to-know basis. Just as I'd learned years earlier with the kids, people will tune you out if you talk too much. If you give them more information than they need, it elicits questions and concerns you neither need nor have time for. Either he would be an awesome dad, or I ran my house like a business. I think perhaps both.

Our leader guided us out of the hotel and into a white extended cab passenger van decked out in DFAD stickers. We pulled out of the circular drive and into the beautiful luxury retail district. The IDG and CCA Global group had been in the city all week preparing for our arrival. Frank was at the wheel, Mark was in the passenger seat, and the rest of us quietly looked out the windows as we passed Michael Kors, Kate Spade, and L'Occitane, all still sleeping off a busy Friday of shoppers. The air was crisp, although at least fifteen degrees warmer than my Motor City, and the sun was shining softly on the concrete, steel, and brick cityscape. Within ten minutes, we were parking in the back lot of an old JCPenney. It was surrounded by run-down buildings and felt very much like Detroit if you wandered a few blocks in any direction from Woodward Avenue. This was Operation Breakthrough.

Over the next couple of hours, we were escorted through the non-profit, a daytime shelter for pre-school children of poverty-stricken families. It was founded in the 1970s by Sr. Berta and Sr. Corita, who decided to open their home to provide daycare to single moms. Throughout the years, their outpouring of love grew so large that what seemed like a miraculous vision materialized into the real deal. This old department store had been converted into a phenomenal facility that provided day-care, education, warm meals, medical care, dental care, and counseling to over 450 children in Kansas City. I'd never seen anything like it and walked a thin line between wishing that every metro area in the country could host such a program and being grateful that I was not one of these moms. Stephanie led us through the medical rooms and the food pantry, explaining how dire these moms' situations were, and how an antibiotic and a jar of peanut butter could make the difference between a good and a bad day.

I silently prayed for these inner-city moms who were experiencing my worst nightmare every day. While I used to fear ending up in a cardboard box, they could only dream of my life with a loving spouse who wanted to care for their family. I didn't feel guilty, but I was bleeding empathy at a level I'd never before experienced because I knew that this could just as easily have been me, had I not had the support of my husband, parents, and "angel" friends. As my mind wandered, we arrived at the lower level of the old store and were situated behind a giant wall of Visqueen. Stephanie, Mark, and Krista wore proud smiles, and I knew we were about to experience some DFAD magic.

"Behind this tarp lays over 2,000 square feet of space, which used to be a multi-purpose community space. Stephanie and her team have designed and transformed this from a dreary basement to what will be a bright and cheerful multi-purpose environment for moms and their children," Mark announced. "Are you ready to get to work?" he asked to build our excitement. We were ready, and we could hear the camera crew and the rest of our dinner party buzzing like busy bees on the other side. Mark pulled back the tarp to reveal a large, bright, happy community room, half artistically crafted with bright green floor-covering to mimic a grassy playground, the rest covered in earthy gray commercial wood plank flooring, similar to what we'd installed at Lahser. The walls were covered in a whimsical wallpaper of geometric trees with bright white field color and beautiful bright shades of blue, red, orange, and yellow.

Stephanie and Mark led us in. It smelled fresh and clean, and the hard labor had been done. Stephanie shared her vision and described the rest of the area. There were sliding barn doors off the main gathering room that would reveal a seasonal giving room filled with donated items for the moms. The room adjacent to the playground was a computer lab with workstations around the perimeter and a small conference table in the center. There was a volunteer who spent time helping clients with resumes and job searches to get them started as independent providers. The responsibility of a single mom has to be the hardest task a woman has ever encountered. I couldn't imagine being me without Tom. I wanted to hug every one of them.

The final room of the makeover was off the lab and one of our favorites, a boutique for the women and children. When we were finished, it would be filled with outerwear, clothing, shoes, accessories, and toys donated to the charity as well as a little retreat for a weary mom to shop for her needs. Stephanie had brought a phenomenal design to transform the dreary basement, and even though I'd only met her the night before, I was proud of her giving heart.

"And now it's time to get to work!" Mark cheered with a big smile. We gathered around the center column in the "grassy" park area, ready for his next reveal. "While it looks like most of the work is done, I promise you that we have a full two days of work ahead. We'll need you to each take a job. First up, this column." We shifted our focus to the white 18-by-18-inch post in the middle of the room. There were flagpole brackets screwed into the top third of it at varying heights. "We need to recreate the pattern of the wall paper onto it and paint the horizontal stripes to match, but at a much larger scale." I shrunk down amongst my statuesque peers. Anything math related under pressure would bring on a bout of anxiety, and I didn't need that.

"I'll do it," Lucy casually said with a smile, like she'd painted thousands of linear patterns on columns over the years. I quietly sighed in relief. I'd rather pull hair out of a shower drain. Mark smiled, confident that Lucy would love the challenge of painting color for the day.

"Great! When it's finished, we are going to pop spray-painted tree branches into the brackets, and it's going to be a large tree in the park to mirror the walls—the focal point of the space." We smiled. The camera crew was busy setting up a track behind us. I wasn't sure about being on film. "Okay, next. The barn doors to the seasonal pantry. We need someone to paint the center panels with chalk paint." Now *this* I could do! I'd painted half of our main floor with an unwavering hand in the last year. Me. Chalk paint. Two doors. Easy.

"I'll do it!" I sprung forward. Mark smiled.

"Great," he confirmed as he moved on. Dani took on the hanging of artwork. Nicole joined Lucy. Stephanie was working in other areas of the building with Mark and the camera crew.

"Okay, the most important thing for you as you get to work is to grab Brett or Howard to let them know when you are beginning the first part of your job. The first stroke of your paintbrush. The first print going on the wall. Whatever it is, we need that moment in front of the camera." We nodded in agreement. "And I'd like to introduce you to Donna Marie. She's the Art Director; if you need anything, she's your go-to." I didn't notice her before, but out of nowhere had come his fabulous friend with a smile. She was everything you'd expect an Art Director to be: late forties, caramel blonde boho layered hair, a nice tan, perfectly draped tunic, dark washed skinny jeans, large artsy jewelry, and cool open-toed wedges that made my feet hurt with just a glance. Glamorous Boss. I was in. Ready to soak up all the California vibes they brought to the heart of America.

And that's where it all started. Mark and Stephanie disappeared behind the giant tarp to interview staff members and homeless moms, and I stood in front of my track-driven single-panel barn doors buzzing inside like a bee. I had no interest in design. I was simply task-driven and ready to work my butt off to experience some more makeover magic. The other designers and crew were busy too. They seemed to know what they were doing. Lucy and Nicole were hashing out a design plan for their tree, and Dani was already holding oversized prints in the hall. Did I have stage fright? Why was I standing in front of these white doors wasting time? It was like standing in front of someone else's kitchen sink, ready to get the dishes done, but having not a clue as to where they kept the dish soap

294 · HOLLIE GYARMATI

or where the silverware drawer was located. For the first time in a

294 · HOLLIE GYARMATI

294 · HOLLIE GYARMATI

or where the silverware drawer was located. For the first time in a long time, I was not in charge.

Donna Marie must have sensed my disorientation and swooped over to get me started. "Hollie, right?" I nodded. She smiled. I loved her hair. "All the supplies are in the office over here," she trailed off as she led me to a small office/control center. It was messy and crammed with paper, plans, snacks, paint, Home Depot bags, coats, handbags, camera guy stuff, and my favorite, Sharpie Markers. Lots of oversized Sharpies. There was a giant roll of paper hanging on the wall with Donna Marie scribbles. The letters were soft and flowed across the page like her drapey wardrobe. I was in designer heaven.

"Here is your chalk paint," she handed me two quarts, "a roller," she plopped a tiny foam roller on top, "a brush and, oh yes, some tape!" I stood there holding my supplies and a sense of relief that I could get to work.

"Thank you," I smiled and headed back to my doors. Lucy and Nicole were still discussing a plan. I wasn't behind after all. I set up camp and seconds later was meticulously taping the inside trim, using my thumbnail to ensure it was secure. I never tape but wanted this to be spot-on, so I took extra care, extra time, and extra designer everything to ensure Mark's and Donna Marie's approval. I could see Lucy and Nicole measuring their column. The camera crew had disappeared, and the IDG part of the team was busy in the other rooms with other jobs. Without drop cloths in sight and a new floor under foot, I found a couple of garbage bags to cover my area before opening the thick charcoal paint. This should be a breeze—a couple of heavy coats and I'd be on to other jobs. I gave the camera crew a heads up for my "first stroke."

Within minutes, I was holding my edging brush along the lower half of the right door waiting for the "go ahead" from Brett to get started on my scene. I know, it wasn't a "scene" per se, but I was prepared to look like a pro, so I was getting into character. "And...rolling," Howard said, his giant lens pointed at my profile. I ever so carefully dipped my brush and ran it along the edge of the thin blue tape. My hand was shaking inside, but to the camera it probably looked normal. It was the longest thirty seconds of my career. It took every fiber of my being not to start laughing or crying while holding back the blood from rushing to my cheeks in spotlight embarrassment.

"Perfect!" Howard praised, and the crew, satisfied with my expert chalk stroke, moved on to their next pro. I was relieved to get my "first" out of the way. The next time would be much easier, and before the weekend was over, I'd be expecting calls from HGTV. I continued painting the edges as I critiqued my first appearance on film. Within a couple of minutes, the first door was edged, and I moved on to the next. Painting, along with drawing floor plans, is my therapy—my escape from all stressors, my mental yoga. I immersed myself in my charcoal outline and did my thing. When finished, I straightened up and stood back to admire my work. I'd have these doors done in no time and be off to assist or take on more work! The paint looked great; it was drying fast and had a nice flat finish. I didn't worry too much about precision lines since I'd taped the crap out of it to be extra safe.

Then I noticed it. As my beautiful brushstrokes absorbed the basement air, the tape began to bubble up, leaving little gaps of white trim exposed to my thick layer of paint, rendering the tape completely useless. Just minutes earlier, I was worried about the blood rushing to my cheeks. Suddenly, it was flushing *from* them as I slowly peeled back the thin blue outline of tape. With little effort, it nearly fell off the large doors. I was horrified.

The tape didn't stick. It was edging tape, and not the brand I typically used, but nonetheless made to stick. Maybe it was the finish on the door? Maybe it was the specially formulated chalk paint? Or maybe it was the thick air of this old JCPenney building? Whatever it was, it set me back an hour and elevated my stress levels to the forty-five-realtors-showing-up-in-five-minutes kind of day. I worked fast, collecting the wet tape in my garbage "drop" bag that I'd laid on the floor. Nobody noticed my panic, as they were all engrossed in their own tasks. I wanted to scream. Lucky for me, there were only a few blotchy edges of white trim, and it was fresh enough to wipe away with a wet cloth. I could handle it. And I did.

When I had my mess cleaned up, I prepped my area for rolling. The hard part was done, my edges were crisp, and now I just had to roll without drips. I unwrapped the small roller. It was foam, which meant it had no nap. If you've ever painted with a roller, you know that in order to get good coverage you need a nice, thick nap foundation. The one I had to use was the opposite. It was covered in tiny porous holes; it would cause the paint to roll on thin. I dipped it in my tiny matching tray. At least it was cute; I love all things small. I'd make it work. The first dip quickly soaked into the foam, and I dipped again. And again. And again. I was trying to get enough to transfer onto the panel. When I did, it rolled on like a translucent nail polish, the kind where you paint two nails and realize it's more than a two-coat job and a nice finish sans blemish might be impossible.

"Make sure you roll that paint on nice and thick," Donna Marie directed as she breezed by. I smiled. Inside, I screamed. I *couldn't* roll it nice and thick! I was so frustrated! I was doing my best, which usually brings about great success, and this was anything but that. It was going to take all day to get these doors covered. It would take an hour for each coat to dry, and by the looks of it, it would need four. If I could have, I'd have aborted the job, driven to Home Depot, and purchased a big thick Purdy that would roll that point on without a peep. "You have to *really* roll it on thick; load that brush up with lots of paint," she instructed again in her next pass. Donna Marie probably thought I was incompetent.

The rest of the workday continued to be a challenge. I was embarrassed when I stopped into the office to ask Donna Marie for another job while I waited for my paint to dry. Three times. I'd hoped to contribute to this project in a meaningful way, yet it seemed like every task she gave me took three times longer than it should have. She handed me two little brushed silver frames and a Sharpie and asked me to make a couple of signs for the seasonal room and the boutique. When I sat down to get started, I realized the frames were held tightly together with screws and brackets, each needing a mini screwdriver and a lot of patience. No screwdriver available, but I used my time-tested mom skills and a coin to get the job done. Lucy and Nicole were still in the other room carefully drawing lines around the column. Dani had moved on to spray painting branches outside, and after my second coat of paint (and more direction to "roll it on thicker") I joined her in the chilly November air.

Stephanie would pass through the construction every now and then, each time in deep thought about one thing or another. We'd see Mark meeting up with Donna Marie, and everything seemed to be moving along well. I decided to keep my frustrations to myself and worked to the best of my ability. When 6:30 rolled around and Mark announced that we needed to wrap it up for the day, I was relieved, emotionally exhausted, and very interested in a shower. We arrived back at the Raphael with just thirty minutes to get ready for our evening event at a local barbeque. I was happy to have some time alone in my room. I turned on ABC for some background noise and retreated to the white-tiled bathroom to figure out how to pull off some kind of look for dinner without washing my still straight, dirty, and paint-splattered hair. It stayed in a ponytail, my least favorite style, and I washed up and wore a pair of black J. Crew leggings, a drapey gray T–shirt, and a long black Tahari cardigan with dolman sleeves—very DM (Donna Marie). Wardrobe approval might be the only kudos I got from my tough Art Director. I pondered her for a moment. She reminded me of me.

She was The Mom, responsible for getting a big job done, one that came with sneezes, hiccups, spilled milk, and a bunch of unforeseen issues that push you to your limits. I was reminded of my frazzled moments trying to guide my five through a busy morning of breakfast, brushing teeth, making beds (when I really had my game on), packing lunches, and loading on winter gear to walk down to the bottom of the hill to catch the bus. When I've run out of milk, splatter toothpaste on our shirts, are too tired to get to the beds, forget to put the water bottles in the lunch bags, and can't find the left boot as the minutes creep closer to departure time, it's easy to go from sweet and nurturing to short-tempered and a little nutty—even within two hours of my first sip of coffee. Donna Marie seemed much nicer than I in these supermom moments, but I could see it in her eyes, that things were maybe not running as smoothly as she'd planned, or that we all had different styles of getting the job done, or just being annoyed that the designer in charge of the barn doors was whining about her wimpy roller.

Whatever the case, I had another Captain Morgan and Diet Coke with a lime that night and thanked my mentor for a job well done, expressing my gratitude for her patience and hard work at Operation Breakthrough. When I got back to my barn doors the next day, I found a small Purdy roller waiting with my supplies. Donna Marie did me right.

CHAPTER 27

OLD, NEW, BORROWED & BLUE

The showroom. It had been a long time since I'd fallen in love with a showroom. The first time, I was just three years old. I was at the old Wick's Lumber near Flint, and my parents were building our house on Hensell. I don't remember why we were there, but I recall being antsy in the hardware aisle, my dad telling me to "hold my shorts," grabbing the frayed edge of my little cut-offs (it was 1978), and somehow ending up in the lower level which was lined with kitchens. From there, I moved to floor-covering stores, mom and pop furniture retailers, conversion van interiors, and finally, the JL Hudson furniture floor. Once I'd graduated from college, I had the pleasure of visiting the design center and luxury hotels during my early years with Tom. I appreciated it all, but the Hudson's furniture floor made my design heart happy. That's how I felt as we followed Patrick Madden through his 1920s white Dutch colonial situated in the rolling hills of Leawood, Kansas. It was traditional. It was modern. It was filled from top to bottom with beautiful furniture, art, accessories, and floor-coverings. We *oohhhed* and *aahhed* at the turn of every corner. There were offices nestled into what were once old bedrooms, multiple living rooms, and a designer's dream sample studio in the basement.

I had passed Patrick in the hustle and bustle of painting my barn doors the day before, assuming he was a floor guy like Matt. One step into the elegant foyer of his commercial residence screamed that he was not. Mr. Madden, although clad in his jeans, DFAD T-shirt, and sneakers, *was one of us.* He was in his late forties, had brown hair, sported thick brown rectangular glasses (think Brooks Brothers ad), and a twinkle in his eye as well as a smirk that either led to witty sarcasm or a conversation that revealed his love for philanthropy and design. Either way, he was a gentleman to say the least, and he had the entire design team wrapped around his finger as he shared his late father's legacy with us. Madden-MacFarland was the standalone version of the JL Hudson Interior Design Studio. Luxury living was part of Patrick's livelihood, and I was intrigued by his story.

I reminisced those days shopping as a three-year-old and romanced this kind of showroom being part of my everyday life. I thought about what it would be like to watch the rooms change every season and the privilege of viewing fine art as it traveled in and out of the front door. Certainly, the clientele would dress for the occasion, and I would get to admire ladies in their 1960s Sunday best and gentlemen with Mad Men hair and three-piece suits. I'll bet there were many cigarettes smoked while testing white George Washington style sofas and cocktail tables. I imagined setting up my own little studio with the real designers and hanging onto every tasteful declaration they'd make throughout the day instead of making forts under the dining room table while eavesdropping on Grandma Foss's telephone calls. My mind continued to daydream as Patrick led us from room to room, answering questions about marketing, vendors, and his design staff. We landed in the front living room with the camera crew. Mark had joined in, and my focus shifted to his conversation with Brett and Howard.

"We'll have them sit around Stephanie as she presents her design plan, then they can volunteer for their jobs while using the samples that are spread on the cocktail table," Mark planned. Brett nodded in agreement.

"Perfect. Then we'll shoot them arriving in the van and have them greet Patrick at the front door," he added. Mark looked pleased. Brett turned to Howard and Joe, who were making final adjustments to their tri-pods and umbrellas, to confirm that they were up to speed with the plan. Mark gathered us to the two cream sofas, and we settled in close together, Stephanie in the middle. I sat on the very edge so I could keep my presence amidst my peers.

"Okay, we are going to shoot a couple of scenes while we're here. Stephanie, I want you to run through your design plan and then the jobs needed to get done at the site." He looked at the rest of us. "When she gets to your job, volunteer for it and add a little something personal. This is all stuff that actually happened yesterday, but we wanted to include the showroom, so we are shooting it today." We nodded and marveled at the talent standing before us. These guys were amazing. They were artists. They made something hard look easy, and we got only a glimpse of how much time and effort their process involved! They were shooting over eighteen hours of footage and knew exactly what they needed to be able to edit it all into an eight-minute makeover video that would take Design for a Difference into 2015. As designers, we inherently know what our end result should be, and we work from there. Brett, Howard, and Joe were doing the same. It was so exciting to see them in action!

We shot the scene as planned, loaded and unloaded into our decked-out celebrity design van at least three times, each time with a greeting from Patrick on his covered front porch, and then loaded up one last time to drive to our next destination. Mark had thoughtfully planned the day with the camera crew for the five designers to spend together, and we were enjoying every minute of it. Sarah, a local crew-member, was in the driver's seat, and Brett was at her side. I was in the middle right behind them, flanked by Stephanie and Nicole. Mark was in the back row with Dani and Lucy. We continued chatting about our lives. We talked about our businesses, our families, our homes. Mark shared more about his childhood with us and his journey entering into the design industry. Before color, Lucy loved fashion and had a first career run in the industry. Stephanie landed clients by default when she became a mom who already had impeccable taste, and Dani and Nicole specialized in custom kitchens and baths which, in my opinion, requires the most technical yet rewarding skill within our profession.

As I sat in my middle seat surrounded by these amazing people, I felt small inside. As much as I owned my story and all the trials and tribulations that filled it, I felt entrapped by my circumstances and hopeless about achieving the only thing that kept me going through the poor house. My 3 AM dream. Then it happened.

"I wish I could design kitchens."

I said it. I didn't mean it. I didn't want to design kitchens. I wasn't exactly sure what I meant. I think I was expressing my admiration for the level of work they do. However it came out, they thought I wanted to design kitchens (logical, right?)

"You CAN design kitchens!" Dani encouraged with a kind smile. I wished I hadn't blurted that out. *Horrible* communication skills on my part. I managed a smile back. Nicole nodded, feeling the need to cheer me on. "It's not hard. And there's a lot of profit to be made," Dani continued. "I know it looks overwhelming, but the most important part of the design is to keep it all symmetrical." By this point, I had a lump in my throat. What I was feeling was the frustration of knowing what I was capable of and having a plan, I didn't have the time or the resources to act on it. My eyes filled with tears.

"I didn't mean that I literally want to design kitchens," I blubbered. "I just wish I could have a career like all of you." My eyes were now wet, and Dani's design excitement quickly turned to compassion. The only two people who regularly witnessed an overwhelmed mom meltdown were my mom and Claudia. And usually by phone. I wanted to rewind my lump and the tears, but I couldn't. I continued. "These last couple of years have been so hard, and any design work I do is added onto a sixty-hour work week. All I've done for the last year and a half is clean my giant house for realtor showings, take care of my kids, and take on design jobs that come my way so I can help pay the bills."

I hung my head, much like my little Natalie—the baby of the family—when in distress, and took a moment. I heard some shuffling around in the van. Brett had moved to the very back seat behind Mark and had a camera lens in my face. Great. Now I was the epitome of a staged reality TV show. I felt Dani and Nicole give me a hug, and everyone did what they could to console me. I lifted my face, my mascara slightly smudged, and tried to regroup to the best of my ability, something I usually did alone in the pantry or in my closet while the kids were screaming. Mark, having been through over 1,000 teary-eyed client moments, gave me the pep-talk I needed.

"Hollie. You are being too hard on yourself. (My mom has also told me this many times over the years.) You are doing something *none* of us has done. You are raising *five* kids. You've been through some really hard times. And look at where you are! You are here!" I gave him a weepy, pathetic, brown-eyed thank you.

"I just want to get out of our house and write a book," I replied in a weak voice. He gently put his hand on my shoulder.

"Then write your book," he said. "I did." I used the back of my hand to wipe away the tears under my eyes. Mark wrote a book. If he could write a book, then I could write a book. I then returned to design land with a smile.

"I will," I stated. And that was it.

A few minutes later, we arrived at the Nelson Atkins Art Museum, played in the crisp November sun, and had a picnic in the grass. I was embarrassed about my van moment for a multitude of reasons, but in the end, I trusted Mark, Lucy, Dani, Nicole, and Stephanie. I later learned that most of us had been through some pretty tough battles, and I just so happened to be emotionally on my last leg when I arrived in KC forty-eight hours earlier. I decided to give myself the break. I was the only one who would ever know how many hours I'd devoted to my husband, my kids, my business, and pushing that damn Dyson back and forth in my 7,500 square foot home. Add a charity makeover installation to all that as well as the time it takes to prep my family for my five-day absence, and I think anyone in my situation would have done the same thing.

We arrived at Operation Breakthrough to find the IDG and Madden-McFarland design crews hard at work. My barn doors were almost done. Many of the other small jobs were finished. Furniture had been placed. There was still quite a bit of staging to do, but we could tell that many had put in a full morning of work. Donna Marie was still scurrying around making sure everyone was on task, and there, in the middle of the park, was Lucy's half-painted-like-the-wallpaper column. Minus the branches. It stood out like the giant pile of clean clothes in the middle of my bedroom floor, needing to be folded and put away—right before a house showing. It needed to just get done. We spent the entire afternoon, all of us, including Patrick, squashed around the giant post, painting staggered horizontal stripes. What seemed like an easy job the day before had become a time-consuming, tedious one. Much like my chalk paint mystery, simply painting bright colors on a white background seemed impossible. We were using tiny foam brushes and experiencing sheer nail polish syndrome. I must have painted six coats of red to get the coverage I needed in many spots. We worked all afternoon and into the evening on that post. On tall ladders, on step stools, butts in faces, and drips of paint on the shoulders of those standing on the floor. The five of us plus Patrick grew some design roots of our own as we gathered around that tree, roots that would later grow into lifetime friendships we'd cherish forever.

In between coats of stripes, we hit up every room of the makeover, asking Donna Marie for direction on what needed to get done. Still feeling a little out of our element, yet eager to please, we all worked together to finish the park, which included a library of children's books, small kid tables and a park bench, the seasonal pantry, the resource area, and the very fun boutique. At one point, Lucy and I found ourselves in an overflow storage room amongst heaps of children's outerwear, clothing, rolling racks, and yoga mats. Donna Marie ran in, pointed in fifty different directions at once, then disappeared. I looked at Lucy and she at me.

"Do you have any idea what she wants us to do with this?" I asked, almost ready to laugh. Lucy was calm and collected as usual.

"I have no idea," she replied. I decided to take charge. This was a mom job if I'd ever seen one. It looked like the boiler room in my basement with hand-me-down clothes from Patti and old ski gear. I quickly created categories. We made piles and hung everything by size and color. I asked Lucy about her design process as I took on the DM persona, and we laughed, sneezed through some old air, and found our Zen for the day in what was supposed to be the yoga room for moms.

We didn't shut down until 8PM. Krista, in her most generous too-young-to-be-our-mom-but-we-love-her-like-a-design-mom way gave us gift cards to use on our own for dinner that night. Eager to continue our girl time, we unanimously agreed to eat at the hotel again because we were tired and extremely grubby, wearing our bright blue DFAD T-shirts, two-day old jeans, and appetites for steak, seafood, and at least one round of wine. As we dragged ourselves into the luxurious entrance of the Raphael, we decided to go straight to dinner. Lucy, however, gave it a second thought.

"I think I'm going to go take a bath. I'll be down in ten minutes," she stated, as if taking a ten-minute bath was something she did on a regular basis. I looked at Nicole, she at me, and we busted out laughing as we watched Lucy casually walk to the elevators. Lucy made everything look easy. Sure enough, she joined us ten minutes later at the head of the table. The same one we met at on Friday night. It was the first time we'd been alone, and boy, did we enjoy a fabulous meal and stories that brought us all to tears, and not my big-girls-don't-cry tears, but the kind that only true friends exchange in once-in-a-lifetime moments. I soaked in my own tub late that night with no regret. I loved these women and would be loyal to them until the day I died.

The next day, I got to wear real clothes and didn't have to re-create my straight hair. I let it find comfort in its natural wave and felt comfy in my J.Crew ensemble of cream silk blouse, Deco-style necklace, dark-rinsed skinny jeans, and heels. It was reveal day, and our time at Operation Breakthrough was coming to an end. As I finished gathering my bag, I thought about how different I felt compared to the previous morning. I wasn't worried about barn doors or chalk paint. I wasn't worried about expectations. While the charity was getting ready for the tarp over the project to be pulled back, I think the real makeover happened the day before between the designers. I can't describe it, but I was as happy as the day I had my 3AM revelation. Something inside me was complete.

The five of us were like a wedding party. Stephanie was the bride; we were her bridesmaids. We had experienced something amazing and formed a bond that could not be broken, and we would walk into the lobby of the Hotel Raphael on our third day with a united confidence that could move mountains—and large tarps hiding the renovated basement of an old JCPenney. I pulled my hotel room door closed behind me and pondered my wedding party analogy while walking to the elevator. That basement was very *old*. The makeover was over $75,000.00 worth of *new*. The time and talent of our team was something *borrowed* that we would insist our bride keep; we did not expect her to give anything back. And last, for our something *blue*, how appropriate that Mark signed off on the 2014 DFAD T-shirts to be printed in the most energetic bright blue you've ever seen.

The elevator doors opened, and I glided through the lobby with joy as I saw Dani and Nicole wearing their CEO best, and not far behind them, Lucy, queen of the tunic and easy breezy cool. As we joined together in front of the complimentary coffee buffet, the elevator doors opposite mine slid open, and out emerged Stephanie, her hair shining like a Kansas City sunrise, wearing a stunning taupe sleeveless Tory Burch dress and pointed toe pumps that made us proud. We gushed over one another as if we'd forgotten that, yes, we were designers, we were fabulous, and combined, we had a style that could own the room.

That day went down in my book as one of the most endearing of my story. When we arrived on site, we walked into the made-over basement with the awe of Dorothy as she opened the old rickety door of Aunt Em's tiny farmhouse into the land of Oz. The tree we'd labored over the day before proudly wore its brightly painted branches. The grass was greener than it had been all weekend, and my barn doors had been decorated with a whimsically handwritten invitation to find a warm winter coat. The paint brushes were put away, the dust was swept away, and Operation Breakthrough was glistening from the inside out. Brett, Howard, and Joe had an interview chair set up, and we were corralled into the yoga room that Lucy and I had organized to get hair and makeup done and enjoy our catered lunch. This really *was* like a wedding day!

Stephanie was up first to sit in front of the cameras. We watched with excitement as the crew worked simultaneously on her hair and makeup while she asked our opinions on cardigan or bare arms. She was beautiful and confident, and ready to share her Operation Breakthrough story. Once she was finished, Mark escorted her out, and she was gone for a long time. We had to keep our volume low and chatted about everything and anything while getting our makeup done. About half an hour later, Stephanie returned.

"How'd it go?" I asked, a little fidgety about my upcoming spotlight.

"Really well," she said as she pulled up a folding chair. "Your makeup looks wonderful!" The tiny Tinkerbell-esque stylist was applying a layer of pink gloss to my lips. It had been years—six to be exact—since I'd had my makeup done.

"Thanks!" I replied, taking a quick look at Lucy, Dani, and Nicole. The makeup was laid on thick, but it would look great on camera. "Who's going next?"

"I'll go," Lucy offered with sultry, smoky eyes. A moment later, Mark popped in and away she went. The interviews took a couple of hours. I went after Lucy and, to my surprise, it was one of the easiest fifteen minutes with Brett and Howard. By that point, they knew me, my personality, what I was passionate about, and what would break me into a cold sweat. So thankfully, they didn't go there! They set me up in a director's chair, told me which camera to talk to, and guided me through some very personal yet easy questions regarding my makeover, my business, and what life was like as a mom of five. I was so impressed with their skill, and I trusted them with all my footage, knowing that they would find the best of my blab to share with the world. Nicole followed me, and Dani went last.

We all became a bit antsy to get out of the yoga room. It seemed like everyone on the crew had wandered in and out over the last couple of hours, and I thought about how much time guests had to wait backstage during morning shows, talk shows, and late-night television. My deep thought daydream was interrupted when Dani returned to the room with tears in her eyes.

"What's wrong?" we all asked, hoping it was nothing.

"You're never going to believe what happened just now!" she smiled as she wiped her cheek. I had no idea. But emotions were running rampant in the basement those last couple of days, so nothing would have surprised me. We gathered in closer.

"You know how everyone was watching us from behind the camera?" We nodded. "Well, Donna Marie was standing next to Mark (who we hadn't seen since the day before) and in the middle of my interview I noticed that she'd walked away, returning with a Kleenex. I assumed she was moved by the story of the sisters and all these single moms, so I didn't think much of it." She had our full attention. "When I finished my interview, we had a minute while Mark and

Brett went over a few things for the reveal. Donna Marie came over and told me how moved she was by the Operation Breakthrough story and how wonderful DFAD is, but do you know why she was teary-eyed?" The four of us leaned in a little closer still, a couple of us expressing our *why* out loud as Dani continued. "She told me that the five of us spoke *so* highly of each other that she couldn't believe that we just met this weekend." Our eyes widened in shock as she went on. "She teared up even as she was talking to me and told me that she'd never seen women bond like this and that she was honored to be part of our weekend."

"She really said that?" I asked, feeling warm and fuzzy inside. *This makeover process really can do a number on you,* I thought, as I ran a fast play of all the emotions I'd been through in the last couple of weeks.

"Wow," Stephanie glowed with satisfaction and relief. I could tell that we all felt the same way. "That's pretty powerful. And here we were, all so worried about meeting up to her expectations."

"I know," Dani said. "She was really sweet about the whole thing." More unanimous nods. If Donna Marie had been standing there with us, we would have smothered her in design love and appreciation. Some of my favorite people over the years were the ones who intimidated me at first or seemed hard to get to know. But once I got past the first layer, they became some of my most loyal friends. I viewed our glamorous director in this way. She was from California, she was an artist, she was the boss, and she was Mark's friend. I think we let those surface facts get to us along with our wet paint. But I was grateful for the DM dynamic. She was the catalyst that brought our vulnerability to the surface over the weekend. Big projects are hard. Bringing a bunch of strangers together and guiding their work is even harder. This woman survived this difficult task, which I'd compare to air travel with five kids under four in my mom book, and for that, she deserved a gold medal of honor in DFAD history.

That afternoon, we watched as Mark, Krista, and Stephanie pulled back that giant tarp and the Sisters, staff, and a select group of moms with their young children saw their new space for the first time. Local newspapers and news crews joined Brett, Howard, and Joe, and we experienced the power of giving from the heart.

Our "wrap party" was held on the second floor of a local restaurant near the hotel. The entire group, along with spouses and some special DFAD alumni, added even more personality to our night. HGTV's design star Jennifer Bertrand graced us with her signature black-rimmed glasses, platinum hair, and gut-busting humor. Local designer Lisa Schmitz added even more contagious laughter to the evening. Our fourth and final night together was much different from the first. We laughed, we cried, and we marveled at what can happen when people come together as one. We clinked glasses during multiple toasts, shared one large table, and ate cake.

There was DM bonding at the bar, the mastering of the perfect star-quality selfie (thanks to Mr. Brunetz himself), and more rounds of hugs. As our celebration came to an end, Brett and Howard pulled the five of us in close for a special moment. Brett's blue eyes glistened in the dim light, and Howard wore an inspired smile.

"I have something to tell you," Brett began. "In all the years I've been in the film industry, I have NEVER seen THIS (he moved his hands in a big circle in front of us) happen." We thanked him as he went on. "We are not sure what exactly took place last night, but something changed. We all see it. And I'm going to say something that I want you to think about, because I am *very* serious. Think about what you want to do next. The five of you together are a Dream Team, and you can do anything from here." We were once again moved to tears, and that concluded our night. We moved back to the hotel bar, and while it was only after midnight, it felt as though it was 3AM. We were all exhausted. Our night ended with one more walk through the beautiful lobby of the hotel as we made our way to the elevators, back to our rooms, and back to real life.

CHAPTER 28

BUYING AND SELLING

"Meet Tom and Hollie. They live in a beautiful estate home in the prominent city of Bloomfield Hills, Michigan. They've hired award-winning and top-producing real estate agent, Cindy Kahn, in hopes of selling their million-dollar-plus property and buying a smaller home that will fit their large family of seven. They've given Cindy a tall order, as they'd like to stay within the same school district, gain as much square footage as possible without sacrificing the quality they are accustomed to, have a three-car garage, lots of storage space, a small yard requiring little maintenance, and a safe neighborhood for their elementary-school-aged children to grow up in..." I daydreamed the voiceover as I sat in the middle of my master bedroom separating clean clothes into piles during another episode on HGTV. I couldn't believe that just days before, I was dining with one of the network's prized stars, and now I was back to the pile. On this day, however, it was my pile of peace, the end of my rainbow, and circling around me were my five munchkins and little Otto.

I came home from Kansas City with a new sense of calm. It was like the good, happy hormonal calm I had when Natalie and Kate were born. Life had handed me more than I could humanly handle, but by that point I was extremely seasoned in overwhelmed "momness," and with my big design project complete, I could focus on my family. I

312 · HOLLIE GYARMATI

decided not to take design clients until the first of the year so I could enjoy the simplicity of being the homemaker. Even though I was still making over the house every week for strangers to walk through, I no longer cared. We'd dropped the price to the "sweet spot" Cindy had mentioned months earlier, and now that we could squeak by, I decided to let it go. I welcomed every realtor call and showing as if it were a gift to march my family through "house-showing clean." For the first time in years, I had a clean house.

While I was making over spaces, Tom was on a mission to find every property in Bloomfield Hills that could possibly work. I snubbed my nose at every house he had in mind, and he gave me the "stop being ridiculous" look whenever I'd flash my laptop his way. My houses were too small, too old, needed major renovations and, in my frugal style, ones that we could pay cash for to take a breather on a mortgage. For a long time, I had asked him to consider a different city, but I resolved to staying in our school district for the kids. I thought I could move anywhere and be happy, however after many piles of laundry and trips to Costco or the post office (where they know me by name), I realized I was no longer a small-town girl. I had been here for fifteen years. Bloomfield Hills was my home, and I was ready to live as modestly as I needed to in order to keep my roots here. I envisioned a nice 1950s two-story colonial with four bedrooms and a finished basement. I could make anything work. I pictured my kids lined up to use the bathroom and double bunk beds. It made me smile.

"I can't end up in anything built before 1980," Tom griped as we sat at the kitchen island with our laptops one evening. He was so closed-minded on this topic. "It's not that they are too small, which they are, it's that they need massive renovations, and if they don't, they will. And the nicer ones within our budget are almost the same price as larger homes built in the 90s. It's a joke." I ignored him as I continued to scroll through listings. He had a valid point, and I thought about all the Sunday Open Houses we'd toured and the smell factor alone. From must and mildew to stale pantry and cat urine, we'd encountered our worst fears in homes that looked perfectly normal on the outside. I added "odorless" to my wish list for Cindy.

"Your just too picky," I retorted as I envisioned my spouse renting a storage unit to stash his collection of childhood, bachelor pad, and deceased father's keepsakes. That was my wildcard. I had cleaned out every square inch of our home over the last year, and we *still* had a lot of "stuff." He'd just have to figure it out. At least this move, when it happened, would be normal. We'd have sixty to ninety days to pack. And when we ended up in my small colonial, he'd have to sell off all that "stuff."

"I want you to look at this house with an open mind," he perked up as he opened his new case.

"Okay" I agreed, spinning in my seat and resting my feet on the side of his counter stool.

"I've been watching this for months. It's in the neighborhood we love, it's big, but in our range," he began the slideshow. He knew I loved this neighborhood. The houses were big but not outrageous, nestled close together, and situated close to our old starter home near the lake I used to jog around. I watched the slideshow of dated rooms. They were empty, had lots of windows, and mostly white walls. There was also a finished basement. It was a brick two-story with double bay windows flanking the front door and a side-facing three-car garage attached to the right. The roof was tall, had black shingles, and looked European in style. It was nice. I wasn't excited because I knew it was out of our budget.

"Yeah. It's a beautiful home, but it's still big and comes with a big price," I stated with wifely authority.

"I'd really like to see it in person. It's been on the market for as long as ours; they've dropped the price a few times, it's November, and they are probably willing to make a deal." I gave him a "have at it" look and closed my laptop as well as the topic of house hunting for the night.

Oh-blah-dee. Oh-blah-dah. Life went on for the next couple of weeks. I made breakfast, packed lunches, sent kids off on the bus, did laundry, ran errands, cleaned, staged, and vacated for a few more showings. One group of businessmen from overseas supposedly had a lot of interest, but I'd learned to go Jerry Maguire before getting my hopes up at that point. I'd now prepped for over seventy-seven showings in the last year and a half. At least fifteen were second- or third-time showings, and for one family, there were four. Whatever the case, I rolled with it, keeping my mind focused on the day-to-day routine.

Tom *did* in fact inquire about his dream house, but to his disappointment, Cindy returned his call to tell him that it had been sold. I guess it just wasn't meant to be. I kept my mouth shut and turned my attention to my latest adoration, becoming the godmother to Todd and Claudia's number six, Isaac Michael. He was born in September, and the first time I snuggled him in my arms Claudia asked if I would do them the honor. I was delighted, and gladly accepted the lifelong responsibility to guide this little guy in our faith. The Zarotney-Gyarmati get-togethers had stood the test of time, and our kid count was now eleven between the two families. They had become our family and becoming godparents (Tom got the girl a couple of years back) sealed the deal.

It was the Friday before Thanksgiving, and I was at the Christian Bookstore purchasing a Catholic Bible for my little guy. It was taking a while longer than normal because the kid at the register was new. I wasn't rushed for time but found it incredibly difficult to get excited about shelves stocked with Precious Moments, Veggie Tales, and little painted plaques when Nordstrom Rack was in the adjacent corner of the plaza. I stood looking out the front window, calculating the time it would take to make a fast run through the shoe department, but did not give into temptation. Just then, my phone vibrated in my J.Crew leather tote. I loved this bag but also appreciated my mom's old lady purses with their compartments in moments like this.

Fumbling through receipts, gloves, cosmetics, and Trident, I found my mobile and slid the answer icon. "Hello," I said, knowing it was Tom. I turned to supervise the kid hunched over the embossing machine.

"Are you sitting down?" he asked in his good news voice.

"No. I'm in a store. What's up?" I said. I hoped this kid didn't mess up my Bible.

"Cindy just called me. Those men from out of town are making an offer! She'll have it by the end of the day!" My heart skipped a beat. We hadn't had a *real* offer in months. I was doubtful.

"Really? I don't even WANT to get excited. But I'm EXCITED!" I whispered, now turning back to the Rack. I should go try on shoes. I should not.

"I know. Me too," he said in a low voice. I could tell he was walking down a hallway at the office. "Ok, well, I'll let you go, I just wanted to tell you!"

"Ok, Thanks! Love you, bye," I said, sliding "end call" before he could respond. I am horrible that way. An offer! I couldn't believe it! I envisioned how this could all play out. We would be house shopping for Christmas, packing boxes instead of wrapping them. It would be a dream come true! I had no idea where we would live, but just the idea of this finally materializing was thrilling.

"Ma'am, you're all set," the young teen boy's voice broke my thought.

"Oh! Thank you," I smiled as I walked back to the register. I opened the box to find Isaac's name neatly embossed in gold leaf three quarters of the way down the cover. Spelling correct. Done deal. I slid it back into the box and left the store, walking straight for my minivan, not even glancing at Nordstrom. I didn't have time for shoes. I had to start packing.

On Sunday afternoon, I held my Godson in my arms at Our Lady of Good Council, then proceeded with Tom and the kids a mile south to Todd and Claudia's one-hundred-year-old farmhouse for an early dinner with extended family. It would be an understatement to say that Tom and I were a little distracted. On Friday night, the real offer came through, we countered, and the game began. We were optimistic about it all, and the real question was, where would we go should this offer go through? Cindy seemed confident that it was a done deal, and we had her walk us through a house the day before just for kicks. We hated it. It had the smell. It needed work. There weren't enough bedrooms. and there wasn't one thing about it that felt like "us." As we stood in the kitchen with a glass of wine after dinner, Tom took a call from Cindy. There were at least six adults gathered around the granite island, and the basement was rumbling with kids underfoot. Tom is really good at taking phone calls in a crowd. I can't hear a thing, so I was glad she was calling him. He sounded surprised and locked eyes with me as he was listening to her. Something had changed.

"I can't believe it," he smiled enthusiastically. What couldn't he believe? "Well, we are about forty minutes from home right now and at a family baptism. Can tomorrow work?" Ugh! The suspense was killing me! His blue eyes were bright. "Oh," he continued. She was like a bloodhound. I loved her. What was she chasing? He finally held his iPhone up and whispered, "The house I love—*the deal fell through*! It's open today. Huge price drop. Multiple offers. She said if we want a shot at it, we have to meet her in forty-five minutes. Can we do it?" My heart skipped a beat. This house, at a lower price, was in our range, yet twice as nice (I thought) as anything else on the market! Would Claudia mind? I was the Godmother! But she would be the first person to tell me to go. She'd held my hand through the phone every Wednesday afternoon for ten years!

"Let me ask Claudia," I whispered, and in a split second, I pulled her away from the kitchen sink, debriefed her, and got the blessing to get our butts out of there! I gave Tom the thumbs-up and we were on our way!

Exactly forty-five minutes later, we were parked in the driveway of my husband's dream house. Cindy arrived five minutes later, and we gave the kids the "best behavior" pep talk and followed her along the paver sidewalk to the front porch. The house was dark, and Cindy had an excitement in her voice I hadn't heard in over a year. Well, before two days ago, but Tom got it from her on Friday. As we discovered, realtors—the really good ones—lay low until the game is on. And once it is, they are there for you every step of the way. It took us a while to understand this approach, but once we did, we appreciated the expertise we were investing in. Cindy was just as busy closing deals with other clients as she was with us. And finally, our turn had finally arrived.

"I left a family dinner to get here. That's how strongly I feel about this house for you," she confided as she opened the lockbox on the front door. I know Tom's tail was wagging with gratitude. I have to admit, I was intrigued yet guarded as she pulled the key out of the box and slid it into the keyhole. After quick turn, she squeezed the handle and the heavy oak door opened into the foyer. We followed her in as she turned on the lights. It was at least 6:30, and it was dark outside. The worst time of the day to look at a house.

A second later, the eight of us were standing in the large foyer with our coats on. I looked down at the marble floor. It was 1990 peaches and cream. I could get over it. Above my head was a crystal chandelier that was a quarter of the size of the seventy-two-inch diameter brass, dust-covered beauty on Pine Gate. I loved it. I took a quick panoramic of my surroundings from left to right. Nice oak paneled library with bay window in the front. Step down into formal living room. Amazing split sixty-inch-wide staircase straight ahead with a fifteen-foot wall of windows from upstairs to down overlooking the backyard. It looked like something out of the *Frozen* castle, and I pictured the girls turning in circles on the landing. On the other side was another step down into a small family room with a double-sided fireplace shared with the kitchen, and to my right was a hallway to the garage and a formal dining room with another chandelier, hardwood floors, and a bay window overlooking the front walk. A dining room in the front of the house! I'd always wanted one, and I envisioned my design projects spread out on the table.

I looked at Tom and he at me. Our eyes met over the five little faces standing patiently in their socks and winter coats in between us, and we felt it. *This was our home.* I can't explain the overwhelming sense of peace I had in that moment, but I immersed myself in it while Cindy told us the story.

"They had a done deal. This couple from Jersey bought the house, they had the inspection, the closing scheduled, and wouldn't you know they noticed the homestead property tax and flipped out," she explained. "They backed out of the whole deal, the homeowners are beside themselves because they want to be done with this whole thing, and they dropped the price over six figures this morning, holding an Open House. They are DONE," she took a breath as we took note. "So, do you have any idea what a steal this is? In THIS neighborhood? They've received over ten offers today. It's a good thing I go way back with this realtor or they wouldn't have waited for this showing." My stomach turned. I looked at my husband, he looked at me, and we both looked at Cindy. We were speechless. "Let's take a quick look," she said, as she turned on the library lights.

We followed her through the 11x12-ish room, which would be Tom's office, admiring the hardwood floor and beautiful paneled walls. It was timeless. There was a wood pocket door on the west wall that led through a cute wet bar with a beautiful full-length window. Through the door was a step down into the formal living room. There was a fireplace on the south wall, and it was surrounded by windows. I would turn it into our family room.

"Isn't this a great space?" our realtor asked, and in coded marital cool, we just smiled. It's like buying a car. We never gave our opinions openly, even with Cindy, and had to pray the kids' mouths shut. Usually a McDonald's drive-thru in exchange for silence bribe did the trick. We followed the leader back through the foyer kiddy-corner into my coveted dining room, through a butler's pantry, hallway, and into the kitchen. It was 1990s white. It wasn't state of the art, but it was void of wallpaper, wallpaper borders, dark green marble counter tops, and it was filled with more beautiful windows as it opened into a cozy breakfast nook, the fireplace, and a step down to the small family room, which would be our hearth room. It was much smaller than Pine Gate, and I could see my family sitting around the table every night sharing our "highs and lows."

"This would work for you, right?" our realtor continued, with childlike excitement. She sensed our love of the home even through our silence. We toured the upstairs next. I adored the staircase. Not only was it wide and glamorous with its three-story windows, but there was only one set in the entire house. No more of this double staircase baloney! Cleaning four sets of oversized stairs had been exhausting over the past seven years; this would be a piece of cake! The master suite felt like a hotel room. It had a lot of character, a beautiful bathroom that overlooked the street, his and hers vanities on opposite sides of the room (no more man clutter), and a nice closet for the two of us to share, complete with more full-length windows—four to be exact. The north side was a dream come true for the kids. The front room featured the bay window that sat over the dining room, a Jack-and-Jill bathroom with a sweet gable-roofed ceiling running its length, a tiny little room for the water closet and another for the shower. It felt like we were in a Swiss chalet.

Emma's and Isabelle's room was a little bigger, boasting a classic dormer window to the north and a sizable walk-in closet. Noah would have his own suite, complete with bathroom, that overlooked the backyard which, as we dreamed, was very small yet looked like it came right out of a storybook. It was filled with mature pines, oaks, and maples. There was a beautiful pond with a waterfall that dropped into a larger body of water and ran under a large custom-built gazebo that came complete with a screened-in door.

As I walked through each room I didn't wonder if this could work. I *knew* it would work. I knew it was our home. I knew it was meant to be. The kids were starting to chatter, and Tom and I were nudging each other as we walked back down the staircase to the basement. When we got to the bottom, there was a tiled landing area with a large, heavy wooden door, complete with a lock, that opened into the finished basement. As Cindy pulled it open, I wondered if this lower level was soundproof. I imagined our small, black piano nestled under the stairs and wondered if my rendition of Fur Elise would echo up to the bedrooms. She reached to the left and turned on the lights. And there, opposite a custom oak wet bar and nubby Berber, was Switzerland. Seriously, it was a vintage wall mural of the Swiss Alps. The colors were faded, and it had a harvest gold and olive tint to it, so I assumed the actual photo had been taken in the late 60s or 70s. It was an obvious design trick to tackle a tight entrance. Beyond the mountains was a classic living area, bathroom, and what was staged as a guest bedroom, although I'd never let anyone sleep down there without an emergency egress. The room would make the perfect office.

We scoped out the rest of the basement, which was three quarters storage with one large room on the north and one on the south side. His and Hers. Perfect. My stuff could sit nicely on my side, and his could collect on his side. The kids could have the run of the lower level, and I could lock the door if it got overwhelmingly messy. As I was busy already living in my new home, we followed Cindy back up to the foyer. The entire house was lit up, and it felt even darker outside just fifteen minutes later. Tom and I exchanged another "We know this is it" look, and Cindy said, "What do you want to do? If you are interested, we have to act tonight because it will be gone tomorrow." (No pressure.) The three of us knew exactly what needed to happen and that it would take a miracle to pull it off. My eyes filled with tears as I stood in "our" foyer surrounded by our future without the means to make it happen.

"This is our house." There. I said what we were all thinking out loud as a giant tear dripped down my cheek. Tom's eyes watered up. Cindy's eyes watered up. We had been through so much and couldn't believe that this moment was here. Tom was beaming; I think he was experiencing his own male version of hormone happy because he was confident, calm, collected, and added, "This IS it. There is nothing like it for this price. This is unbelievable."

"There is nothing, you're right. And this deal on your house *is* happening with one more signature," Cindy said, still caught up in the emotion of it all. "We need to put down a deposit, and I want you to send them a personal email sharing your story. This owner can sell to whomever they want at this point, and you need to set yourselves apart from the rest."

We both agreed and parted with our realtor, who confided that she was going to pray that this worked out and told us to do whatever Catholic rituals we could think of to ask for help from the Heavens. On the way out, we circled through the cozy neighborhood. It was private. There was only one entrance. There were cul-de-sacs. Beautiful architecture. Nice landscaping. And our home looked like a perfectly balanced manor in the French countryside. It was more than we could ever have dreamed of, and all we could do was pray.

Tom stayed up until well after 1AM that night composing our email. It was professional. It was honest. It told this homeowner all about our big house, big family, and big financial loss over the last seven years. It shared our dream of raising our children in Bloomfield Hills, our commitment to our school, and our community. It was perfect. Now it was time to pray some more. And wait.

Monday came and went and was filled with more ups and downs than a game of Chutes and Ladders. The buyers of our house wanted us to drop the price. We did. Then they wanted us to drop it again. We fearfully did not. Then they demanded a fast closing and wanted us out before Christmas. We even *more* fearfully, especially on my end, agreed. I couldn't believe that we could very possibly be pulling off another big move, and we weren't even positive as to where we were moving *to*. I don't think either of us ate that day. Tom was at work and I plugged along with my regular routine. But it was like waiting for a twin delivery. We just wanted the answers out, and we wanted everything to be okay. IMMEDIATELY!

Tuesday followed suit, and I was emotionally exhausted from answering phone calls detailing the latest request from the buyers and the lack of communication from the owners of what was hopefully our new house. The kids were all invited to an after-school play date at a new friend's house, and as much as I despise the pick-up line (bus rules forever), I loaded them up in the late November chill to get to the host's house on time. It turned out that the nice family who looked at our house almost a year ago, the ones who found Tom's master sink "under construction," ended up in a beautiful home over by Cranbrook. We'd met them at school and were happy to get together for indoor basketball and snacks.

I decided to stay for the play date so I could help out this brave new mom friend. There were at least twelve children running around, and there were snacks to make, which kept my mind off buying and selling. I sliced apples, spread cream cheese on mini bagels, and set up crafts for almost two hours. It was a little nuts. I am not a natural kid-lover. It's horrible, I know, but mine alone are enough. This mom put me to shame with her ever-joyful smile and endless patience for other people's offspring. I was happy when pick-up time arrived.

"Gyarmati kids, it's time to clean up!" I belted out over the railing. Everyone but my own looked up at me in shock. I'd gotten louder than the average mom over the years. When I turned around, there were the cutest little toddlers I'd ever seen running around the oversized island. A little preschooler with big blue eyes and a thick head of dishwater blond hair was chasing her baby brother. He had big brown eyes, a matching crop, and looked much too young to be running as fast as he was. He had stolen some glue sticks off the table, and his mom had joined his sister in the chase. She was younger than I, by at least three

to five years, and had thick blonde hair like her babies, except hers
was brighter and naturally curly. Ringlet curly. She had eyes like her
daughter and was in a tizzy over her sprinters.

"Nate!" she yelled. "Give me that glue stick right now!" I liked this
mom. She had lungs like mine. Nate zipped around the corner, and I
snatched up his cute little diapered butt and handed him to her.

"Oh, thank you so much," she greeted with a sigh of relief. "I'm
Sara. I don't think we've met."

"Hi, Hollie Gyarmati. Who are you picking up?" I asked, hoping it
was someone my kids were friends with.

"Jonny and Maddy. They are in Shaftner's class," she smiled, as
her mini-me disappeared into the formal dining room.

"They are with my youngest, Natalie and Kate," I said, smiling
back. Now their names were familiar. Jonny was Kate's "boyfriend,"
per her twin, and she never denied the label. Kate was my sensitive
one; if she was friends with a boy, he was a great kid. This opened up
the usual mom chatter, and I quickly forgot about my crew as I talked
with my new friend about twins, more babies, being at home full-time,
and growing up outside of Bloomfield Hills. I liked Sara. She was my
kind. I did all this while chasing Olivia and Nate around the kitchen
and lounge area by the balcony.

"What area of Bloomfield Hills do you live in?" I finally asked out
of curiosity. I knew every neighborhood, side street, dead end, and
most of all, For Sale sign in the city.

"We live in the neighborhood behind Target," she said, "My house
is a mess; we'll need a designer when these little rascals get into
school." She lived in the same neighborhood our new house was in!
My tummy knotted up as I realized that we had no idea if it would
actually be our house. We were still waiting for one signature from
our buyers and the "Yes, we accept your offer" communication from
the seller. I wanted to scream. Instead, I stood at the island wishing I
could share more details about who I was and how I wish I had time

for new friends. I finally responded to her "How about you?" response, which I heard in the background of my frustration.

"We live off of Woodward and Long Lake. We'll have to get together sometime," I said in a chipper voice, genuinely meaning it. She agreed as she disappeared into the expansive estate to round up her four under five. My kids were lined up in the foyer (proud mom moment), fully dressed, with backpacks on, and we were off to return to the Big House and all the uncertainty dwelling within it.

That evening, Tom called me on his way home from work. I stepped into my office, closed the door behind me, and sat on the step stool. It had been a couple of hours since I'd heard from him, and I knew that tensions were high with our buyers. There was still no word from the sellers, and Cindy as well as her assistant had been on the phone all day trying to line up both deals. It was just like us to end up in some crazy predicament that we had no control over.

This time, he didn't ask if I was sitting. I could hear that he was driving, and I could sense the excitement in his voice. I braced myself. Was this it?

"I just got off a call with Cindy and you are NEVER going to believe this!" he exclaimed. My pulse quickened, and I said nothing. He knew what I was feeling.

"She said, 'Tooommmm…are you ready for this? The sellers finally came forward and they not only want to take your offer, but they said that the moment they read your letter, they knew you were the family they wanted to live in their home. It's yours! *And,* your buyers have also agreed to the finalities of this entire deal; both parties want to close in two weeks!' Can you believe it?"

"This is *real?*" I squealed, joining his party. The new house was more than we could have dreamed of. Everything about it—the location, the architecture, the floor plan. And there wasn't even a *smell!* "This is too good to be true! Is this really happening? Can we tell the kids?"

"Get them together, and I'll tell them on speaker!"

Two minutes later, I had all the kids standing eagerly around me, and I was holding my finger to my lips signaling them to be very quiet to hear what Dad had to say.

"Kids? Is everyone there?" Tom asked. I could hardly keep a straight face. My palms were sweaty, and I felt like I could sprint around the house faster than the dog.

"YES!" they yelled.

"Remember the house we looked at with Cindy on Sunday night?" he prepped in his Dad voice.

"Yeessss," they answered in their "What's coming?" voices.

"We are buying that house and selling this house to the nice guys from Japan."

In that moment, it was pointless to try to communicate with my spouse. I left the speaker on but directed my full attention to the five beautiful children standing around me. Actually, they were no longer standing. They were jumping, they were screaming, they were cheering so loudly you could have heard them all the way to Woodward Avenue. I soaked in their joy and was amazed at their reactions. They were thrilled about the new house, but what they were *more* excited about was the simple fact that it was over! They were singing praises of gratitude that we sold the house! That we no longer were being held captive by financial woes and an impossible standard of living. That we could move forward with our lives and just *be*...without hardship.

Noah fell to his knees and threw his hands up in the air, yelling, "Thank you God!" I couldn't believe the emotions dancing around me. Emma began crying, my poor dear, my oldest, who had been my right hand over the past couple of years. She was always there, humble and kind, acting on my every need. She'd taken the brunt of sacrificial nine-year-old pleasures, and I promised her over and over that once we sold the house, she could start going to parties again and participating in after school activities. She was an angel.

326 · HOLLIE GYARMATI

Isabelle followed her lead, her giant blue eyes glazed over as she wrapped her arms around my waist. Natalie and Kate were jumping up and down, I think releasing the excitement of the new house dreams for their group. Even Otto was running in circles; I think he knew all those bedtime prayers had finally paid off. Contest. Job. House. Each answered in bigger and better ways than we could have possibly imagined.

CHAPTER 29

HEAVEN IS A PLACE ON EARTH

On December 12, 2014, Tom and I walked into the Max Brook real estate office in Bloomfield Hills ready to close on our new home. It would be the final step in our new beginning, and the entire day had been surreal. My husband was on a Boeing 747 at 8:30 that morning. I was rushing the kids through what would normally be the busiest and most stressful part of my day—getting them out to the bus stop on time without mishaps or meltdowns. On this day, I didn't care so much about the kid details (with the exception of getting them out on time). Twenty minutes after they stepped onto the bus, I bravely drove to Birmingham to close on the Pine Gate Big House all by myself. It was the biggest financial transaction I'd ever tackled on my own, but with Tom's thorough business skills and attention to detail, he made it "closing on your estate for dummies" style, and Cindy held my hand through the endless required signatures.

I was exhausted. Tom had traveled each of the two weeks leading up to the closing, which left me once again packing most of the house on my own (with the exception of the garage and basement storage). I was grateful for any help that came my way which, to no surprise came from those with the names Patricia, Patti, and Patsy. I made it without drugs. Without panic attacks or mommy dearest moments.

Moving my family away from the home that had owned us for almost a decade was the greatest gift I could have received that December.

Tom got back into town just in time for the new house closing. We were on time for our meeting, maybe even a little early. A receptionist escorted us to the conference room, which was situated in the center of the new office building. It was decorated in modern whites and ebony woods with bright abstracts of Detroit on the wall.

"You may have a seat in here; Melanie will be with you shortly," she said. We entered the room, surprised to see a nice older couple already sitting at the conference table. The sellers. He had white hair and was dressed in business casual, wearing khakis, a button-down, and a sport coat. He looked friendly, like the kind of gentleman I'd chat with in line at Costco and leave feeling happy. She was sitting up straight with a slightly stern expression, her thick brown hair cropped slightly over her earlobes. She well dressed, complete with heavy jewelry and a very large, round diamond wedding ring. She matched from head to toe, and had she been in line behind me at Costco, I might have kept to myself for no other reason than mild intimidation by her Bloomfield Hills glam. I felt my pulse quicken. Her husband stood up as soon as we walked in and started introductions while he made his way around the table.

"Hello, I'm Franz Boos, and this is my wife Alice," he smiled, shaking Tom's hand.

"It's nice to meet you, sir. I'm Tom, and this is my wife, Hollie."

"Ahhhh, I thought you brought your young girlfriend..." Franz replied as we embraced in a friendly handshake. He was good at this; Tom and I both laughed as we sat down. Franz had a heavy European accent. I couldn't quite make it out; maybe German? It was familiar and sweet. We greeted Alice as we sat down, and she smiled as she said "Hello," keeping her perfect posture. Her accent matched. She almost sounded like it would be more natural for her to sing as she went up in pitch with her "H." I could tell that she was naturally loud, very much like me. I have to make a conscious effort to speak quietly, and I think that Alice was doing the same. Our chairs had castors, and I gently pulled myself in as Tom and Franz continued their conversation. They confirmed that they were, in fact, the original owners of our dream house. They had raised their three children there through both high-school and college, and had downsized a few years earlier, renting the home for about a year before it went on the market.

They took turns sharing their story, and I was overwhelmed with a sense of comfort with and familiarity in their presence. It was like having a combination of Grandma, Papa, and Tom's parents sitting across from us. And it wasn't just their accent; it was their Euro way. I can't really explain it, but this generation has a work ethic and sense of integrity that Tom and I very much respect; it ran through our Hungarian-Belgian gene pool. I nudged my husband's foot with mine from under the table. He looked at me and I at him. Franz and Alice paused as they noticed our spousal exchange. We smirked.

"Are you thinking what I'm thinking?" he asked me quietly.

"Do you feel like you're sitting here with your parents?" I smiled, as I felt my cheeks flushing with emotion. He nodded, his eyes tearing up as well. I wasn't sure if we were really having a moment or were both exhausted beyond measure. He turned back to Franz and Alice.

"I'm sorry, we are just taken with your accent; it reminds us of my parents, who were from Hungary and Hollie's grandparents, who were Belgian." They both smiled. I envisioned Tom's dad sitting there with us. When we were faced with many of our impossible decisions over the last few years, we often missed him and wondered aloud what he'd say if he were there.

"We are Swiss. Born and raised in Switzerland," Alice proudly announced. The mural in the basement! Then she looked at me as I fought back my emotions. These were good people; I could feel it. "Hollie, is it true that you have twins?"

"We have two sets of twins, plus one in-between." Alice promptly pushed back in her conference chair, stood up, walked around the table, and embraced me in the biggest hug I'd ever received from someone who knew nothing about me. Obviously, motherhood qualified? I wasn't sure, but she hugged me hard, and as she pulled away, she had her own tears streaming down her cheeks. This was more than motherhood.

As she got situated back on her side of the conference table, I looked at Tom and Franz. They were having this moment with us. "We knew that you were the family we wanted to live in our home the moment we read your letter," Alice confided. That was all I needed to hear before I officially needed a Kleenex.

"I am an engineer and parts supplier. We went through the crash in '08 and understand what you must have experienced as an eliminated dealer," Franz added. Our realtors were rounding the corner with the young lady from the title company trailing behind. What they expected to be a normal meeting was anything but. As Cindy and Melanie joined us, we all began to discuss our difficult journeys through the Michigan economic struggle and the stress of selling our homes, a process that took well over a year for both parties. After five minutes of connecting the dots on how miraculous this was, we were all reaching for tissues instead of our pens, and the poor title company girl was sitting at the head of the table wondering if she'd been placed in a therapy session by accident.

"In the twenty-five years I've been selling real-estate, I've never had a family or story touch me like this," Cindy said with a sniffle. "This is absolutely the most wonderful family, Melanie, and after everything they've gone through, I can't think of a more deserving one to buy this home." Melanie, whose picture is plastered on every shopping cart at the Kroger across the street and whose middle name is "SOLD" blotted her eyes, careful to not smear her liner.

"I feel like I'm sitting in the middle of a Hallmark Hall of Fame movie," she blubbered. "And just twelve days before Christmas!" Melanie was right. It was only twelve days before Christmas. I thought I'd figured out years ago not to put God in a box. Not to just ask for what we needed to get by, but to pray for bigger things. To pray for the dream. This was more than a dream. We were getting the dream house and with it this wonderful couple who would "adopt" our family as their own.

"Our house is always happy," Alice said, as we gained composure. "Even on the gloomiest days it is bright, and Tom and Hollie, it is filled with *love*." Really? Two weeks prior, I was worried about house smell and old kitchen grout, and here I was getting the keys to a new home filled with love. I noticed Alice's contemporary cross situated neatly on her chest. They were Catholic. We were Catholic. "And today, you are my new son and daughter-in-law, and I now have twelve grandchildren instead of seven." And she meant every word of it. That closing went down in the books as the most inspirational meeting between two Jewish realtors, two Catholic families, and one single twenty-something from the title company, who was moved either to tears by our happy ending or to find a new career.

The movers came one week later to Pine Gate Drive. By then, I had every room in the house boxed up, the Salvation Army donation bins full, and a pile of garbage bags by the driveway that looked like...well...like we were moving. It took three full days, and I only had one meltdown when my husband decided that the Direct TV guy should come on moving day, trumping his supervision and packing of the basement and garage. I had Big Bill and his three guys standing at Pine Gate amidst the piles of man stuff counting on me to know how I wanted them to move it. When I got Tom on the phone, he said, "They said they'd pack it," and Big Bill said, "We are not packing it," I broke into a little Hollie Foss sweat and started crying. Big Bill decided, after three days with me by his side, that I needed a hug, and I let him provide it. They then proceeded to move the big stuff, leaving the piles for the love of my life, who was in that garage until...wait for it...3AM.

He redeemed himself when I realized that we could not live without the Disney channel for a day and thanked him for his attention to detail on the TV matter. He also stepped up to the plate that weekend when I decided to take an Ambien at 1:30AM after a busy day on the job, then realized that I left my bite guard in the bathroom. At the old house. Somewhere in the master bathroom. He knew I couldn't sleep without it (or drive on drugs), and reluctantly got out of bed at the new house, took the dog, and drove to the old house to find it. He ended up getting pulled over for driving through a yellow light. When the nice officer asked him what he was doing out at 2AM, Tom said, "You wouldn't believe me if I told you."

"Try me," the kind patrolman offered. And Tom gave him the story.

"Welcome back to Bloomfield Township," the officer replied with a smirk, and sent him on his way.

Never a dull moment.

My favorite moving day moment: I was standing on the front porch, directing furniture up the steps, and I heard a mom yelling, "Jonny, Maddy! Get back in here. You need your coats on before you can ride your bikes!" (it was unseasonably warm). Wouldn't you know, I squinted across the cul-de-sac and saw two cute little twins running back up to their curly-blonde bombshell mom. I grinned, and my heart skipped another beat at the realization that we'd moved in next to my new mom friend, Sara, who agreed upon my first shout-out over the grassy island in between our driveways that we were the luckiest moms in Bloomfield Hills. It was an encore happy ending! First, we meet the stand-in for the in-laws I'd missed so much over the years, and now the Betty Rubble I'd always dreamed of having in my life was only fifty steps from my front door.

* * *

When I strutted through the terminal in Detroit that morning, skinny latte in hand, pulling my tiny black carry-on with the designer bag hitching a ride, I looked like the woman I'd always wanted to be. And everyone thought I *was* her: the successful interior designer with almost two decades of high-profile clients in her portfolio, happily married to an automotive exec, mom to a couple of kids with a well-paid nanny at home who kept the pace while she was traveling the country. My on-lookers had no idea that I was actually flash mobbing to Alicia Keys in my head and would later be having secret conversations with St. Peter about walking through fire and the amazing grace that I'd been granted in the last six months. A full day of travel had brought me to the stuffy back seat of a yellow cab almost 2,000 miles from a story I kept hidden deep in my heart. "I don't deserve this much of a happy ending," I thought, as I pondered the new house, the closing, and my new neighborhood while gazing past the skyline of Las Vegas Boulevard into the rocky dessert. It was getting hot, and while it felt as though I'd been sitting back there for hours, the meter on the dashboard read only thirteen minutes. The driver caught my eye, stepped on the gas, and made a quick right into the front entrance of the hotel.

"Mandalay Bay," he announced. Three mirrored towers stood tall and proud in the afternoon sun, glistening like gold. I tightened the grip on my Prada, its two worn-out handles holding the story of over ten years of my life. I couldn't help but hear my theme song, the one that got me through some of my hardest days.

She's living in a world and it's on fire, feeling the catastrophe, but she knows she can fly away...

As I took in the grand entrance, I remembered Mark Brunetz telling us that he had planned many special events at this luxury hotel and casino. Tonight, he was actually hosting one such event, where I would be reunited with my design sisters: Stephanie, Dani, Lucy, and Nicole for the premiere of our Kansas City makeover. The cab halted to a stop. This was it. The driver kindly opened my door. The warm sun beamed on me as I stepped onto the shiny marble drive. Maybe I did deserve my happy ending, but I didn't feel like this was the end. I felt like it was the beginning. Of my after...

ACKNOWLEDGEMENTS

About seven years ago, my husband handed me a MacBook Pro and said, "Here. Go be Carrie Bradshaw. Go write your book." I promptly retorted that "the book," the one I would refer to in the midst of an unhinged mom moment, stating, "another one for the book," didn't mean I was actually going to *write a book*. How in the world would I find time to write a book?

Fast-forward two years to the back of the Design For A Difference van, where I was surrounded by awesomeness (my design sisters + the ever-inspiring Mark Brunetz) yet crumpled in a desperate state of exhaustion, tears, and a weakly stated, "I just want to write my book." In response, Mr. Brunetz ever so gently placed his hand on my shoulder and offered some heartfelt encouragement, enough for me to get a grip and *keep on*, even though I was uncertain of what the future would bring for my equally exhausted family as we faced the possibility of losing our home. Thankfully, the end was near, and within a few short months I had finally landed in a place where I made the decision to just *make it happen*.

And so, having nothing but the creative writing skills I'd learned in junior high, a deep desire to share my story, and a newly opened fortune cookie from PF Chang's that read, "You are a lover of words. You should write a book," I bravely opened up Word and started with chapter one. And then I told everyone I knew that I was writing a book, because I figured I should start the buzz sooner than later, and I'd feel like an idiot if I failed this new mission.

With that, I somehow managed to keep my family from disowning me over my writing and publishing obsession, which, for the record took a grand total of four years. And, undeservingly, I had the ears of a small army of friends, family, and colleagues, who never tired of book talk (at least that I know of and thank you for shielding me if you did) and always offered their honest opinions, excitement, and support as I fumbled through a process I knew nothing about.

I couldn't have made any of it happen without my pack.

Noah, Emma, Isabelle, Natalie, and Kate—every day, the world tells us that we are blessed. I want *you* to know that *I know it* and understand it beyond measure. You are the greatest gift in this life, and I love you all with all my heart.

Tom—I give you the highest of praises for your willingness to play the best supporting actor to my lead. To let me share our story. To be the Raymond to my Debra. And for your call from the Tampa airport when you told me you felt like you had just devoured a bestseller. Your review will always mean the most, and I love you.

Mom—thank you for being my biggest fan. You have always believed in me, no matter how big and ridiculous the dream. If I speak it, you seem to be able to pray it into existence. And Dad, while you are a man of few words, the fact that you read mine in less than two days speaks volumes in terms of how proud you are. Less is more, always. I love you and am the luckiest daughter on the planet.

To my grandmas in Heaven—I may not have known it when you were here, but I am the culmination of your talents, skills, hopes, and dreams. Your testament as strong, independent women continually impacts my life and I owe all of who I am to you both. I miss you and love you more every day.

Claudia—for almost twenty years, you have been the sister I never had. Thank God For Wednesdays.

Patsy—I had no idea that what started as mall walks would turn into one of my favorite friendships in the world. You've been with me since the starting line, and the fact that you've listened attentively to my blab for what feels like Forest Gump marathon distance may be the kindest gesture I've ever received. I can't wait to see where our next journey leads.

Soni—little sister, twin sister, you have given me the ultimate suburban housewife dream. My life is better with you in it, and your unwavering support keeps me grounded. Thank you for embracing me, my crazy story, and my big ideas with new enthusiasm each day. XO.

Kelly—thanks to that expired Groupon ad, I not only found a beautiful friend, but one who's helped me in so many ways throughout this process I wouldn't even know where to begin--thank you.

Patti McCalmont—you are the epitome of a loyal friend. I'm so happy you saw a twin mom in need of diapers in the drop-off line and much thanks for proofing the final script.

Matt Pfeiffer—thank God the pastor's wife needed carpet in 2013. My story has been "rolled out" because of you. XO

Mark Brunetz—I can scroll through my entire book of blog words but will never find just the right ones to tell you how thankful I am to call you my friend and mentor throughout this journey. Who else would actually agree to be the first to read my stab at writing a book *and* agree to receive a FedEx box filled with an almost 500-page, double-spaced, printed manuscript that had been blessed with holy water? *You are a saint.*

Stephanie, Dani, Nicole, and Lucy—meeting you was like finding my design home in the world. You will forever be my design sisters and I love you all.

And Patrick—I never thought that waiting for an airport taxi on a crisp Vegas morning would reveal my "what's next." For your friendship, I am eternally grateful.

Cindy, Franz, and Alice—the day of the closing will always be one of the most emotional, memorable, and heart-warming days of my life. Cindy, thank you for believing in us; you have a heart of gold. Franz and Alice, I knew we were getting the key to the front door, but not the key to your hearts. I love you both.

To the brilliant and talented women who stepped in to help a first-time author make her dream come true: Marni Jameson and Carmen Renee Berry—how lucky am I to have had a nationally syndicated home columnist and author and a *New York Times* bestselling author as beta readers right from the start? Your feedback gave me the direction I needed to shape this story into something worth sharing. I am humbled and eternally grateful. And Nicole Jarecz—you are truly an angel sent from Heaven. Your ability to capture the essence of my story in your cover design will never cease to amaze me. I will never have enough NJ art in my life. Thank you for saying yes.

Elizabeth—I don't even know where to begin, except to say that you were, unknowingly, with me from Day One. When I was a hot postpartum mess and ready to quit, your words gave me the confidence I needed to be the mom who made it work. And years later, when I felt hopeless and swallowed up by five kids under four and a to-do list three years long, your passion and strength inspired me to be the woman I have become today. And when I finally searched for you to tell you how much your book impacted my life, you took me under your big-hearted wing as if I were your twin-mom-creative-entrepreneur-author-little sister in a way that brings me to tears imagining how I would have made any of this happen without you. You are forever my hero and I will forever be your biggest fan. XO.

And finally, I must give all the glory to Jesus, the alpha and omega, thank you for giving me this life, this purpose, and the constant reminder that every day I am loved and have the choice to make every moment beautiful.

ABOUT THE AUTHOR

Hollie Gyarmati is a designer, author, and National Ambassador for Design For A Difference, the first-ever community-driven design movement that gives makeovers to charities in need. Since 2014, she has made appearances as a panelist at numerous conferences, been featured in Design For A Difference promo videos and media, and been active in multiple charity makeovers at both national and local levels.

As a writer, she most recently loaned her voice to several campaigns in the upscale design space as well as Revealed, the official Design For A Difference blog (designforadifference.com).

Attributing her creative talents to her Flemish roots, Hollie embraced her love for design and makeovers at age seven, when she spent an entire Saturday decluttering and rearranging her best friend's bedroom in lieu of enjoying a backyard filled with kids and kickball.

She is a Magna Cum Laude graduate of Central Michigan University and received recognition for her design portfolio from the International Interior Design Association (IIDA), ranking among the top three in the state. She went on to pursue her dream career as a residential designer for the once-prestigious Dayton Hudson's Marshall Field's Corporation, where she thrived on creating dream spaces while building long-lasting relationships with her clients.

Today, Hollie is the publisher of #MakingBusyBeautiful, and after cultivating her unparalleled skills as the "get it done in style" stay-at-home-mom and entrepreneur, has made it her mission to teach her "less is more" approach to create simple, stylish, and practical lifestyles for perpetually busy, high-performing women.

She lives with her husband and five children in Bloomfield Hills, Michigan. You can connect with her on Instagram @HollieGyarmati or visit her website at HollieGyarmati.com.

Made in the
USA
Middletown, DE